FROMMER'S

BEAT
THE HIGH COST
OF TRAVEL

FROMMER'S

BEAT THE HIGH COST OF TRAVEL

Travel More, Travel Better

by Tom Brosnahan

A FROMMER BOOK
Published by Prentice Hall Press
New York

Copyright © 1988
by Simon & Schuster, Inc.

All rights reserved
including the right of reproduction
in whole or in part in any form

Published by Prentice Hall Press
A Division of Simon & Schuster, Inc.
Gulf+Western Building
One Gulf+Western Plaza
New York, NY 10023

ISBN 0-13-402132-0

Manufactured in the United States of America

Design by Stanley S. Drate/Folio Graphics Co., Inc.

Although every effort was made to ensure the accuracy of the travel and product information appearing in this book, the author does not pretend to have tested every product and service mentioned.

Prices though accurate at the time of research, can and do fluctuate in the course of time.

Contents

6 Hold That Bag!   121

7 Scouting for Airfares   129

12 Bring Home Something Memorable   298

13 What to Do If Anything Goes Wrong   321

14 Special Travelers   356

Introduction

I love to travel. In fact, I love it so much that I make my living at it, as a travel writer and photographer. Each new trip is an exciting adventure, even if I know the destination so well I could (and probably *did*) write a book about it. And when I travel, I like to enjoy the city or country I've come to see. I want to get maximum enjoyment, but without wasting my money. Because if I don't waste my money during one trip, I can spend it on another.

But I used to waste a *lot* of money. On a journey, I would do the expected things, and travel the way the majority of people traveled. I thought this was normal and that everything was just fine.

Then I made a discovery: there were people who traveled more than I did, to more exciting places, in greater comfort—and they paid less money to do it! The first time I came across this phenomenon, I could hardly believe it.

The discovery was this: I walked into a hotel and asked the price of a room. The clerk's answer was the high, unhappy figure I had expected. I took the room anyway; hotel prices are high these days. But as I was filling out the registration card, I noticed other cards on the desk. Many of them had lower room prices on them; some were substantially lower, and more like the amount I wanted to pay. So some of my "neighbors" in the hotel were enjoying the same type of room on the same day, but paying a good deal less for it! What a shock!

We've all had the experience of being on an airplane and knowing that the person on the left might have paid more for a ticket than we did; and the person on the right may have paid less. We accept it. What we *should* do is ask ourselves, "How is this possible?"

I became fascinated with the reasons for these discrepancies. There is much, much more to it than just a short-term promotional airfare, or a package deal at a hotel. There are certain economic laws which govern the workings of the whole huge travel industry. I was determined to discover these rules.

I did. I learned about how the brand-new phenomenon of deregulation has affected the transportation industry in the last year or two; I learned about occupancy rates at hotels, and about how travel industry professionals target specialized markets.

As I was doing this research, my own "rules of the road" were evolving.

I sat down one day to put it all together. I was surprised to learn that my "rules of the road" had outrun my travel industry research. I found that I did not really have to know all about travel industry machinations to travel more and to travel better. It was only necessary to follow my four simple, easy-to-learn "rules of the road," and the travel industry would work for me. I was glad I had done all the technical travel industry research, however, because that research showed me *why* my rules worked.

Something else happened during this time, something much more important than saving money. I found that I felt more *in command* of myself and of my journey. Rather than being filled with uncertainty and unexpected happenings, every trip was a boost to my feeling of self-worth. I learned a lot on each trip, I felt good about myself, I wasn't afraid of unexpectedly high prices, and I converted this good experience into a renewed sense of confidence. This is why:

I grew up believing that restaurants belonged to waiters, that hotels were ruled by desk clerks, and that reservations agents had to tell me what sort of ticket I could buy. You can imagine my surprise when I discovered a way to put waiters completely at my service, to make hotel clerks do what I asked, and to find out true bargain fares from reservations agents or travel agents. And it was all so easy and painless, and made me feel so good.

There's *no reason in the world* why you can't do the same. It really is very simple. All it takes is an acquaintance with my "rules of the road" (which I've called the "Four Laws" in this book), some examples of how they work, and some hints on how to get started. The rest is up to you. The first time you use this information, it will change your entire outlook on travel—and perhaps on the way you conduct your life.

HOW IT WORKS

Here's an example of what I'm talking about.

I was asked to appear on a television talk show to discuss my book and how its principles could save travelers money, and at the same time provide them with a more adventurous and exciting travel experience.

"Let's give it the acid test," the talk-show host told me. "Let's plan a trip to a certain destination. We'll show our viewers what the normal cost would be, and then what the cost would be using your method."

I agreed. The talk-show host suggested the name of a city, which many of the viewers might choose as a business or vacation destination, and we made our plans. First, I did the normal, expected things:

I called a few airlines offering flights to the destination, asking about discount fares and excursions;

I also dialed the toll-free numbers of several hotel reservation services, asked about rates, packages, and weekend specials;

I found out what it would cost to rent a car so I could take excursions outside the city;

Then I went back and did it all again, following the principles in this book.

In front of the television cameras, we compared notes and prices. The first, normal way of planning the trip ended up costing $410 per person for flight, hotel, meals, and rental car.

But the price for doing it my way was $250 per person.

Remember, this was an *unrehearsed* example. I did not choose the destination because I knew of a cheap way to get there, or a cheap place to stay because of my work as a travel guidebook writer. The talk-show host chose the destination, and I simply planned the trip from scratch following the principles in this book. And I shopped for comparable services—I did not lower the standards, or lower the price by buying less expensive goods.

So what accounted for the big difference in price? How did I do it?

Well, I followed the "First Law" when I booked my hotel room. The First Law states, "Don't take 'no' for an answer until you're sure the answer is 'no.' " I called the toll-free hotel reservation number and asked for prices, including special weekend packages. The reservations clerk gave me the room prices, which were quite moderate; as for weekend specials, the answer was "None offered." I asked, "Are you sure?" The clerk answered, "Yes."

But I decided to follow the First Law. I called the hotel directly (a toll call) and asked for Reservations. "Sure," was the answer, "we'll give you two nights for slightly more than the normal price for one night." So there it was! The hotel only wanted to offer this deal to local people, or to those in the know. They didn't want it widely offered, as it would be through their reservation service.

The other big savings came with the flight and the rental car. For these, I followed the Third Law, "Look beyond the Obvious." After calling the airlines which flew to the destination, I asked myself, "What's the alternative? What else can I do?" The city in question has two airports. I looked into flights to the other, less-used airport. No luck. Then it hit me: Why stop there? A city just an hour's drive to the south had a big airport. I looked in the Yellow Pages and found new regional airlines which flew there. I called. Fares were lower. "Anything else?" I asked the airline's reservation agent. "I really want to save money." "Well," she said, "we do have an off-peak flight every day at lunchtime." The fare for that off-peak flight was *60% less than the excursion fare* directly to the destination, and 85% less than the normal round-trip fare.

But when I got to the alternate city, I was still an hour away from my destination. That's where the rental car came in. Because the alternate city was a less popular business and vacation destination, car rental rates were lower. I ended up getting flight *and* rental car for only $7 a day more than what I would have paid for the flight alone had I taken the "low-priced" excursion fare directly to the destination. And the drive to the destination city was through pleasant farming country, along an uncrowded four-lane highway.

These laws work, and they work for everyone. Reader Rich Green, of Indianapolis, Indiana, wrote to me, "I have been amazed at the money I've saved following your tips when dealing with hotels and motels. Usually the request for the commercial rate does the trick. And I've saved hundreds of dollars by not taking the supplemental insurance offered by rent-a-car companies. With your advice, traveling is more of a sport for me as I try to beat the high cost of travel." (For full details on how to save on these items, see Chapters 8 and 9.)

GETTING STARTED

"Okay, that makes sense," you may say. "It's all logical, and easy enough. And the savings are certainly spectacular. Next time I plan a trip, I'll look for regional airlines, and I'll call hotels directly about special discount rates."

No. You've missed the point.

Those two tips—calling a hotel directly, and finding out about regional airlines—are excellent travel tips. You'll find hundreds more, just as good, in the pages of this book. But the point is not just to give you tips. Can you memorize all the information in this book? Do you want to? Relax. You don't have to.

The Laws explained in this book are easy to learn and to remember.

They will change your entire way of thinking about travel, and about how you direct your life.

They will show you the situations in which you should do things differently.

They will help you to find your own money-saving methods and tips.

They will make the old ways of doing things look silly and wasteful.

Each Law is illustrated by enough examples so that you can easily grasp its meaning. In addition, there are plenty of good travel tips to get you thinking on your own.

But after you've read this book and absorbed its simple lessons, there will still be one thing to do: *try it out*. When you've done it once, you'll experience that thrill of power and independence, that wonderful feeling of being in command of your fate, that can make travel so exciting and fulfilling.

Don't even wait for your next trip to use the Four Laws. You will be amazed at how well they work right at home. When the time comes for your next big travel adventure, you'll be well prepared to take control and enjoy it to the fullest.

1

Wise Travel: The Four Essential Laws

I don't think you'll believe me until you've tried it yourself. You'll think, "It can't be that easy to get other people to do what I want and to get better prices."

But it is.

Trust yourself. Learn to recognize which of the essential laws applies in each travel situation. Each time you come upon a problem or difficulty, go over the Four Laws in your head to see which one will solve the problem.

The Four Laws will not solve the problem without *you*. You must solve the problem. But the Four Laws will lead you to the solution. And when you have solved the problem yourself, you'll have greater confidence in your power to meet problems head on and to solve them quickly and painlessly.

Here are the Four Laws. Read them slowly and carefully.

THE FIRST LAW

Don't Take "No" for an Answer until You're Sure the Answer Is "No."

Most of us will accept a "no" without question: Do you have this in stock? Is there a cheaper flight? You have no rooms available at all? In lots and lots of situations the "no" has nothing to do with reality, but rather with the personal preferences of the one answering "no." "No, we don't have it" can mean "I don't feel like going to look for it." And "No, we have no rooms at all" can mean "We've got a few rooms, but I don't want to rent one to a single traveler—I want to get the double rate."

Your job, in obeying this Law, is to discover the true significance of the negative answer. Get more information, don't just walk away. This is actually quite easy, and not unpleasant. No need to threaten or berate, just keep talking. At the point when you would normally turn and walk away, stay and ask a few more questions. What can it hurt?

"You must have something similar or interchangeable in stock."

"Perhaps there has been a cancellation or a no-show, and a room is free."

"Maybe if I come back just before flight time there will be a seat open."

By staying, you'll demonstrate to the other person that it will be easier to satisfy you than to get rid of you by saying "no." This Law works. It works at home and it works abroad.

Notice that you are supposed to stick like glue "at the point when you would normally turn and walk away."

Over half the time, it will solve your problem right then and there: you'll find the thing you want, or that elusive charter flight, or that spare room.

If it doesn't, you'll know that the true answer was in fact "no," and you can proceed with alternative plans. But you'll go on with confidence: you took control of the situation, you discovered the true answer, you know you're not missing anything.

THE SECOND LAW

Search Constantly for the Point of Mutual Advantage.

The Point of Mutual Advantage is that point where the interests of the buyer and the seller come together, and both make out well.

The clearest example is a partly filled hotel. The clerk says a room costs $100. You only want to spend $60. The clerk knows that if the room goes empty (as it will, without you), the hotel earns $0. If you rent the room, you'll engender a few dollars' expenses: a few gallons of water, a kilowatt or so of electricity, a set of sheets to wash. The expenses are marginal, and almost any room price will exceed them. So the Point of Mutual Advantage is $65 or $75 for the room: you win and the hotel wins.

Remember, both sides must stand to gain from the arrangement, or there is no Point of Mutual Advantage.

Here's another example. In a curio shop in Florence, you see a painting you like, and also a little statue. You want to buy one or the other as a souvenir. Prices are marked, and the shopkeeper won't budge. It doesn't matter to you which one you buy, you like them both. Now, ask the shopkeeper for a special price *for the two items combined*. What does he gain? Two sales where there would have been only one; he takes in a slightly smaller markup on one item. What do you gain? Two lovely souvenirs for a bit more than you expected to spend, but a bargain nonetheless. It doesn't have to be in Florence. I bought two Japanese prints in San Francisco; I suggested a discount; the owner said, "But this guy's work is expensive!" He did agree to pay the sales tax himself, though. All I did was suggest it. In this case, for a small expenditure he got himself a very satisfied customer.

The Point of Mutual Advantage is all around us, all the time. Look for it, find it, and everyone benefits.

THE THIRD LAW

Look Beyond the Obvious.

Accept it as fact: What you need exists, and all you must do is locate it.

Here's an example of the Third Law: I arrived at Paris's Gare de Lyon, got off the train, and headed out to have a good Parisian lunch. Now, around a major station there are always dozens of cafés and restaurants which aim to serve travelers just like me. I didn't know this area of Paris. The normal, obvious thing to do was to walk out the station door, spot a restaurant, sit down, and hope for the best. The prices seemed high, though, so I decided to find a neighborhood place where the locals dined, not a place designed to catch travelers. I explored a few streets *behind* the obvious restaurants, and within ten minutes I found what I wanted: a small, friendly neighborhood restaurant that featured a daily business lunch. I had soup, pasta, meat and vegetables, salad, dessert, and wine—all included—for the price of "steack et frites" (tough beef and french fries) in a crowded café facing the station.

Airport buses are another common subject for the Third Law. In many cases a few well-placed questions will reveal that the airport is served by a municipal bus at a fraction of the fancy airport bus price. You may have to walk a few minutes to a bus stop (how long did you just walk down those endless airport concourses?), and the city bus may take a bit longer. But you'll probably save enough money to treat yourself to some little luxury, and you'll plunge immediately into the life of the city or country you are visiting.

Don't Take "No" for an Answer until
You're Sure the Answer Is **"No."**
Search for the Point of Mutual Advantage.
Look Beyond the Obvious.
Commitment Saves Money; Flexibility
Usually Costs Money.

Sightseeing tours are still another Third Law subject. Some sort of public transport has got to go close to your sight, and since local people use it every day, it must be relatively cheap.

Look Beyond the Obvious, because the Obvious is often put there by someone who'd like to make a few extra dollars from you.

THE FOURTH LAW

Commitment Saves Money; Flexibility Usually Costs Money.

We pride ourselves on the amount of personal freedom we enjoy. But when it comes to travel, flexibility is expensive because of the uncertainty involved. Hotels, airlines, rental car firms, and other businesses want to sell their services to you. But until you've actually paid for and used their services, they can't be positive of a sale. You might change your mind at the last moment, leaving them with nothing after weeks of planning. So these businesses heed the adage "A bird in the hand is worth two in the bush." They'll go a long way in lowering price if you will only commit yourself to them. Here's a humorous example.

Fulton Flyboy is a reservations executive for Aeolian Airlines. On October 23, his line has a flight from Chicago to Miami with 200 seats on it. Fulton's job is to fill those seats. It is just after the busy Labor Day weekend when we look in on Fulton in his office. He is worrying about the Chicago-to-Miami plane for October 23, even though it is seven weeks in the future.

"For that flight last year I had sold 180 seats at the full fare. But then at the last minute 100 people cancelled, didn't show, or traded the ticket for that of another airline. The plane flew less than half full, and even the 80 full-fare tickets didn't pay the bills. This year I'll try a different tack. I'll offer big discounts if people will only *promise* me they won't cancel, that they will show up (or at least pay), and that they won't switch to another airline. That commitment is worth losing a bit of money for; at least there won't be a repeat of last year's debacle."

Soon the ads appear: "Fly to Florida on Aeolian! 30% off if you buy and pay now!" It's a real bargain, and Florida-bound passengers respond by buying lots of seats. The offer expires three weeks before flight time, when business and last-minute travelers start booking seats. They have to pay full fare because they didn't help Fulton out in his plane-stuffing task, and because they wanted the freedom to change their minds at the last moment.

The day of the flight, Fulton is ecstatic. "Whoopee! I've sold 100 discount seats and 80 full-fare seats. I'm almost home free. Now, how to get people into those last 20 seats. . . . I know what to do! I'll offer a standby fare."

So Fulton's final passenger list was composed of 100 discount-rate passengers, 80 full-fare passengers, five full-fares who arrived breathless at the airport and simply *had to* get to Miami on that flight, and 15 standbys who were willing to take pot luck.

"That system works!" Fulton said to himself in self-congratulation. "If people will only commit themselves, I'll give them a good deal."

Airlines are an obvious example of businesses that are willing to give a discount in exchange for a commitment. If you think a minute, you'll realize that hotels, restaurants, and car rental firms have similar problems. They want to use their facilities to the fullest extent. They want as much time as possible to gather customers. And they want to be sure you'll come and patronize them. No-shows, who exercise their flexibility by deciding not to show up or pay for the promised service, cost the hotels and airlines plenty. These firms often routinely overbook, hoping they can guess correctly and match the number of no-shows with the number of overbookings to achieve an even 100% occupancy. If their guess is off, they lose money. It makes sense that they're happy when someone makes a commitment and pays in advance.

Restaurants work this way too. The very difference between table d'hôte and à la carte menus shows it. The chef is saying, "I'll plan a nice, balanced, delicious meal. It will be easier and less expensive for me to plan, buy for, and prepare this meal than it would be to prepare a hundred different meals based on diners' immediate desires. So I'll sell this table d'hôte meal a little cheaper to tempt people. People can also order from the à la carte menu, but it's more trouble and involves more expense to keep all that food on hand just in case somebody wants it, and to prepare it on a moment's notice, so the à la carte diners will have to pay more for the privilege of selecting exactly what they want at the moment."

More important than the information on guesthouses, discount airfares, and free traveler's checks are the mental exercises and thought patterns that you will learn by using this book.

With hotels, the Weekend Package leaps to mind as an example of the Fourth Law. "Come on Friday, Saturday, or Sunday," they say, "and we'll give you a special rate. But come on any other day and you'll have to pay more." If you sacrifice the freedom to arrive any day you choose, you will be rewarded with direct cash savings. The hotel management knows that some travelers, particularly business people, have to arrive on business days. These clients demand the right to arrive whenever they choose. "Sure," the hotel people say, "come whenever you like—but be prepared to pay." The business travelers have no choice, so they pay.

The point of the Fourth Law is not to hem you in with regulations, uncertainty, and inconvenience. It's to make you think in terms of flexibility vs. money. If a certain type of flexibility is not important to you, take it and turn it into cash, which will buy you a type of flexibility which probably will be more important to you. Book a Super-APEX flight in advance, and you'll save enough over the ordinary airfare to upgrade your hotel accommodations, or to dine luxuriously.

The aforementioned examples are straightforward and familiar. But to keep to the Fourth Law, you should combine it with the Third Law, "Look Beyond the Obvious."

A friend of mine cut the cost of renting a car in half by combining these two laws. Her travel plans were firm and established well in advance, and she was willing to commit herself to the car and the exact rental period weeks in advance. Carefully examining the car rental brochures, and questioning the rental agents, she learned that special rates could be applied for firm commitments made well in advance—just as with the airlines. Instead of signing up for a "reserve at any-time" rental, she found a way to trade a bit of flexibility (which she was not going to use) for substantial savings on the rental.

Try it. The next time you must make a hotel reservation, ask them for a special price in exchange for full payment a week or two in advance. Sure, there is risk involved, and if your plans are not firm you may not want to risk it. But if your travel plans are good and firm, take advantage of the savings. What you save will easily cover a Cancellation Insurance policy (see Chapter 5), with money to spare. Your risk with such a policy is reduced to virtually nothing.

Flexibility vs. Commitment

One of the criticisms leveled at our society is that people find it difficult to commit themselves for the long term. Whether it be a marriage, a mortgage, or a meal ticket, we're frightened of pinning ourselves down. In such a fluid society, how do we know that a better mate, or interest rate, or career is not just around the corner? And if it is, how can we grasp it if we're already committed? How can we give up the freedom to change our minds?

Finding the easier, or quicker, or less
expensive way doesn't require genius.
What's required is creativity, ingenuity,
clear sight, and a willingness to explore
new possibilities.

The answer is that you're not giving it up. You are taking control, deciding what you're going to do, and then doing it. You set definite plans when this is possible and wise. You preserve your flexibility when this is called for. If, at the last moment, you *must* change your mind, it's not a disaster. And once you're in command of your own destiny, this rarely happens.

2

Where Are You Going? When? Why?

A journey can be fulfilling only if we know what we're doing and why we're doing it. But we often plan an important trip with as little thought as we would use to select a television program or a fast-food snack.

It's not difficult to guarantee the success of a trip. It involves learning something about our destination, and—more important—about our own motives, sometimes hidden, for going there.

This takes no extra time at all. Everything you discover by asking yourself the three questions above, you would find out eventually. But by then it may be too late. You may have committed yourself to a trip, a destination, or a season which is bound to leave you disappointed and unhappy. This is needless, and easily avoided.

Take a minute to read through this chapter, and then another minute to reassess your travel plans. You may be fascinated at what you'll discover.

At first, virtually no one has a clear picture of what traveling is, where they want to go, why they wish to go there, and what it's going to be like. Instead of a clear picture, our minds are cluttered with outdated information, stereotypes, prejudices, unfounded fears, flights of fancy, and simple ignorance. Without proper information, and a proper frame of mind, it's impossible to have an enjoyable trip; and an unpleasant or disappointing trip is the most expensive trip of all.

WHY ARE YOU GOING?

Keep your goal in mind. Why are you off on a trip? If the reason is just to get away from home, see new sights, meet new people, learn new things, then you're sure to succeed. "I've never been to Switzerland (or Arizona, or Tangier, or South America) and I just want to see what it's like." Bravo. But watch out for the hidden reason: "I'm an Anglophile and I'm lonely, so I'm going to England to meet the perfect mate." That may happen, but don't expect perfect mates to flock to the airport arrival gate. It's no easier to meet perfect mates on a trip than it is at home, and if you're confined to a ship, bus, or train for long periods and there's no one eligible aboard, it may be considerably harder. And did you expect England to be the land of your fairytales? All bowler hats and cozy pubs and Shakespeare? Don't be disappointed if it turns out to be a real country, with real people much like yourself, full of beauty and ugliness you never expected, and which never appeared in the fairytales.

Travel literature does little to help dispel stereotypes, simplifications, and false hopes. In fact, all travel brochures and most travel magazine articles and some guidebooks do all they can to encourage hazy visions of beauteous climes and cheery Munchkins: Rome without drizzle, Cairo without dust, Hollywood without smog. Did you know that Acapulco has more rainfall than any other place in Mexico? That weather in the Aegean is sometimes so bad that ferries to the

Greek islands may not run for days? That visiting airy Phoenix can be bad for your asthma? All of these places are beautiful, and all are worth visiting, but they are real places with bad as well as good points. To know where you would like to go, you've got to have a clear idea of a place's true character—or at least throw out the stereotype—tell yourself "I *really* know *nothing* about New York (or Turkey, or Bolivia, or Québec)" and suspend judgment until you arrive.

It's important that you keep your goal in mind so you can avoid disappointments; and avoiding disappointments—plus saving money—is the subject we take up next.

WHERE DO YOU *REALLY* WANT TO GO?

It may seem silly to bring up the question of destination. "I know where I'm going, thanks very much. My mind's made up."

But WHERE? is very closely associated with WHY? You've always wanted to see San Francisco or Switzerland, so you're going. Fine. Skip below to WHEN?

If you're still unsure about your destination, however, you have an even greater chance to be adventurous. An example: you live in the western part of North America, and you'd like to see some of the East. You could go to New York, Boston, or Montréal and have a wonderful time. But the price structure in these cities is quite high. Although inexpensive lodgings and meals are to be had, they're much more difficult to uncover. Substitute Halifax and a tour of Nova Scotia, instead of Boston and New England or Montréal and the Laurentians, and you'll have cut your expenses before even setting foot outside your front door. Or go to Portugal instead of France. Why did you want to go to France? To live in the midst of a storybook dream filled with boulevardiers, Hemingway and Fitzgerald, bistros and bonbons? If you were going to France to learn about French culture and to practice your French, then go, because you can't do that in less-expensive Portugal (though you *could* do it in less-expensive Québec City). If, however, you just want to get away from home, dine on excellent food, experiment with some of the world's great wines, relax on sunny beaches, explore medieval fortresses and great museums, get to know an ancient and fascinating culture and its people, then go to Portugal and the savings over a comparable trip to France will astound you. On your next trip, head for Québec, or fly off to a French-speaking Caribbean island in "shoulder" season or off-season, and you'll get your French practice at bargain rates.

Don't get me wrong. Paris is Paris, and when you truly want to go to Paris, nothing else will do. It all depends on WHY? you travel. Examine your travel objectives, choose your destination based on your true reasons for traveling (and an honest assessment of the destination), then move on to the all-important question of WHEN?

WHEN IS THE BEST TIME TO GO?

Everyone knows that there are "high" seasons and "low" seasons, and that one can save incredible amounts of money by visiting a country, city, or resort during the slack time. But this is not as easy as it sounds, for there are very good reasons why most people travel in high season. When it's freezing in Toronto, Hartford, and Seattle, that's the perfect time to head south to Mazatlán, Miami, and St. Thomas. We're back to the old question of WHY? you are traveling. To get away from the cold? Then you must go when it's cold up north and warm down south. Take off and enjoy it, follow the advice given later on in this book, and you'll still save money.

You might be surprised to learn, after asking yourself WHY?, that your true reason for heading to Florida is to take the kids to Disney World; that you're actually taking off to Mazatlán or Acapulco because it sounds exciting and foreign and the beaches are supposed to be so nice and the water so warm; or that you're headed for the Caribbean because for all these years you've wanted to see what these emerald islands looked like, rather than simply to get away from the cold.

Did you know that Acapulco has more rainfall than any other place in Mexico? That weather in the Aegean is sometimes so bad the ferries to the Greek islands may not run for days?

Go to Florida from late spring to late autumn and you won't believe how cheap everything is: airfares, motels, special services such as deep-sea fishing or tours of the Everglades. The highways aren't crowded. Miami Beach is all yours. The seafood is cheaper. The same sort of inexpensive, leisurely, uncrowded travel is yours to be had in the Caribbean during this time.

With many destinations it's not so easy to determine the best, most cost-effective time to go. Austria would be lovely in August, yes? No. Sometimes it rains hard for days, particularly in August. The Greek islands are pretty far south, so it must be like the Caribbean there in February? Wrong again. It's damp, and it drizzles, and many of the inexpensive small pensions have no heat, or are closed altogether. Québec City would be a dull icebox in winter? Actually, Québec's Winter Carnival is one of the most exciting, exhilarating, and enjoyable events of the year, well worth the trip. Forget Mexico in the summer, or Northern California in January? Not at all. You can go to Mexico City, or San Francisco, almost any time of year so far as the weather is concerned, because the climates of these two cities are equable year round.

How, then, does one choose a time to travel? By looking closely at information about climate, holidays and festivals, hotel prices and airfares. Every guidebook deals with the subject of when to go, and guidebooks are more trustworthy on this subject than are many materials produced by the local travel offices (which tend to want tourists to come even if the weather is terrible and all the museums are closed).

Ask friends who have been there. Study guidebooks, newspaper and magazine articles until you *have a sense* of what it will be like. Of course no friend, guidebook, or article can guarantee the weather. But with some research you can determine what your chances will be, and you can discover the climatic quirks of the area: rainy seasons and dry seasons, typhoon seasons and scirocco seasons, sunstroke seasons and black fly seasons.

UP-TO-THE-MINUTE WEATHER REPORTS: The computer age has brought several new ways to determine the weather anywhere on earth. One of these is WeatherTrak, a service of Airdata Inc., P.O. Box 7000,

Dallas, TX 75209 (tel. 214/869-3035, or toll free 800/247-3282). To use this service, you simply dial a local number in any of the cities served by WeatherTrak, and listen; the number for New York City, for example, is 212/355-1212. A computerized voice will ask you to punch in the telephone area code of the major city for which you want a weather report. Once you punch in the code, you'll get an up-to-the-minute report on the time in that city, the temperature, current weather (including wind speed and relative humidity), and also the weather forecast for tomorrow. WeatherTrak is free, except for the cost of the telephone call, which is a local one if your city has a WeatherTrak number, or a long-distance one if you must call the nearest WeatherTrak city. Cities with local numbers include Atlanta, Chicago, Dallas, Denver, Houston, Minneapolis, New York, Omaha, Phoenix, San Antonio, San Jose, and Tampa. WeatherTrak gives reports on 235 cities throughout the world. For a list of these cities, request the list from Airdata at the address above, and send a self-addressed stamped envelope.

Another innovative weather service is the Climate Desk established by Banana Republic, the travel and safari clothing company. Call the Climate Desk toll free at 800/325-7270, on any business day between 8:30 a.m. and 5 p.m. Pacific Time, and you can ask for climate facts on 500 different locations around the world. Besides weather information, agents at the Climate Desk can give you updates on travel conditions and dangers, and on the political situation where you're going. They'll also suggest appropriate clothing, guidebooks, and background reading for your chosen destination. To get a copy of Banana Republic's catalogue, request one by writing to Banana Republic, P.O. Box 7737, San Francisco, CA 94120.

Local Customs Affect Travel Plans and Costs

To get the most out of your trip for the least amount of money, you will have to study carefully more than just the weather at your destination. Look also at a calendar of holidays and festivals, and learn what importance they have. For instance, if you arrive in Israel on Friday evening, most everything will be locked up tight for the next 24 hours—it's the Sabbath. You'll be able to get to your hotel (but only by taxi or shared taxi, not by bus); the hotel will be open (but not the bar, and perhaps not the restaurant); to go to a museum the next morning, you must have bought your ticket in advance, before the Sabbath began. It saves time, trouble, and money to arrive in Israel on a day other than Friday or Saturday.

A trip to France in the summer may sound great, but you can't try out all those little neighborhood restaurants (or many other attractions) in Paris in August, because virtually all of those little neighborhood restaurateurs—and their customers—have headed south for the traditional Parisian month on the Riviera.

Going to a Moslem country? The holy month of Ramadan, determined by the lunar calendar, comes at a slightly different time each year. In all Moslem countries—Morocco, Egypt, Turkey—daily life changes completely during the holy month. Business and museum schedules, restaurant hours, transportation timetables, all change to accommodate the daily fasting (from dawn to dusk) of the faithful. Want a cold Coke to lay the dust on a hot Cairo afternoon? Sorry. But come back at nightfall and you can have all the Cokes you want—even dine on pigeons and figs until 4 or 5 o'clock in the morning.

Even less exotic destinations have quirks and foibles that can affect your travel plans—and costs— dramatically. In any French-speaking country, June 24 is a day to note. It's St. John the Baptist's Day (St-Jean Baptiste), and trains will be packed, hotels jammed, and restaurants mobbed as young French, Belgian, and Swiss people take part in a midsummer frolic, the roots of which date back far beyond the beginning of Christianity. What it means for you is that you had better have a reserved seat on the train, a confirmed reservation in that inexpensive little Left Bank hotel, and the ability to deal with crowds. If not, you may find yourself paying a first-class fare for the only seat on the train, or staying in a fancy hotel at breathtaking prices.

A similar phenomenon closer to home is Columbus Day in New England. Virtually every room in every hotel, motel, inn, and guesthouse is booked in advance for this weekend, when the maple trees are usually in the full radiant blaze of their fall color.

If you just want to get away from home, dine on excellent food, experiment with some of the world's fine wines, relax on sunny beaches, explore medieval fortresses and museums . . . then go to Portugal, and the savings over a comparable trip to France will astound you.

But you get the idea. Anyone can tell you a time—perhaps only a day or two—when a local event changes daily life drastically and makes things difficult, or more expensive, for the casual traveler. These events may have little to do with the weather, or the normal tourist season, or any other predictable aspect. You've got to find out about such phenomena before you plan your trip. In finding out, you'll learn a tremendous amount about the place and the culture you're about to explore. In short, you'll be prepared to take full advantage of your travel opportunity.

Weight + Weather = Money

Another aspect of WHEN? is packing, and in this respect weather equals money. You simply cannot travel heavy and travel wisely at the same time. You must travel as lightly as possible so you can walk the several blocks from the terminal to your hotel rather than taking a cab; so that you won't need to tip porters, or pay for luggage lockers; so that you won't waste time dealing with *things* when you should be out on the beach, or in a museum, or trying the local delicacies. And the weight of your bags is directly related to the weather. Go to Rome in the summer and all you'll need is a few drip-dry things, sandals, and a sun hat (when you wash your clothes, they'll dry in minutes in the arid Roman air). But go to Rome in the winter and you'll need a sweater, a raincoat, perhaps an umbrella and rubber boots. There's more to come on the subject of packing, but for now, keep in mind that "weight plus weather equals money."

It's a great pleasure for me to get letters from readers of my books. This valuable feedback helps me to help other travelers, and it allows me to keep in touch with you. Please! If you have a thought or an idea while reading, jot it down and drop me a note. I'll do my best to write back as soon as possible if I'm not out on the road. My address is: Tom Brosnahan, Prentice Hall Press, One Gulf + Western Plaza, New York, NY 10023-7772. Many thanks.

Information Pays—and Much of It Is Free

Information is better than money. Sometimes money alone can't get what you want. In those instances where money is necessary, having the right information *always* saves significant sums of money.

Certain sorts of information are useful when traveling wisely. By using the Four Laws, you can get the information you need. In most cases, it will cost you very little time or money.

In travel, information is crucial and immediately useful, because if you've never heard about that cheap charter flight, you will certainly end up paying the higher scheduled airline fare, and if you don't know that Mrs. Smith operates a delightful bed-and-breakfast on Main Street you will end up checking into the noisy motel out on the highway. Most of the information you will need on your trip—no matter where you're going—is available to you right now, very cheaply, at home. The rest is available near your destination, and it too is mostly free, or very inexpensive.

You must take the time to get information and then

you must take the time to absorb it. As we've seen, knowing in detail about weather, high and low seasons, and local holidays, can affect your travel budget directly and immediately. But you've got to learn about these things *before you go*. Don't pick up a guidebook on the way to the airport, planning to read it on the plane. By then it may be too late to take advantage of the information the guidebook provides. When you get to your destination, you may spend several dollars for a local map when you could have had a much better map *completely free* by writing to the local tourist office in advance of your departure. (When you get to where you're going, the free maps may not be available. Local map vendors may put pressure on the tourist office not to give maps away; besides, the tourist office would rather send you a map, thereby helping to convince you to come, than provide you with a free map once you're there.)

Start planning for your trip early. Choose your guidebook; send away for information, maps, schedules, and brochures; meet with friends who have been there; and visit a travel agent. Do all this months before you leave.

If you plan to travel with others, especially children, one of the smartest things you can do is to involve them in the information-gathering process very early. This takes some of the burden off you, and builds their enthusiasm as well. For more on this idea, see Chapter 14—Special Travelers, under "Pleasant Family Travel."

SOURCES OF FREE INFORMATION

Virtually every city, state, and country wants to encourage tourism. Tourists bring money and they take back memories that are a valuable public relations resource for the city, state, or country concerned.

Every tourist destination—down to tiny villages in remote places—generates tourism information, mostly in printed form, but sometimes also in the form of a person (more or less knowledgeable) who staffs a booth or a desk and provides guidance to visitors in person or by phone. Virtually all of this information is free, though for a few items you may have to pay a nominal charge to cover printing costs.

Information is better than money.

Tourism jurisdictions usually overlap. For instance, if you're planning a trip to Montréal, you could get lots of information from the Canadian Government Office of Tourism, which has offices throughout the United States and Canada. Also, the Province of Québec would be glad to provide you with lists of accommodations, parks, activities, and special events. The City of Montréal would happily send you a detailed street plan, a plan of the fabulous Metro system, a list of good restaurants, a guide to museums (with hours of operation, telephone numbers, etc.), and perhaps a few discount coupons to this or that. You can even delve deeper. Every hotel will gladly send you a brochure, and a price list, plus news on any special deals currently available. Many restaurants have reduced-format sample menus, which they'd love to tempt you with. The museums will send brochures, notices of special exhibits, floor plans. In fact, the quantity of information that's yours for the asking is so great, you'll have the delightful problem of *too much* information, rather than not enough.

How do you get all this? Often you don't even need the proper address. If you know the right city, just make up an address if you can't find the right one easily. Something like "Tourism Information Office, Department of Commerce, Commonwealth of Pennsylvania, Harrisburg, PA," will no doubt get you whatever you want: a good Pennsylvania map, list of state parks and camping areas, details on hunting season, on local vineyards (there are lots!), walking tours of Philadelphia. If you don't get the information itself, you'll at the very least obtain the exact address from which the information may be had.

Foreign addresses are no problem. "Ministry of Tourism, Ankara, Turkey," may result in a slim envelope with exotic stamps, or a thick information-crammed envelope from the Ministry of Tourism office in New York. You could have written to New York in the first place, had you known. But if you didn't, no matter. Given time, some official in Ankara will translate your request and see that it's passed on for action.

Be aware that the quality and amount of information available from tourist offices will vary. For example, Canada and Britain both provide first-rate and abundant information, as do New York state and Tennessee. Other countries and regions may not supply as much or as detailed information as they do, but it will still be helpful.

And when you're on the road, remember to stop in at the local tourist office, even if you already have information about the area. City and regional tourist offices usually have much more detailed materials about local lodgings, dining possibilities and sights, than do state or national offices. Don't be afraid to chat and get acquainted with the folks running the tourist office. They'll take it as a compliment that you're interested in their home area, and will offer all sorts of juicy tidbits of information you never expected. You may even make some friends. Then if problems develop, you'll know where to find a helping hand.

What to Expect from a Tourist Office

What can you get if you send a card to a city, state, or national tourist office? That depends on the particular tourist office: some are astoundingly efficient and well prepared; others are woeful holes for petty bureaucrats, somebody's relatives, and time-servers. If you have specific desires, always *ask:* request the basics specifically, and *give a deadline* by which the information must reach you. Here are the basics:

MAPS: Quality and detail may vary, but every office hands out maps. Ask for a country map and city maps as you need them. If you want special interest maps— nautical maps of the Maine coast, hiking routes in Nepal, railroad lines in Switzerland—ask where you can get them. Often these small-scale, locally produced maps are better than the commercial ones.

HOTEL INFORMATION: You may get a short list of names with telephone numbers and official class rankings (Luxury, First Class, etc.), which is next to useless; or you may get a thick book with everything you could want. Prince Edward Island puts out a provincial lodgings guide that gives a description of every single lodging place on the island, with its exact location, mail address and phone number, prices, number and type of rooms (cabins, housekeeping, etc.) other facilities (swimming pool or whatever), and tips on reservations or what to do nearby. This book is free. Nova Scotia's is almost as good, and it too is free. Both guides also include lists of campgrounds.

The British Tourist Authority also provides exemplary materials. Write to them and you can get a "Map and List of 100 Inexpensive Hotels," or a directory of sumptuous castles and manor houses that have been converted into hotels, or a list of homey bed-and-breakfast lodgings in Stratford-upon-Avon.

The only problem with such hotel information is that it is impartial. Choosing a hotel is one situation in which partiality is a virtue. Whereas a travel writer, in an article or guidebook, will advise you that some hotels are overpriced and others offer great value-for-money, an official information source will stick to bare statistics and will not—indeed is forbidden to—offer an opinion about a hotel's relative value.

RESTAURANT INFORMATION: It is much less common to receive detailed restaurant data, and restaurant recommendations made by official people suffer from the same weakness as official hotel data: impartiality. Of two restaurants which meet the same official criteria for three stars (or three forks, or whatever), one may be rather scruffy and one may be superb, though both charge the same prices. Again, a travel or dining guide is of much more value, providing that it's opinionated and exclusive (i.e., it puts some restaurants in and leaves others out).

DATA ON WHAT TO SEE AND DO: You'll receive lots and lots of this, and most of it will be excellent. Booklets that outline walking tours—with maps—are a common item. Auto itineraries are also popular. Read them carefully before you set out, because impartiality comes into play here too. The tourist office wants to spread out the tourist dollars as evenly as possible, so they'll map out routes into the boonies where there is little of real interest to see or do—they want to get you out of the major attraction centers (where you'll probably go anyway) into the backlands, which could use some infusions of cash.

OTHER INFORMATION: The miscellaneous information you will receive may be the most important: weather data and temperature charts, lists of festivals and holidays, train and bus schedules, cruise ship itineraries.

Other Sources of Free Information

Use your library. Once you've decided on your destination, read about the country, city, or resort. At the local library consult the *Readers' Guide to Periodical Literature* for a listing of the latest articles that have been published by magazines like *National Geographic Traveler, Condé Nast Traveler, Travel & Leisure, European Travel & Life, Travel/Holiday, Gourmet,* and *Sunset* about your destination.

Another good source of almost-free information is the State Department, which publishes backgrounds on particular countries throughout the world. Write to the Superintendent of Documents, U.S. Government Printing Office, Washington, DC 20402 (tel. 202/783-3238), for a list of available backgrounds. The department publishes one background per month containing useful information about a specific country's government, people, climate, and health hazards.

About the best all-around source of travel information is the same it has been for centuries past: other travelers.

And don't forget the newspapers. Admittedly the travel sections of the smaller newspapers may not be too useful, but at your library you should be able to find your closest large metro daily or the *New York Times,* the *Los Angeles Times,* the *Washington Post,* or the *New York Daily News,* all of which carry excellent Sunday travel sections.

Some travelers even subscribe to the leading newspaper or local magazine of the destination city for one month at least. By writing to the tourism office, you can find out if the major city—Athens, Bogotá, Paris,

New Delhi—has an English-language newspaper (it usually does). Get the address from the tourist office, subscribe well in advance, and specify air-mail postage. You may want only one paper a week, perhaps the Sunday edition (but the Friday edition of the *Jerusalem Post,* etc.)

By getting a local paper, you can take advantage of excursion flights offered *only* by advertisement in the local paper. And that's not all; you might spot several hotels that are less expensive and pretentious than "the only hotel fit for an American tourist," according to your travel agent. You can read ads from restaurants that are running specials. You'll know about the weather and what holidays are coming up.

WHAT ABOUT TRAVEL AGENTS?

The use of a travel agent follows the Second Law: Search constantly for the Point of Mutual Advantage.

Travel agents are retail merchants who sell travel. They will sell you a product or service provided to them by a wholesale travel packager, or they will custom-design a trip for you. In either case, you obtain their services—consulting with you on travel plans, making reservations, troubleshooting—virtually for free.

How can this be?

They obtain a percentage of return not from you, but from the airlines, hotels, car rental companies, and travel wholesalers whose products they sell. They charge you nothing, directly, for their expert help and assistance, which many times goes far beyond the call of duty.

In many cases, you cannot get the same product for less if you bypass a travel agent and buy directly from the source. Airlines, for instance, charge you the same amount for a seat whether you buy through a travel agent or directly from the airline. They do not want to ruin the travel agent system, which is an excellent way for the airlines to sell their services to the public. And if you bypass a travel agent, you lose the benefit of the free, expert counsel and advice.

Actually, a travel agent will save you a lot of money and time. Agents are trained and equipped to use computerized reservation systems for airlines, hotels, rental cars, cruise lines, and many other travel services. They can do in a flash what might take you hours of work.

The best agents are professionals who take pride in keeping abreast of all the fast-breaking developments in the frenetic travel industry. They'll gladly give you tips on the most cost-effective transportation and lodgings, visa requirements, currency regulations, and travel advisories. (The U.S. Department of State issues travel advisories for countries and areas where unrest may threaten tourism, and your travel agent should be on their mailing list.)

In general, then, travel agents provide very valuable services to you, at no cost.

But you must remember that travel agents *work for you*, that you are the customer. No good travel agent should attempt to pressure you into taking a cruise, or a flight, or a hotel room, that is too high for your budget, just so the agent can pocket a bigger commission. And you must not let this happen. You can be in complete control of the situation. Without you, the travel agent earns nothing. You must *use* the services provided by the travel agent to get what *you* want.

If you get poor service from a travel agent, you can write to the Consumer Affairs Department of the American Society of Travel Agents (ASTA), P.O. Box 23922, Washington, DC 20006 for satisfaction. All reputable travel agencies are members of ASTA.

At the same time, keep in mind that a travel agent does live by commissions. If an agent frequently spends a lot of time with customers but they buy nothing, that agent won't stay in business very long. You needn't feel that you must buy something every time you visit an agency. In fact, you *shouldn't* feel that way, and good agents will not make you feel that way. They want good, long-term relationships with customers, because that's the Point of Mutual Advantage. You both benefit wonderfully from a good, long-term relationship. You provide the agency with business, and the agency assures you of expert advice, extra consideration, and service above and beyond the call of duty.

You'll know a good travel agent when you meet one. A good agent will be familiar with your proposed destination (if not, you will probably be directed to another agent, who does know). A good agent will use computerized data links to provide you with up-to-the-minute information wherever possible. You can also expect to receive many small courtesies and time-saving services such as delivery of tickets, help in completion of official forms, and personal advice. An example of this helpfulness: When you fly to Mexico, an agent should obtain the required Mexican Tourist Card for you along with your air ticket. You give the agent your passport number, or a copy of your birth certificate or voter registration card, and the work will all be done before you even get to the airport.

Sometimes it's better to make arrangements yourself, however. Agents may not be familiar with the very lowest-fare airlines, inns, pensions, etc. Even if they are, it still may be wise to make the arrangements yourself. The reasons for this are purely economic. For instance, an agent will sometimes write your ticket on a very inexpensive flight if you are a good customer, even though the agency is actually *losing money* to do so (the cost of preparing the average airline ticket, in terms of agent's time and office overhead, is about $20; a commission on a very inexpensive air ticket may be only $10 or $15). You should not ask them to do this too often. It is strictly a favor. If an agent seems reluctant to spend a half hour searching for an extremely low fare, this is why: for the agent, it's definitely a losing proposition.

So if your agent can't afford to find out about the very cheapest flights and other services, it's up to you to Look Beyond the Obvious, to use alternative information sources, to take control of the situation and discover the bargain that you know exists. Later chapters in this book will give you guidance on just how to go about it.

Pay-As-You-Go Travel Agents

A travel agent's normal commission from an airline, tour operator, hotel, or cruise line, varies from about 8% to 15% or more, depending on the circumstances, and so if an agent sells you an airline ticket for $200, the agency keeps about $20 and sends $180 to the airline.

This system works fine as long as airline tickets cost $200 or more. For expensive first-class tickets costing upwards of $4,000, it works wonderfully, because the more expensive fares pay bigger commissions ($400) for the same work, or for even less work. It's no wonder travel agents prefer big spenders.

The problem arises when many travelers are flying on discount airline tickets, as is the case today, when 85% to 90% of all passengers use discount fares of one sort or another. Not only do the lower discount fares pay lower commissions, but the agent must do much more work to get them. Restrictions abound, and so the agent must spend lots of time rummaging through computer databanks looking for a cheap fare that applies in your case. At the end of it all, if the agent is really successful in finding the lowest fare, the reward for all of this hard, skillful work will be a pitifully low commission; and the harder and more skillfully an agent works, the lower the commission!

In response to the tidal wave of cheap fares which yield very low commissions, travel agents have begun to change the way they do business. In short, many agents now charge for what they used to give you for free. But this may be to your advantage. It's called "fee-based pricing," and it works like this: you go to a travel agent, ask for advice about where to go on vacation, you buy a ticket, later you change your flight dates, and finally you decide you can't go after all, so you cancel the ticket. Then a bill arrives in the mail from your travel agent. You owe the agent $35, even though you're not going anywhere.

In agencies which use this system, the customer pays for each service used, and the fee is the same no matter what the price of the ticket. For instance, that bill for $35 breaks down like this: $25 for consultation on a good vacation destination, $5 for rewriting the ticket when you change your flight dates, and $5 for cancelling the ticket. Under fee-based pricing, the agent will be paid for time and effort no matter what you decide. Under the old system, if you cancel your ticket at any time, the agent receives nothing whatsoever for all of that work.

A fee-based agent is happy to help you, and to spend as much time as necessary, even if you're looking for the lowest of low fares, because compensation is no longer based on commissions.

Is this good or bad for you? Mostly good.

First of all, you often get your tickets at a discount right in the beginning, as the agency might not skim off a commission; so a $200 ticket would be sold to you for $180. If you're decisive and know what you want without asking for the agent's advice, you may only have to pay $10 for the writing of the ticket. If you make your own reservation, the fee may drop to $5. You save $10 or $15. And if you need the agent's help in finding a low fare, you know the agent will work hard to find you the lowest one. You save again.

The fee-based pricing system works to the disadvantage of those who want lots of advice on where to go, where to stay, and how to get there. It also is disadvantageous to those who change their minds a lot.

So far, few travel agencies have adopted fee-based pricing completely. More often, an agency will adopt a hybrid plan. For instance, there are agencies that charge $2 to make a reservation on a promotional-fare ticket, $2 to cancel a ticket, $2 to reissue a ticket, and $25 per hour for advice and help (though the first ten minutes of help are free). Ticket prices are standard, with the agent keeping the commission. The agent charges fees to customers who only use the agency occasionally, or to customers who demand lots of services and buy only low-priced tickets, but waives the fees for good, steady, regular customers, or for customers buying high-priced tickets that will generate large commissions.

Don't be afraid of fee-based pricing. If a good agent can save you $100 on a deep-discount ticket, it's worth it to pay $25 for the help.

There are other ways in which a good travel agent who wants your business can help you to save money. See Chapter 7 under "How to Get the Most Out of a Travel Agent" for precise details.

THE MOST ACCURATE FREE INFORMATION OF ALL

About the best all-around source of travel information is the same as it's been for centuries past: *other travelers*. Everyone wants to talk about a recent trip or travel experience. You can approach a total stranger, ask about a certain route, city, or difficult border crossing, and you'll get the stranger's total life story, for free. The trick is not to depend on any one bit of information. Ask numerous other travelers until you have confirmed the data you first received.

Don't leave this source of information unexploited; don't leave meetings with other travelers to chance. Seek out people with fresh experience of the place: ask travel agents, and friends, and local cultural societies to put you in touch with someone who has recently returned. Remember, everyone wants to talk about a trip. You're doing a favor (to them and to yourself) by listening.

USE YOUR TELEPHONE!

In the realm of low-cost information, the telephone is tops. And you can make most of your important calls absolutely free.

The travel industry's lifeline is the telephone, and so almost every big company has toll-free lines. You can get a listing of all these toll-free lines at once by ordering a copy of the *AT&T Toll-Free 800 Consumer Directory* or the *AT&T Toll-Free 800 Business Directory*, 500-page phone books filled with nothing but toll-free numbers. They have both white pages and yellow pages sections, so you can search for an information source (tour operator, airline, cruise line, travel agency, discount ticket broker, etc.) by name or by category. Here are some of the categories useful to travelers:

air ambulance service
automobile rental and leasing
automobile transporting and driveaway service
banks
barter service
boat rental and charter
bus lines
credit cards
cruise lines
government offices and agencies—
    federal and state
health insurance
hotels, motels, and resorts
luggage
magazines
maps and charts
newsletters
newspapers
passports and visas
photography
railways
recreational vehicles
ride sharing
steamship agents
telegrams
tour operators
tourist bureaus
travel agencies
travel assistance organizations
yachts

You can order the Consumer Directory ($9.95) or the Business Directory ($14.95), or both, by calling toll free 800/426-8686, extension 222. A postage, handling, and tax charge of a few dollars will be added to the cost of the books.

Another useful phone book to have is *Calling On North America,* "the complete source book of business and leisure travel information," published by Rand McNally. This large-format, 100-page glossy book includes the attractive, well-known Rand McNally maps of North America, plus a good deal of travel information broken down by region and state or province. Names, addresses, and telephone numbers of the major sights and attractions in each U.S. state and Canadian province are included, saving you the expense of calling long distance for directory assistance. Want to know the phone number of the Fort Laramie National Historic Site in Wyoming? It's here. What about the Canton/Stark County Convention and Visitors Bureau in Canton, Ohio? That's here, too. The book is published as a joint public relations effort among American Telephone & Telegraph Company, the American Society of Travel Agents, and the National Tour Association, and is often given away for free as a promotional "gift." Call toll free 800/225-5288, extension 12, for information on getting your copy.

An even cheaper source of toll-free information is the *Toll-Free Travel/Vacation Phone Directory,* published by Celebrity Publishing, 185 Route 17, Mahwah, NJ 07430 (tel. 201/529-4339). At $6.95 + $1 postage, it gives you almost 400 pages of travel-related information sources in a "Yellow Pages" directory format.

But even if you must pay for some toll calls, the information will still come to you at a very low real cost. Look at it this way: every other source of information—guidebooks, free travel folders, advice from friends, even queries by mail—is one-way (they give you data, and you pick out what you want), or more or less out of date, or both. With the telephone, you can go instantly to the prime source of the information, and you can pump that source of information in detail; furthermore, you can request action. "Send me some brochures," "Make my reservation," "Let me know when the date is set," and *you can hold someone responsible*: "I spoke with Mr. Quiensabé on March 3, and he said the price was $79"; "Mrs. Noncomprendo, of your office, told me the festival had been cancelled."

Obviously, you don't want to use the phone when there is a cheaper way of obtaining the information; one wouldn't call London to ask about the *QE2*'s cruise schedule when any local travel agent would have it. But you can call the U.S. Department of State Citizens' Emergency Center (tel. 202/647-5225) and ask if there has been a Travel Advisory issued for this or that country, and get an official opinion on the safety and comfort, and advisability, of travel to any disturbed area. No more fretting over ominous newspaper and radio reports; you'll *know*. Or you can call that little hotel in Paris, tell them you've heard rumors that everything there is booked solid for next week, and ask if they have a room: "How much? Is that the only one? Is there anything else nearby that you know of? Would you tell them I'll mail a deposit? What's the weather like? How many francs to the dollar these days? My name is Tom, I'll see you in a week."

You must take the time to get the information and to absorb it. . . . Knowing in detail about weather, high and low seasons, and local holidays can directly affect your travel budget.

All this would cost about $4. To call London is even cheaper. The alternative is to fret, and worry, and send letters (at 44¢ a shot), and arrive after a long flight in Paris with no information on the room situation and less than 12 hours in which to locate one in your price range. Once you're on the ground, you can take care of everything locally. But for planning, nothing beats the telephone.

Please, please note that I recommend using the telephone this way only when calling from the United States and Canada. In most of the world, telephone charges are still absurdly high for long-distance or international calls. A three-minute call from Detroit to Athens might cost $4; the same call dialed from Athens to Detroit might cost $40 or more. For full information on using telephones in foreign countries, see Chapter 13 under "Turning Mountains into Molehills."

TIMETABLES AND NEWSLETTERS

It takes training and experience to become a competent travel agent, someone who can dip into the complex airline reservation systems and find the best fare for a flight at the right time. But you can improve your chances of dealing successfully with a travel agent if you know something about the various schedules that a travel agent uses. Also useful are the many travel newsletters.

Good Old-Fashioned Timetables

Though they seem obsolescent in this computer age, the familiar timetable, a thick book of schedules for bus, rail, or air transport, is still a supremely useful traveler's tool. Some of the information in a printed timetable will undoubtedly be out of date by the time you read it, but most of it will be accurate, and the timetable will give you a good sense of frequency of flights, convenience of routes, and complexity of ticket restrictions.

RAILWAY TIMETABLES: Perhaps the most familiar and useful railway timetables are the ones published by Thomas Cook in London. The timetable for Europe is called the *Thomas Cook Continental Timetable*; for the rest of the world, you want the *Thomas Cook Overseas Timetable*. They are available for less than $20 apiece from Forsyth Travel Library, 9154 West 57th Street, P.O. Box 2975, Shawnee Mission, KS 66201-1375 (tel. 913/384-0496, or toll free 800/367-7984).

A railway timetable often used by travel agents is the *Official Railway Guide to North American Travel*, published by International Thomson Transport Press, 424 West 33rd Street, New York, NY 10001 (tel. 212/714-3100). The "passenger edition" (you don't want the "freight edition"!) costs $32 for a single copy, $54 for a one-year subscription. Send your request to the attention of the Circulation Manager.

BUS TIMETABLES: The "bible" of the bus business is *Russell's Official National Motor Coach Guide*, covering the United States and Canada, published by Russell's Guides, Inc., P.O. Box 278, Cedar Rapids, IA 52406 (tel. 319/364-6138); Russell's offices are at 834 Third Avenue, S.E., Cedar Rapids, IA 53403. The timetable is published monthly. A single issue costs $7.60 plus 50¢ postage and handling; a one-year subscription costs $63.20.

AIRLINE TIMETABLES: Besides the computer reservation systems, many travel agents use the *Official Airline Guides*. You can consult the OAG at your travel agent's, or you can order the pocket edition, considerably smaller and more compact than the bulky, phone book-size regular edition. A one-year subscription to the *OAG North American Pocket Flight Guide* costs $41 plus postage (which can vary from $3 to $10, depending upon how fast you want each month's issue delivered). The timetable is published by Official Airline Guides, 2000 Clearwater Drive, Oak Brook, IL 60521 (tel. toll free 800/323-3537; in IL 800/942-1888, extension 8572).

Travel Newsletters

Newsletters are an excellent way to get various sorts of travel information to the public quickly, while the information is still fresh and useful. A newsletter can be written and compiled faster, printed faster, and mailed faster than a guidebook or timetable, which makes a newsletter the perfect vehicle for conveying the most changeable data such as fares, special offers, and schedules.

Other articles in newsletters may deal with subjects of importance to the serious traveler, such as strategies for dealing with travel agents or how to avoid telephone surcharges in foreign hotels. These topics are useful, and they serve to educate their readers, but the information could just as well be published in a book or article.

Newsletters tend to be expensive compared to guidebooks. Considering that you can buy a guide book for less than $20 that is virtually an encyclopedia of facts to a given travel destination, a newsletter's yearly 50- or 60-odd pages of information might cost twice as much. In newsletters, it's freshness and pertinence that count. If you subscribe to a newsletter, and find that only a fraction of the information is of interest to you, then reassess your needs, and perhaps cancel the newsletter.

Here are several of the best-known and respected travel newsletters:

• *Consumer Reports TRAVEL LETTER* is perhaps the most highly-respected newsletter of all because of its reputation for unbiased, factual reporting in the tradition of *Consumer Reports* magazine. A one-year subscription costs $37; order from the Subscription Director, Consumer Reports Travel Letter, P.O. Box 53629, Boulder, CO 80322-3629 (tel. 303/447-9330, or toll free 800/525-0643). Each issue contains valuable information on topics of interest to frequent travelers, such as what to do in case of flight delays, the rights of smokers and non-smokers, and how to choose the best travel club. Reports on popular travel destinations (Rome, Budapest, Acapulco) are thorough, but even a year's subscription might not yield any destinations of interest to you. This information is perhaps better gotten from a guidebook. Still, this newsletter is one of the best ways to keep in touch with rapid changes in the travel industry.

• *Travel Smart* has been around for a while, and has been well regarded all of that time. Besides late-breaking news on opportunities and things to beware in air travel, car rental, lodging, and cruises, it offers subscribers' deals on numerous travel expenses. In effect, the newsletter acts as your broker, using its mailing list as bait in order to obtain discounts for you from travel suppliers. This is an excellent way to keep up on what's hot in the travel industry. A one-year subscription costs $37, but an introductory offer may lower the price of your first year to $29. Order it from Travel Smart/Joy of Travel, Dobbs Ferry, NY 10522 (tel. 914/693-8300).

• *Arthur Frommer's Travel Letter* concentrates on locating discount and last-minute travel deals for its subscribers rather than on advice and caveats. Arthur Frommer, who writes the newsletter, is the famous travel writer whose book *Europe on $5 a Day* revolutionized travel to Europe, and who also founded the famous series of travel guides which includes the book you are reading at this very moment. Mr. Frommer negotiates special deals with travel service suppliers such as airlines, car rental companies, cruise lines, and tour operators, and then offers these deals to newsletter subscribers. In effect, he becomes a sort of consolidator (see Chapter 7), and his readers save lots of money. A one-year subscription costs $19, and is available from Arthur Frommer's Travel Letter, 10076 Boca Entrada Blvd., P.O. Box 3007, Boca Raton, FL 33431-0907 (tel. toll free 800/231-2310; in FL 800/433-5565).

● *Best Fares Discount Bulletin* is a monthly newsletter, available from Best Fares, P.O. Box 171212, Arlington, TX 76003 (tel. 817/261-6114), compiled by researchers who pore through the airline reservation systems looking for unusually low fares or special deals. The newsletter is a goldmine for anyone fascinated by the intricacies of the airfare system. It can save you hundreds of dollars on a single fare, should your travel plans match up to one of these special bargain fares, which is perhaps why it costs so much ($68 for a one-year subscription).

TRAVEL DATABASES AND TELEVISION

The electronic revolution in our society is especially well designed to serve the travel industry. Computer databases let anyone with a personal computer probe into airline reservation systems and call up the latest travel advisories on areas to avoid because of political unrest or epidemic outbreak. Travel videos allow prospective travelers to see and hear a hotel, restaurant, cruise ship, or travel destination in their own living rooms before they commit themselves to the big expense of an actual journey. And television marketing brings a wealth of travel products—including last-minute bargains—right into our homes.

Databases and Information Utilities

By signing up with an information utility such as CompuServe, The Source, GEnie Online, Delphi, etc., you can get up-to-the-minute information on visas, health requirements, hotels, car rentals, and airline schedules and fares. You can even make your own reservations for these things, and arrange for tickets and vouchers to be delivered to you. In effect, you can become your own travel agent.

Using the databases takes some skill and experience, but use is getting easier all the time, and the rewards of learning database use are certainly substantial. And the way it looks, we'll all have to learn to use databases sooner or later, in any case.

Costs for using a database can be substantial, however. The charges include subscription to the information utility (anywhere from free of charge to $40 or $50), "online usage" (the amount of time you are connected to the information utility's computers), and surcharges for use of some of the services. You have to be careful that using the database to find a cheap flight doesn't eat up all of the savings garnered from that cheap flight! But the more familiar you become with the databases, the faster (and cheaper) your searches will become. And some of the best and most useful services of a particular information utility cost nothing extra.

Anyone with a personal computer and a modem (a computer's "telephone") has heard of CompuServe, 5000 Arlington Centre Blvd., P.O. Box 20212, Columbus, OH 43220 (tel. toll free 800/848-8199), the information utility with hundreds of databases to choose from. It's the largest and most popular of the information utilities. Here are some of its travel-related offerings:

● *ABC Worldwide Hotel Guide* has descriptions and prices for over 30,000 hotels and other lodging places in many parts of the world.

● *Eaasy Sabre* is a simplified version of American Airlines' reservation system database. Besides all American Airlines' flights, the database includes information on flights by 650 other airlines throughout the world, as well as data on 13,000 hotels and 25 car rental agencies.

● *Official Airline Guides Electronic Edition* gives you all of the information in the thick printed books, but it's more accurate because the database can be updated daily.

● *State Department Worldwide Travel Advisory* is a service of the U.S. Department of State, advising travelers of dangers in various parts of the world. The dangers may range from irritating official red tape to outright revolution, but, in any case, travelers should know about them.

● *Travel Forums* is a service whereby travelers exchange information, tips, and experiences with one another. If you have a question about travel or a particular destination, you can post it on this electronic "bulletin board," and, in some cases, receive an answer in a matter of hours.

● *Travelshopper* is a service of Trans World Airlines. It lets you make reservations and arrange tickets on TWA and 750 other airlines, world wide. You can pick up your tickets from your local travel agent, or at the airport, or have them mailed to you. Hotel and car rental reservations may be made as well.

● *Visa Advisors* is a Washington, DC, company that arranges passports and visas for prospective travelers. They list visa and health requirements in the database.

Information utilities other than CompuServe offer some of these same services, or similar ones. Contact Delphi, 3 Blackstone St., Cambridge, MA 02139 (tel. toll free 800/544-4005); GEnie Online Services, 401 North Washington St., Rockville, MD 20850 (tel. toll free 800/638-9636); and The Source, 1616 Anderson Road, McLean, VA 22102 (tel. toll free 800/336-3366).

Travel Television

Cable television has just barely begun the revolution it will bring in delivering information to our homes. In the future, it may be that no one will visit a travel agency at all. Instead, the travel agency will be available right at your television set, at any time of the day or night.

Several cable television companies have started off in that direction. There's the Shoppers Travel Network's "VTV" show, produced by TV Travel Marketing, and shown in Florida. Viewers can watch the show for free, but if they want to take advantage of all the special vacation deals available to club members, they must pay an annual membership fee. A quarterly newsletter also keeps club members informed, and a toll-free telephone hotline is available for checking last-minute availability of trips.

More ambitious and widespread at this writing is The Travel Channel, founded by a division of the company which owns Trans World Airlines. The Travel Channel is a cable television channel broadcasting nothing but travel information and commercials, 24 hours a day. About half of program time is devoted to "editorial" content such as news, opinions, and fast-breaking developments. The other half of the time is commercial, providing advertisements and information on various travel companies, products and services. Anyone can watch as long as The Travel Channel is available on their local cable TV service, but to take advantage of the various offers and opportunities seen on the channel, a viewer must be a member of The Travel Channel Club. Membership costs $49.95 a year, and includes a newsletter, discount card, books of discount coupons, and a chance at winning free flights in a TWA sweepstakes. For information, contact the club at 2250 Butler Pike, Plymouth Meeting, PA 19462.

4

Some Guidebooks Are Worth It, But . . .

Any trip may cost hundreds or even thousands of dollars. On the average, a guidebook accounts for 1% or less of this cost. Yet having the right guidebook can double the pleasure you get for your money, and can cut the actual dollar costs of the journey. It is crucial to have the right guidebook. But it takes careful consideration to make sure you choose the right one. In the pages that follow, I'll help you in your choice. To do this, I've drawn on years of experience and thousands of discussions with other travelers.

WHO WRITES THESE GUIDEBOOKS, ANYWAY?

My adventures as a travel writer have taught me a lot about how guidebooks are written, about which ones are worth the money and which ones are not. Approach the "Travel" section in any bookstore and you'll see dozens, perhaps hundreds of titles. Some are parts of a series of guides; some are independent;

some cover entire continents; others concentrate on one city, or even on a single topic within that city. To understand which guidebook is best for you, it's necessary to understand how guidebooks came into being, and what makes a good guidebook.

Guidebooks have been around for a very long time. Imperial Roman ambassadors and messengers used to carry a *viaticum* ("Take-Me-Along"). This was a collection of documents which described the route, mentioned interesting sights along the way, recommended the better hostelries, warned of dangers, and dealt with such mundane matters as cashing letters of credit and getting medical advice. It's not that they were inexperienced or timid travelers. Rather, the *viaticum* provided them with important, useful information all in one place.

Through the centuries, travelers returning from exotic lands would write their memoirs or edit their travel diaries and publish the results. These travelogues were useful to the next traveler, as well as entertaining to "armchair travelers."

Today, many of the best guidebooks are made the same way: an observant traveler who is also a good writer goes out in search of fulfilling travel experiences, and describes them in detail for his or her readers. In an age of big organizations and bureaucracies, it's refreshing to know that some people are still doing their jobs the good old way: hitting the road with notebook in hand to observe in person, and to pass on important information to those who will come after.

Alas, this sort of one-author guidebook is becoming scarce as the world gets more hectic, more complicated, and more expensive. Other ways of collecting data have been created, and these ways have advantages and disadvantages.

Books written by committee are often found on bookstore shelves. Instead of one travel writer, a number of writers collaborate to prepare a guide to a large area. Each may take a geographic area, in which case the book will have the character of a mini-collection of one-author books. What the book may lack is the unifying overview that a single author can give: a restaurant in Los Angeles can't truly be judged "as good as" a restaurant in New York, because different people have investigated them.

Some guides attempt to solve this problem by having a single set of criteria—a common checklist against which any establishment or travel experience can be measured. Hotels are ranked, and awarded "stars," on the basis of such things as number of elevators, restaurant seating capacity, multilingual staff, or elaborateness of plumbing. Unfortunately, there is little room in such listings for intangibles—ambience, convenience, friendliness, security, propriety—which a single travel writer would have taken into account in a recommendation.

A single travel writer, a committee of travel writers, an army of checklist-bearing data-collectors—there is yet another way guidebooks are put together. This method might be called "stringers and editors." "Stringers," part-time help who live in tourist destinations, send data to an editor in a central office, and the

---

Having the right guidebook can double the pleasure you get for your money, and can cut your actual dollar costs.

---

editor puts it together in a book. Many books are written by this method, and the advantages are obvious: no big travel expenses sending a writer to the destination, perhaps to stay for months; fresh data from stringers who know the territory because they live there; lower overhead through utilization of part-time help (the stringers) and only one full-time person (the editor).

The disadvantages of "stringers and editors" are not quite so apparent, but are extremely important. First, the stringers are not tourists; they live there, and they may find it difficult to see the place through a tourist's eyes. In their daily lives, they may not encounter the many puzzling situations in which a stranger would find him or herself. Also, for stringers the data collection is only a part-time job, which they may or may not think to be important. The editor will probably never know if a stringer sends in data of mediocre quality. The editor may never have been to the place in question, and may inadvertently produce useless recommendations. For instance, the advice to "call for reservations" at a busy restaurant may be useless in a Third World city where the telephones hardly ever work; or "the taxi fare is $3" will do you little good in a resort with a notorious shortage of cabs. The information given is not wrong, it's just useless. Why pay for it? A travel writer on-the-spot would have recommended that you drop by the restaurant the day before to make your reservation, that you take a bus (or reserve your taxi in advance) in that cab-short resort.

In their quest for lower expenses and higher profits, some publishing companies have pushed credibility to the limit. You can pay good money these days for guidebooks that are mostly "boilerplate," rambling prose touching on this or that aspect of the destination involved, more or less entertaining stuff, but hardly what you'd call useful or significant. Boilerplate is timeless, it rarely goes out of date, and it doesn't need to be revised, so it's cheap. Some background information is helpful, but too much is a cost-cutting caper, a way of selling cheap goods expensively.

Other ways in which some publishers lower expenses and raise profits: they don't pay stringers at all, just an editor who garners information of dubious freshness and importance from other published materials—mostly the free tourist-office stuff you can send away for—adds a few maps and some filler copy, and sells the resultant book at a premium price. You don't know you've bought a useless commodity until you're well along in your trip, and by then it's too late.

SECRETS OF FINDING THE BEST GUIDEBOOK

It's not difficult to find the best guidebook, but you must be careful. Abandon all of your preconceived ideas about guidebooks—size, price, series, publishing company, reputation—and enter the bookstore with a fresh outlook and an open mind. Follow the guidelines given below. Trust yourself to *know* the right one when you see it. And remember, the right guidebook can double the success, yet lower the cost, of any trip you take.

Do You Truly Know What You're Looking For?

Guides are written to appeal to specific segments of the traveling public, so the first thing you must do is to locate those guides that fit your trip. Are you going on a two-week charter vacation, with your transportation and accommodations already arranged and paid for? Then look for a series of pocket guides that have details on sightseeing, activities, and the local cuisine. Are you off on a two-month, low-budget vagabond tour? The guide for you is the one chock full of budget travel tips, inexpensive lodging recommendations, and directions to cheap eateries.

How Can You Tell If It's Really "Up-to-Date"?

Now that you've narrowed the field down to the guides that fit your trip, turn to the back of the title page and look for the copyright date. Ignore the dates on the cover. By law, the copyright date is supposed to be that of the year of publication, or up to one month earlier (that is, a book published in December 1990 can bear the words "Copyright © 1991"). In recent years, however, some guidebook publishers have tried to hide or disguise the copyright date; or they have blatantly ignored the law, and have published guides in late summer and early autumn with *next year's* copyright dates. This is unfair, but it should reinforce in your mind the thought that *any guidebook is at least nine months old by the time you buy it,* even if it's "revised annually." Much of the information may be several years old; it is prohibitively expensive to re-collect, re-edit, reprint, and distribute books every few months, and so the book will be on sale for at least a year after it appears, perhaps more.

Is this a rip-off? Not at all. You could have fresh data every three months, but you'd have to be willing to pay hundreds of dollars for it rather than $15 or $20. All guidebooks suffer from this time lag. Your job is to choose the one that gives you the freshest and most plenteous data for your particular kind of trip, all for the lowest price.

What Information Is Actually Useful?

Now it's time to look inside. How much "boiler-plate" is there? A hundred, two hundred pages of background filler? Do you want it? You'll have to pay for it, and then you'll have to carry it!

What about the highly perishable information:

prices, timetables, individual recommendations for lodgings and restaurants. There are none, or very few? This perishable information is the most difficult and expensive to keep up to date, and if a guide has little of it, it may not be of much use to you. It's fine to blather on in glowing tones about a charming restaurant or cozy country inn, but if the guide gives you no idea of the cost, or precise directions on how to find it, what good is it? Actual prices, rather than headings such as "Inexpensive" or "Moderate," are the best, even if inflation has by now left them behind (as it usually has). One quickly learns to compensate by raising the price a certain percentage. But if the charming young couple who run that lovely inn are already charging a "moderate" $200 a night, you probably know what you need to know. Maybe the price is $225 now, maybe it's not. It's hardly "moderate."

In recommending an establishment, does the guide tell you where it is, with driving or walking directions rather than just a mailing address? If there's a paragraph raving about a good restaurant on Ibn Gevirol Street in Tel Aviv, does it give more than the street number? Ibn Gevirol Street is miles and miles long! What about hours of operation, telephone numbers, post office box numbers? It's difficult to say how much of this detailed information you will actually need. But if it's not there in the first place, it certainly won't be there when you need it. You can always find out such little facts somewhere else, but then why pay a guidebook publishing company for work you'll end up doing yourself? Guidebooks should *guide,* telling you just about everything you would want—or, more important, *need*—to know.

Too Many Lists?

Look closely at the book's organization. Are there bare lists of places, or outline-type categorical lists with essential data? These are signs of the clipboard mentality, and out on the road they are very hard to use. A list of every modern hotel in town, with phone number, minimum double room price, and symbols denoting the various facilities? How will you tell the difference from one to the other, except for price and whether or not it has a swimming pool? And those little symbols will drive you crazy! Is there an entire paragraph or page listing all the golf courses, or tennis courts, or museums in the city or country? With a bare list, how will you ever find out which bus to take, or when they're open, or what they charge, or what makes them worthwhile? Remember, editors *love* lists like this: they're simple to compile at a desk miles from the travel scene, they make logical sense, they look impressive—but in fact they're very difficult for the traveler on the spot to use, or even worse, they're entirely useless.

What about finding things quickly? Does the book's structure make sense to you? After a minute or two, can you turn to the information you desire quickly, without much trouble? The book's structure should fit the traveler's actual, practical, on-the-spot needs, and not some editorial requirement or mechanistic system.

How Good Is the Writing?

Now for the final acid test: *Read*. Pick a spot that interests you, something that deals with actual situations you will encounter in daily life—visiting a sight, having a meal, finding a hotel, booking transportation. It should seem as though you're asking a trusted friend who's been there to explain what it's actually like. Soon you will come across the telltale hints and suggestions that let you know the writer has been there and has been through it: "When touring in Burma I strongly advise that you wear sandals rather than shoes—simply because you take them off and put them on so often when visiting temples and pagodas" (Tony Wheeler, in *Burma—A Travel Survival Kit*, Lonely Planet). No editor sitting at a desk, no stringer who had last visited the temples and pagodas years ago, would have thought to suggest such a practical matter. Things that are giveaways to a bad book: lack of prices, phone numbers, and *directions*. I was astounded to read in one guidebook a description of a lovely park, excellent for a picnic, "on the outskirts of Mexico City"! Hundreds of square miles of urban sprawl, millions and millions of people, and the only direction to this lovely park is that it's "on the outskirts"? How much priceless travel time will you have to spend to find it? How much is such a recommendation worth?

It is not difficult to find the best guidebook, but you must be careful.

It isn't just the burgeoning complexity of the world that has made such detailed information crucial. Indeed, it is more important now than ever before to have exact, complete, up-to-date data. But good guidebooks have always given detailed information and hints drawn from on-the-spot observation. In 1907 the venerable Karl Baedeker was advising travelers, in his *Handbook for Travellers: SWITZERLAND* (22nd edition), that "at the second-class inns the average charges are: bedroom 1½–2 francs, breakfast 1–1¼ francs, table d'hôte 2–3 francs, service discretionary, and no charge for 'bougies' " (candles). And another helpful tip: "If a prolonged stay is made at a hotel the bill should be asked for every three or four days, in order that errors, whether accidental or designed, may more easily be detected."

What's So Special about Frommer Guidebooks?

You might think that I, as a writer of Frommer guidebooks, must be prejudiced in favor of our company's books. That's true, I am—and here's why:

Our office is a congenial place where a small crew of travel-mad people edit manuscripts, read letters from travelers who have used our guides, and keep abreast of fast-breaking developments in the travel industry. Our efforts are personal, our contacts are personal, and our approach to travel writing is personal. The guides are filled with the worldly-wise opinions of our writers, who are beholden to no airline or hotel chain, no restaurant or national tourism ministry.

Our books are filled with precise, on-the-spot descriptions of hotels, restaurants, and tourist facilities, with exact prices, timetables, telephone numbers, addresses, and enough background to convey the "mood" of each establishment.

In the years I have worked for Frommer, I've gotten to know thousands of our readers. Many a "letter to the author" has resulted in a lively correspondence that is informative for both parties. From this experience, I have learned that our readers are of all ages, but always young-at-heart and ready for adventure. Most have money to spend, but are very careful to get value-for-money when they spend it. Many are experienced travelers and repeat buyers of our books, and quite a few buy successive editions of a particular guide for successive trips to the same destination. These readers tend to look upon a current guidebook as a cost-effective information resource, not as a guide through perilous unknown waters.

It is extremely important to us to give our readers a value-for-money product, because our success depends on it. We are not an auto club that charges annual dues, we do not accept advertisements, we do not sell stickers or signs that say "Recommended in Our Guidebook." We exist because masses of readers find our guides to be of value—and our readership is the most demanding and aware.

This is not to say that Frommer guidebooks are the only ones that will fit your needs. There are many excellent guides on the market. But there are many, many others that are of dubious value: it's simple to fill a book up with words, but quite another thing to create a book which truly *guides*. A true guide must anticipate questions and problems, and then stand ready to solve them with the right information in the right place. A true guide is beholden only to its readers, for they are the ones who keep it alive.

How Much Is Too Expensive?

Once you've narrowed your choice down to one or two guidebooks, look at the prices. Price is important only in relation to what's inside the book. The book looks great, and it costs only $15? That's an incredible bargain! If it looks great and it costs $20, or even more, it's probably still a bargain. If you've found the precise book that fits your needs, buy it regardless of price. When you're about to spend hundreds or thousands of dollars on a trip, don't quibble about a few dollars. The right guidebook can almost make or break your trip.

If your choice comes down to several books, buy the less expensive one, the sturdiest one, or by weight and size, or by whether or not the book includes photographs. Don't buy more than you need, don't buy less than you need. Buy what fits.

If it seems as though you must buy two, or even

three, guidebooks in order to satisfy all of your interests, do it. Remember that what you spend on good information is a bargain and a tiny percentage of your total trip expenses in any case. The right guidebook can save you many times its own cost, out there on the road.

WHAT TO DO IF THEY DON'T HAVE IT

Your local bookstore may not have the precise guide that you want. To find the elusive book, follow the First and Third Laws. Look in the Appendix to this book, where you will find a list of the best travel bookstores, travel outfitters, and mail order services in the country. These places specialize in travel guides, background books, maps, timetables, and other items such as money belts, water purifiers, and currency converters which can help you to make your trip a successful one.

If by any chance you can't find the book you want in one of these stores, look in *Books in Print*, available in any good bookstore or library, find the publisher's name and write or call the publisher directly. Even if the book is technically out of print or otherwise unavailable, the publisher may have a supply of copies in the office, and may be willing to sell you one. This happens. Most people don't know it, because most people don't know how to follow the Four Laws.

5

Countdown: What to Do First of All

There is somewhere you want to travel, some adventure you want to take, right now. You'd love to just pick up and go, get away from it all, lose yourself in an exciting and stimulating experience away from the familiar routine of everyday life.

You can do it! In fact, you can start the adventure *right now* by beginning to savor the anticipation, the excitement of taking off. The best way to do that is to get involved—early—in the planning stages. The sheer *anticipation* of an adventure is almost as exciting as the adventure itself.

So why not start right away? Begin the Countdown to the all-important day of departure by concentrating on the things that can guarantee smooth sailing during your travels. I've described just what these matters are, and how to take care of them according to the Four Laws, in the following pages. Near the end of this chapter are detailed Countdown Lists so you can effortlessly make sure that everything important has been taken care of.

Read on.

THE COUNTDOWN

First of all, review the following topics. Answer the questions. Then use the Countdown Lists for effortless completion of these important matters.

What about My Camera?

I have not heard of any country where film and photographic supplies are cheaper than in the U.S. Kodak is the world leader, and though foreign films may be cheaper than Kodak in a film store abroad, nothing will be cheaper than film bought in the U.S. Buy what you think you'll need. If you have extra, sell it abroad, or bring it home, store it in the refrigerator, and use it later. The price of film only goes up.

Kodak has processing plants in various parts of the world. Good processing is available (but expensive) in the developed countries. Be very careful about processing in developing countries. If you must get film developed in the Third World, get a recommendation from a consulate, local professional photographer, or newspaperman, somebody who *knows*. Don't just ask a photo shopkeeper if he does good work.

As for equipment, it too can be more expensive, even in the country of its origin. Prices these days have less to do with costs of production than with taxes, duties, and market factors. Before you rush off to Japan or Germany or Switzerland to buy camera gear, have current information on prices.

The same goes for duty-free shops, many of which save you very little. (See Chapter 12 for details.)

Speaking of cameras, consider packing a small beanbag in place of your tripod. Unless you are a professional or a very serious amateur, you can get along by positioning your camera atop the beanbag on a wall, table, or car. The beanbag will allow you to frame your picture just right, with the horizon line horizontal as you want it.

PROTECTING YOUR FILM FROM X-RAYS: On the matter of film, you should know that the effects of airport security-check X-ray examinations are cumulative. That is, you may be able to put your film (ASA/ISO 400 or lower/slower) through an X-ray machine in the United States up to five times without damage, but you risk "fogging" the film if it gets X-rayed more often. This includes all undeveloped film, whether unexposed or exposed. In places other than North America, X-ray machines tend to be much stronger, and could cloud your film in even fewer exposures. And the new very fast films with ASA/ISO numbers above 400 (ASA/ISO 1000, 1600, etc.) should never be put through an X-ray machine, not even once, not even in North America.

Security officials in the United States are obligated to inspect your hand baggage personally, rather than with an X-ray, if you so request. You can make it easier for them if you have all of your film together in a clear plastic bag. In fact, you may want to take all the little film cannisters out of their cardboard boxes and plastic tubes, and just put the cannisters themselves in the plastic bag. Inspectors will occasionally demand that you open every box and plastic tube of film. Besides, leaving behind all that unnecessary packaging is a good way to go.

An alternative is to put all of your film in a lead-lined X-ray-resistant bag, on sale at camera shops, and put the whole bag through the X-ray machine. The inspector won't be able to see through the lead, and may ask you to open the bag, so you get a personal inspection anyway. Or, the inspector may ignore the bag, and you're on your way. You can also just put all of the rolls of film in your jacket pockets. This will set off the alarm in the walk-through metal detector, at which point you can show the inspector your film, and thus get a personal inspection automatically.

In some foreign countries, official inspectors may resist your request for a personal inspection in place of an X-ray. Try one of the aforementioned tricks to get around this resistance. In most countries, however, you will have no problem, and a personal inspection will be easy to obtain. Even Switzerland, the longtime holdout where inspectors insisted categorically that every piece of hand luggage, including film and cameras, must go through the X-ray machines, has now relented and allows personal inspections when specifically requested.

Surprising Discount Offers

Perhaps the best money-saving reason for doing your planning well in advance is so that you can take advantage of the many discount offers available only to those who think ahead. Special discounts on airline fares are often applied if you buy your ticket several weeks in advance; the cheapest seats on every plane are often limited in number and you want to be one of the people who gets such a seat. (See Chapter 7.)

Discounts are also available for other modes of transportation—investigate railroad passes like the EurailPass, BritRail Pass, or the Amtrak equivalent (when it's offered); and bus passes like those offering unlimited travel on Greyhound for one, two, or three weeks at a special low price. Similar plans are offered throughout the world, and if you ask about transportation when you write for tourist information or make your travel reservations, you can find out what's current.

Transportation is not the only field for organized discounts. Lodging discount plans are becoming very popular, especially in Europe during the off-season. National tourist offices, airlines, regional associations, or hotel chains may offer coupons good for a night's lodging at participating hotels, and these coupons will be priced far below the normal room price. Why do they do it? Won't they lose money?

The answer is that the region has excess hotel capacity off-season, and a room unsold for a night is a

---

Perhaps the best money-saving reason for doing your planning well in advance is so that you can take advantage of the many discount offers available only to those who think ahead.

---

room that costs money to maintain but has produced no income. So if they require you to buy five or ten coupons, they'll have guaranteed some income for five or ten days for the room. Finland has such a plan: pay $28 per check for "Finncheques," and you get a night's accommodation for each check in any of 158 hotels in 71 cities and towns. Want to go deluxe? Pay another $13 per check and you've got first-class or luxury accommodations.

One such incredible lodging offer was recently made by British Airways: for passengers flying in winter, rooms in central London were sold at $40 single, $60 double, with tax, service, and continental breakfast included! These rooms were in various Grand Metropolitan hotels; they were priced at $150 or more in high season. (See Chapter 9 for more tips on similar bargains.) The point to be made here is that you must know about such things *in advance*.

Besides transportation and accommodation, sight-seeing and nightlife are often heavily discounted. The Netherlands Board of Tourism, 355 Lexington Ave., New York, NY 10017, will sell you a "Holland Culture Card" for $15. With the card, you get free entry to 170 museums and landmarks, special deals on concert and ballet tickets, even a discount on rail travel. But you have to order the card before you leave home.

All these discounts are normal examples of what is available. The gimmicks change with the seasons, and a special deal for last winter may not be offered next winter—you've got to do some research to find what's current, and then you must order in advance.

SOURCES FOR INSIDE INFORMATION: Obviously, the way to keep track of all the latest promotions offered by airlines, car rental companies, tour packagers, etc., is to scan the major travel magazines and newspapers for advertisements. Or you can subscribe to one of the recent crop of travel newsletters described in Chapter 3.

What to Do about Electricity

Try not to carry too many electrical appliances around with you. After having two transformers melted down by power surges in developing countries, I no longer take my electric razor. I take a safety razor.

Hair dryers must be chosen with care. They may sell you one with "European adapters," and 220-volt current capability, but it may not do all it is supposed to do. For Europe, one needs at least three and perhaps four different plugs to cover all bases. And look for one of the new, small, light models.

Current in Canada, the U.S., Mexico, Japan, and most of Central America is 110–120 volts, 50 or 60 cycles, with the flat-prong American-style plugs. In the rest of the world, current is usually 220–240 volts,

50 or 60 cycles, and the plugs can be anything from the monster three-prong-and-pound-of-plastic British "safety plug" to the flimsy Italian two-round-prong ones.

Want to be certain you're prepared? Call or write the Franzus Company, 53 West 23rd St., New York, NY 10011 (tel. 212/463-9393), manufacturers of currency converters and adapter plugs that can be used worldwide. They can provide you with information on the current in virtually any country. Their converters allow you to use both low-wattage and high-wattage (up to 1,650 watts) appliances anywhere in the world. Even if your appliance is dual voltage (110/220), you may need special adapter plugs. Ask them.

Such converters and adapters are often on sale in luggage and hardware stores, electronics shops, and even travel agencies. Buy your converter before you go overseas, as they can be difficult to find, and much more expensive, abroad. You'd do well to have the adapter plugs you need too, although these can often be found in foreign electrical shops.

What If My Stuff Gets Stolen?

Before you assume that your standard homeowner's insurance policy will cover any losses outside the home, check with your insurance agent. Often you must pay an additional sum for outside insurance; also, the policy may stipulate coverage limits on certain objects: jewelry, cash, and furs, for instance.

Even if your own home policy will cover losses while you're traveling you may still want to take out a baggage insurance policy, because (1) the deductible will be less (often as low as $25), and (2) you may not want to claim against your homeowner's policy and thus increase future premiums. Furthermore, a homeowner's policy does not always cover the loss (as against theft) of your baggage. A baggage policy will, although it will probably exclude such items as money, tickets, documents, etc. The cost of such a policy is based on how long you'll be away and how much coverage you want. Remember—you'll need evidence of any loss or theft to make a claim on the insurance policy. (See below for more about travel insurance.)

What about My Pet?

The Air Transport Association has published a brochure on the subject of flying with your pet, or shipping your pet by air. It explains the various federal regulations and airport policies, and includes useful hints: don't let your pet eat or drink for six hours prior to flight time, and don't give it tranquilizers. Write for a copy of the pamphlet to the Air Transport Association, 1709 New York Ave. NW, Washington, DC 20006-5206.

Can I Drink the Water Over There?

In many countries it's advisable not to drink the tap water, but bottled water is available and usually safe to drink. Other safe beverages are those, such as coffee and tea, made with boiled water; canned and bottled beverages that are carbonated; and beer and wine.

However, there are lots of places, particularly off the beaten track, where you will not know whether any of the water is safe or not. There are several things you can do to make it safe to drink and to use for brushing your teeth.

BOILING: The safest and surest way to purify water is to bring it to a vigorous boil, and then let it cool down on its own (don't add any ice, which may have been made from contaminated water). If you drink from a container other than that in which the water has been boiled, make sure the drinking container is clean and uncontaminated; wash it with hot water and soap. Then pour the water from one container to another and back a few times, aerating it, to improve the taste. A pinch of salt might help, as well.

If you can't boil the water, you can drink tap water that is uncomfortably hot to the touch. Let the water run until it is as hot as possible, and then catch some in a clean container and let it cool. This water is not guaranteed, but it is usually safe.

CHEMICAL DISINFECTION: This is a second-best method to boiling. Iodine is more reliable than chlorine bleach. Add five drops of 2% tincture of iodine (on sale in any pharmacy) to each quart or liter of clear water, or 10 drops to the same amount of cloudy water (but first, strain cloudy water through a clean cloth to remove as much suspended matter as possible). Let clear water stand for a half hour, cloudy water for several hours, after treatment before drinking it.

Several companies manufacture water purification tablets (Globaline, Potable-Agua, Coghlan's, etc.) containing tetraglycine hydroperiodide, sold in pharmacies, travel outfitters, and sporting goods stores. These work if you follow the directions on the package.

FILTERS: These are of two types, those using resins impregnated with iodide, and "microstrainers" which have filters so fine that bacteria can't get through. There is no question that these are effective against many germs, but scientific studies have yet to prove their effectiveness across the board.

What Happens If I Get Sick?

Travelers in Europe, the United States and Canada, Australia, New Zealand, and Japan need not worry much about vaccinations and inoculations against disease. But in the rest of the world, generally speaking, you had better look into the matter closely. Malaria, for instance, is on the *increase*—contrary to the popular belief that disease is everywhere being beaten back. Cholera too is rearing its ugly head, and it's spread throughout the world by people traveling in jet planes. In some cases, as with malaria and AIDS, it's right to fear the disease itself; in others, like cholera, you can be pretty sure of not contracting the illness if you take simple hygienic precautions—but border officials may not let you cross from a cholera area if you haven't had an inoculation. No matter how you swear you're free of the disease, they'll ask for documented proof. You may spend a week waiting in line at a clinic of questionable sanitation, with everyone else in town, to get the shot. When cholera breaks out, pandemonium does too. Few people die, some get sick, many are inconvenienced. You want to be none of the above.

Speaking of malaria, the Centers for Disease Control, Atlanta, GA 30333 (tel. 404/452-4046), note that you must take antimalarial pills *well before* you enter a malarial area. The details of preventative medication vary with the area and the strain of the disease. Often the center's recommendations include an easy and painless regimen: you just swallow a 500-milligram tablet of Aralen (chloroquine phosphate) about two weeks before you depart, then another one a week before departure. You continue with one per week during your trip, and for six weeks after you return home. It's simple. But you must begin at least one week *before* you depart.

Other strains of malaria are resistant to chloroquine phosphate, and to protect yourself from these the center suggests you might have to take something like Fansidar, which may have dangerous side-effects. You've got to be sure of what you're doing.

One way to minimize the risk of illness is to know the health hazards to expect, get as much information as you possibly can, and take the necessary precautions before you leave.

Lots of excellent medical advice is available, for free or at low cost. Being well prepared for a trip does not mean just "getting your shots." You must also know about diseases endemic at your destination, and what steps to take to protect yourself. For instance, though malaria is a huge health problem, you can protect yourself best by knowing three things. First, that mosquitos which carry the disease swarm mostly between dusk and dawn. Second, that if you wear clothing that covers most of your skin, and if you stay in well screened areas during the prime mosquito hours, you can protect yourself very well. Third, insect repellent containing DEET (N,N diethylmetatoluamide) is effective in repelling mosquitos.

BOOKS: All of the aforementioned malaria information and similar information on lots of other diseases is included in the best, most reliable, and most convenient source of detailed medical information on world travel, the 160-page book entitled *Health Information for International Travel*. The book is published annually by the U.S. Department of Health and Human Services, Public Health Service, Centers for Disease Control, Atlanta, GA 30333.

This medically precise and somewhat technical volume provides medical experts, travelers, and patients with information on diseases, diagnosis, treatments, and measures for prevention. Of special interest is the chapter called "Specific Recommendations for Vaccination and Prophylaxis." The book is on file in many public libraries and at some travel agencies, or you can get your own copy by contacting the Superintendent of Documents, U.S. Government Printing Office, Washington, DC 20402 (tel. 202/783-3238), or Federal Reprints, P.O. Box 15301, Washington, DC 20003.

Several other books which deal with travelers' health problems are on the market, and any good bookstore should have one. As for inoculations, the *Foreign Travel & Immunization Guide,* by Dr. Hans H. Neumann, is updated periodically. It sells for $12.50 from Medical Economics Books, Oradell, NJ 07649. You can also get a lower-price 24-page pamphlet from the International Health Care Service of the New York Hospital–Cornell Medical Center, Box 210, 525 East 68th St., New York, NY 10021. Send $1 and they'll mail you the pamphlet, which tells you about common travelers' diseases, inoculations, first aid kits, and the like.

Before going to a Third World country, pick up the little yellow booklet called the *International Certificates of Vaccination.* These are handed out by the U.S. Public Health Service, passport agencies, and the Superintendent of Documents, U.S. Government Printing Office, Washington, DC 20402. Find out from a doctor, clinic, or guidebook what inoculations you should have *according to the season* (cholera, for instance, appears only in the warm summer months). It may take weeks or months to get the full course of inoculation. Also, you can get up-to-date information about any country's political/health and related conditions from the State Department Citizens' Emergency Center in Washington (tel. 202/647-5225) between 8:15 a.m. and 5 p.m. Eastern Time, weekdays.

Similar information can be gotten from the government tourist office of your particular destination.

MEDICAL CENTERS: For shots, advice and problem-solving of travel-related medical matters, you can also apply to any of these clinics which specialize in traveler's health:

Boston: Travelers' Clinic, New England Medical Center of Tufts University, 171 Harrison Ave., Boston, MA 02111 (tel. 617/956-5237).

Cleveland: Travelers' Clinic, Division of Geographic Medicine, University Hospital, 2078 Abingdon Rd., Cleveland, OH 44106 (tel. 216/844-3295).

Miami: Institute of Tropical Medicine and Travelers' Clinic, University of Miami School of Medicine, 1550 N.W. 10th Ave., Miami, FL 33125 (tel. 305/947-1722).

New York: International Health Care Service of the New York Hospital–Cornell Medical Center, 525 E. 68th St., Box 210, New York, NY 10021 (tel. 212/472-4284).

San Diego: Travelers' Clinic, UCSD Medical Center, 225 Dickinson St., San Diego, CA 92103 (tel. 619/543-5787).

Seattle: University of Washington Travel and Tropical Medicine Clinic, University Hospital RC-02, 1959 N.E. Pacific St., Seattle, WA 98195 (tel. 206/548-4226).

Toronto: Travel and Inoculation Service, 200 Elizabeth St., Toronto, ON M5G 2CH (tel. 416/595-3670).

Washington, D.C.: Travelers' Medical Service of Washington, 916 19th St. N.W., Washington, DC 20006 (tel. 202/466-8109).

QUARANTINE STATIONS: These offices of the Public Health Service can answer your questions on travelers' health and international health requirements and recommendations:

Chicago: tel. 312/686-2150, 2 a.m. to 8 p.m. Central Time.
Honolulu: tel. 808/541-2552, 6 a.m. to 3 p.m. Hawaii Time.

Los Angeles: tel. 213/215-2365, 8 a.m. to 5 p.m.
   Pacific Time.
Miami: tel. 305/526-2910, 8 a.m. to 5 p.m.
   Eastern Time.
New York: tel. 718/917-1685, 8 a.m. to 10 p.m.
   Eastern Time.
San Francisco: tel. 415/876-2872, 8 a.m. to 4:30
   p.m. Pacific Time.
Seattle: tel. 206/442-4519, 8 a.m. to 5 p.m.
   Pacific Time.

FINDING A DOCTOR ABROAD: When you're overseas, your consulate can usually provide a list of
doctors and dentists who speak English and who are
used to treating travelers. In addition, several services
provide lists of such physicians that you can obtain
before you go.

IAMAT (International Association for Medical Assistance to Travelers) provides its members (suggested
contribution of $10 makes you a member) with a list of
English-speaking doctors abroad, and also includes a
helpful booklet with health care information for travelers. IAMAT is at 736 Center St., Lewiston, NY 14092
(tel. 716/754-4883).

Health Care Abroad and Assist-Card (see below)
can also help you find a doctor while abroad.

Once you find a doctor, how do you tell him what's
wrong with you, or about your medical history? One
way is to buy a Medical DataCard from the Medicom
Pharmacy Service, P.O. Box 91, Town Center Branch,
W. Orange, NJ 07052. The size of a credit card, the
DataCard contains a microfilm "window" which displays a summary of your medical history. Notes on
urgent conditions can be read with the naked eye; the
rest can be read with a doctor's ophthalmoscope. The
card costs about $20; updates of the information (i.e.,
new microfilm) cost about $8.

A similar service is provided by MedicAlert, Turlock, CA 95381. Life membership costs $20, and entitles you to a stainless-steel necklace or wrist band that provides data on allergies or chronic conditions. You also get a wallet card. Your data is maintained in a file accessible to doctors on a special emergency telephone number.

WILL THEY HAVE THE RIGHT MEDICINE? If you take medications regularly, take a supply that will last your trip, and also take a prescription giving the generic names of the drugs, since trade names vary in other countries. In the U.S., few pharmacies are allowed to honor an out-of-state prescription. Abroad, the drugs may not be available, or may have different names. However, if you know the generic names and dosages of the drugs, chances are good that you will be able to replace them if they are lost. The big drug companies are worldwide concerns now, and the widely used drugs are sold everywhere and are familiar to pharmacists. The pharmacist may not have your specific drug, but may have a very similar product that will do in an emergency.

You should also take along an extra pair of eyeglasses (or at the very least copies of your prescription). If you wear contact lenses, either take a pair of eyeglasses or another pair of lenses.

I GOTTA GET OUT OF HERE: You can insure yourself against an expensive medical emergency abroad for very little money by buying some sort of "evacuation" coverage. If your health insurance policy (or Medicare) does not cover you while abroad, you can buy further coverage, or you can arrange to be transported back home as soon as possible.

International SOS Assistance, Philadelphia Executive Offices, 2 Neshaminy Interplex, Trevose, PA

19047 (tel. 215/244-1500), will refer you to a foreign doctor, transport you home, or transport another person (such as a spouse or relative) to where you are, for $15 per week ($2 for each additional day); $45 per month; or $195 per year.

Nationwide/Worldwide Emergency Ambulance Return (NEAR), 1900 North MacArthur Blvd., Suite 210, Oklahoma City, OK 73127, offers a worldwide evacuation service. They'll get you home by air and land in case of illness, injury, or death, for $120 to $180 per year.

WHO PAYS? Most health insurance plans will cover at least part of the cost of a hospital stay abroad. Look at your policy and check with your employer or insurance agent to be sure. If you're not covered, call an insurance agent and get a short-term policy. Doctors and hospitals abroad often cost as much or more than at home, and visitors cannot depend on being treated gratis even though locals have a national health plan.

If you are taking a tour, get insurance that includes coverage of return travel costs if you become ill and must stay behind when the tour moves on (otherwise, the sad fact is that you're on your own). Senior citizens be warned—Medicare will *not* cover medical expenses abroad, except in *very* limited circumstances in Mexico and Canada.

Many companies offer insurance for travelers. You can buy a simple policy for health coverage, or for baggage loss, or to cover expenses if you must return home unexpectedly. But it makes sense to invest in a comprehensive policy that covers several of the travel-related subjects. This need not cost a lot if you are careful to purchase *only the coverage you need*. For instance, if your homeowner's insurance covers all but $100 of your baggage, and your health insurance covers all but the first $200 of medical expenses, and your automobile policy covers some accident expenses, then you need buy only a little extra protection. *Look at the coverage you already have* before buying more. Check these areas:

- ☐ Homeowner's insurance
- ☐ Automobile insurance
- ☐ Health insurance
- ☐ Automobile or travel club membership benefits
- ☐ Credit card insurance coverage (especially American Express).

The Travelers Insurance Company offers a "Travel Insurance PAK" through travel agents, which provides for accident and optional sickness benefits, trip cancellation and emergency evacuation, and baggage insurance. The cost depends on the number of family members covered, the amount of coverage selected, and the length of time you'll be traveling. You can buy the policy through any Travelers agent, or at most travel agencies.

The Sentry Insurance Company, 1100 Center Point Drive, Stevens Point, WI 54481 (tel. toll free 800/826-1300; in Wisconsin call collect, 715/346-7971), offers a "Travel Guard" policy that covers these areas: personal liability, accidental death, emergency assistance, medical expense, loss of baggage and travel documents, unauthorized credit card use, trip cancellation and interruption. Again, cost depends on number of family members covered, length of trip, and limits of coverage.

International Underwriters/Brokers, Inc., 243 Church St. West, Vienna, VA 22180 (tel. toll free 800/237-6615, or 703/255-9800), markets a policy called "Health Care Abroad" which covers up to $100,000 in

sickness and accident, medical evacuation and repatriation, and accidental death and dismemberment expenses. The cost is a minimum of $40. Trip cancel-
lation and baggage insurance are extra-cost options.
You also receive a directory of doctors and hospitals in
over 100 countries, and an identification card as proof
that you have medical coverage and need not pay
cash. The policy is sold through travel agents, or
directly from the company.

"Access America" is a comprehensive insurance
plan offered by Access America, Inc., 622 Third Ave.,
New York, NY 10163 (tel. 212/490-5345 or toll free
800/851-2800), a subsidiary of Blue Cross and Blue
Shield of the National Capital Area (Washington, DC),
and Empire Blue Cross and Blue Shield (New York).
Protection includes insurance against default of a tour
operator, illness of a traveler, and cancellation of a trip
due to a terrorist incident. The plan covers these
perils, and also medical transportation, hospital payments abroad, medical consultation and monitoring,
and even emergency cash. There's a 24-hour hotline to
provide help and information on medical and legal
problems, including finding a physician abroad. The
Access America insurance coverage is sold by travel
agents (who receive up to 35% commission on the
sale).

**TRIP CANCELLATION AND "RAIN CHECK" INSUR-
ANCE:** If your regular health insurance covers you
while abroad, you may want to invest only in trip
cancellation insurance. Many of the companies mentioned above will provide you with coverage. In fact, it
is possible to buy a policy, often for about $20, that
will reimburse you fully if you must cancel your flight
(even a non-refundable ticket) or tour in an emergency; some coverage will reimburse half of your

ticket or tour expense if you cancel for any reason, even just changing your mind. Ask your travel or insurance agent about such protection.

There are even companies that will insure you against your vacation being ruined by inclement weather! Your travel agent can sell you insurance against tropical storms on your cruise, bad weather on that foreign golf course, or cold weather at your beach resort. Of course, insurance companies are not foolish, and they will charge a high premium to insure you against rain in the damp Northwest or in Scotland. But coverage is available.

Dare I Carry Cash? and Other Money-Related Questions

How can I travel and carry money safely?

CASH: Cash is the easiest and also the most vulnerable. Which is better: to take a chance that some cash will be stolen, or perhaps to pay a gone-forever fee of 1% on your money converting it into traveler's checks so that you can recover it if it's stolen? In some travel situations there is simply no substitute for cash—in that tiny out-of-the-way café, or in the taxi or bus when you first arrive. It is wise to take along some cash, but not so much that you'd be in serious trouble if it were lost or stolen. Use it in cash-only situations— tipping, phone calls, to clinch a bargain deal in a local bazaar—but because traveler's checks are a convenience and insurance against loss, have most of your travel funds in checks.

YOU CAN GET TRAVELER'S CHECKS FOR FREE: Think carefully about how much, and where to buy the checks. Barclay's Bank, with branches in major American cities, does not charge. Several other companies have a similar policy. Thomas Cook, the travel service that started the whole traveler's check business a century ago, often promotes its checks by offering them for free. Note that the free checks offered are usually the company's and not American Express: that is, Thomas Cook's or Barclay's, both of which are perfectly acceptable throughout the world. So remember, always ask at your bank about free checks; also ask your travel or automobile club, or travel agent— they may offer free check deals. That 1% fee is something that's easy to avoid; you need not pay it.

The banks and companies that issue traveler's checks make money at both ends of the deal: they make you pay 1% for the checks, then they take the money you've given them and invest it at the going rate. No wonder they recommend that you "hold onto unused checks for future trips or emergencies." As long as you hold onto the check, they're making interest on your money.

This double-whammy is the reason some traveler's check firms can afford to issue free checks.

Here's a little bonus: You usually get more foreign currency for your dollar traveler's checks abroad than you do for an equivalent amount of dollar cash. If you cash a $100 traveler's check in Paris, for instance, you may get 6 francs for $1, or 600 francs total; for a $100 bill, you may only get 5.9 francs for $1, or 590 francs total. By using traveler's checks, you save 10 francs— not much, but better than nothing.

You may also be able to save money by buying traveler's checks denominated in *foreign currencies* before you leave home. Instead of buying dollar checks, get some checks in pounds sterling, or yen, or Deutschemarks, or French francs. Banks abroad often charge up to 5% to change dollars, whether bills or traveler's checks, into local currency. You will pay some spread when you buy your checks here at home, but it may well be less than it is abroad. And cashing the checks abroad will be a snap.

Who sells checks in foreign countries? American Express does. So does Thomas Cook, Barclay's Bank, and Deak-Perera. Deak offers checks in ten different currencies, and often waives the 1% fee during the spring months when competition among traveler's check companies is intense.

Always ask your bank about free traveler's checks, also ask your automobile club or travel agent—they may offer free checks. That 1% fee is something that's easy to avoid; you need not pay it.

Reader Rosalind Bond of Austin, Texas, wrote to me with an excellent suggestion. To avoid traveler's check service charges abroad when you cash your checks, be sure to cash them at an office or affiliate of the issuing bank. This means that if you have American Express traveler's checks, cash them at an American Express office abroad; if you have Thomas Cook checks, go to a Thomas Cook office; for Citibank checks, find a Citibank affiliate. This allows you to avoid the service charge that is often tacked on if a bank has to handle some other bank's checks.

TRAVELER'S CHECK PERILS: Traveler's checks are "the safe money," right? You always get a refund, right? Wrong! A traveler's check company may deny you a refund if you do not follow the rules for using traveler's checks *to the letter.* "Rules?" you may say, "I didn't know there were rules!" There are.

If you read the legal fine print on the little contract that comes with your traveler's checks, you will discover that you must do certain things in order to qualify for a refund in the event that your checks are lost or stolen.

First of all, you must sign the checks *with permanent ink* in a certain place (often in the upper left-hand corner); the contract may require you to sign the checks immediately, that is, right there at the desk of the bank officer who is selling them to you. Whatever you do, don't use an erasable ballpoint pen. It's best to use the pen provided by the bank, and to mention to the bank officer that you are doing so.

Second, you must make a record of your checks, including their serial numbers, and the date and place of purchase. Of course, making the record is not enough; you must be able to prove to the bank that you made the record by producing it, if and when your checks are lost or stolen. The best method is to make several records. One of them should be left at home or mailed home, the others should be carried with you in various safe places (*not* in the same place as your traveler's checks!).

Third, you must actively protect your checks from loss or theft. If a company can prove that you did not make a good effort to protect your checks, they need not pay you a refund.

Fourth, you cannot use your checks for any illegal purchase or activity, including gambling, bribes, buying illegal drugs, smuggling, etc.

Fifth, you must countersign your checks (usually in the lower right-hand corner) in front of the person cashing them. Don't sign them beforehand. Make sure that the person accepting the check witnesses your countersignature.

Finally, you must notify the traveler's check company immediately of any loss or theft. Some companies require that you notify them within a certain period of time, or you may lose your right to a refund.

All of these requirements are to help the traveler's check company avoid loss and fraud, and to make it more difficult for thieves to cash the checks.

"I'LL TAKE A PERSONAL CHECK": Buying souvenirs at an Arab-run shop in Jerusalem, I asked the shopkeeper what form of payment would be preferable. Can you guess what he said? "Personal check, if you have one."

You may hear just the opposite of that at home, as in "No Personal Checks Accepted—Ever!" but in foreign countries, as a "wealthy" tourist, you're assumed to be good for your debts. Carry a number of personal checks with you when you travel abroad, but guard them as you would traveler's checks. If they are lost or stolen, you should drop a note to your bank so they can be on the lookout for forgeries.

WHAT YOU DIDN'T KNOW ABOUT CREDIT CARDS: A credit card can be a traveler's best insurance and most cost-effective tool. As with traveler's checks, you must understand how the cards work in order to take full advantage of their benefits.

Why have a credit card? There are lots of reasons.

First, a credit card can save you money. By charging expenses on a credit card, you can benefit from what banks call "the float." With inflation an ever-present factor, especially abroad, you can charge an item on your credit card on July 1, and pay for it in dollars on August 1, August 15, or even later. In effect, you've enjoyed an interest-free loan for at least a month.

The range of items you can purchase with a credit card is incredible, yet continually widening. For instance, the discount long-distance telephone companies have installed special telephones in airports and hotels. You insert your bank credit card into the phone, place your call at discount rates, and the charge appears on your monthly credit card statement! You don't have to be a discount telephone service subscriber to use these phones; you just need a credit card.

Second, purchases and cash advances charged abroad on credit cards are normally converted into dollars at the interbank foreign exchange rate, the premium, wholesale rates used between banks for exchanges of a million dollars or more. That's a discount! American Express charges a 1% exchange fee on each currency conversion, but even with this you may still end up making money.

A credit card can be a traveler's best
insurance and most cost-effective tool!

Third, a credit card provides insurance in case of disaster. If something should happen during your trip, and you need a plane ticket, a hospital, a rental car, or a hotel room quickly, you'll have the power to get it. You can work out details of payment later, when it's easy, after the crisis has passed.

Some cards provide even more insurance—literally. If you use such a card to buy your air, rail, or sea tickets, you automatically receive up to $100,000 worth of travel accident insurance for you and your entire family. Some also cover over $1,000 worth of loss or damage to your baggage. This special insurance costs nothing extra, yet it saves you from the expense of buying separate travel accident or baggage policies.

Even if you need cash, rather than credit, a card can furnish it. The bank credit cards (VISA, MasterCard) are honored for cash advances at many banks all over the world. Just show the bank clerk your card and ask for a cash advance.

In the U.S. you may not even have to go to a bank! If your bank is a member of one of the Automated Teller Machine networks, and if your bank credit card is authorized for card withdrawals or cash advances, you can walk up to an automatic teller machine in virtually any big city, many airports, and other travel spots, slide in your card, and extract cash. Even if your bank is in Dallas and you're in Minneapolis, you'll get instant cash and an instant statement of your balance.

The cash advance will show up on your monthly bill, and you will be charged interest (usually 18% per year) on the amount of the advance, but you can avoid this if you're smart. When you ask for your cash advance, send off a check to your credit card company for the same amount, and the check will pay off the cash advance so you pay no interest. (You don't need to receive your monthly bill in order to pay off a credit card charge. You can send a check at any time to the billing address with your name and your card number.)

If you plan ahead, you can always have cash available, at no charge. Before your trip, just send a check for the amount of cash you want available to the credit card billing address with your name and card number. In effect you've opened your own personal "worldwide cash account." You can draw cash out and not worry about paying interest or about mailing further checks.

Here's another trick: if you are one of the many

people with two major credit cards, use one as your "worldwide cash account," for cash advances only, and the other for charging goods and services. This way you can be certain of never incurring an interest charge on your cash advances. But remember, you must pay your monthly credit card bill in full, on time, to avoid interest charges.

The American Express Card actually makes it much easier to get cash while abroad. You don't even have to go to a bank (which may be closed). Your hotel, motel, or airline, if it accepts the American Express Card, will advance you cash on the card, as will any American Express Travel Service Office. You can even get American Express Travelers Cheques from automated Travelers Cheque Dispensers in many airports and other locations worldwide on a 24-hour basis.

There's another money-saving function to charging purchases on a credit card. In many Third World countries where inflation is high, the exchange rate changes daily. You might pay $20 in cash for an item today, and it may only be $19 in a few day's time. But if you pay by credit card, it will take a few days for the transaction to clear. Your charge is exchanged at the rate in effect *when the charge clears*, so you may automatically get a better exchange rate.

"This is too good to be true," you may say. "Somebody has got to pay for all this free service."

Certainly. But it needn't be you.

Except at a few banks (such as European American Bank in New York), you pay an annual fee of about $20 or $30 for a bank credit card such as VISA or MasterCard. This gives you the right to charge purchases and cash advances up to a predetermined credit limit, which is usually $1,500 to $2,000 for new cardholders. You may not even have to pay the fee, because numerous organizations offer credit card privileges as a member benefit. AAA-affiliated motor clubs often provide free VISA cards to members, at no increase in auto club membership dues.

Even if you have to pay that $20 or $30, you needn't pay any more to have the benefits of credit card use.

Of course, many people do pay more for credit card use. They pay 18% per year on unpaid balances. But pay off your balance monthly and you need pay no more than the annual fee.

American Express charges more for their cards. But you get a good deal more for the extra few dollars per year. On these cards there is no preset credit limit. You can cash your personal check by showing the American Express Card at many hotels, airline offices, etc., around the world. There is a good deal of status involved in having these cards, especially abroad, and this status can be a very handy thing to have when dealing with travel industry personnel.

American Express seems to provide many small but helpful services to its Cardmembers, such as bulletins of travel information, handling Cardmembers' mail in foreign countries, etc. One final note: The American Express Card is not actually a "credit" card. It's really a *charge* card. You're expected to pay your bill in full each month. There is no interest charge if you do this. If you want credit, they have special plans such as "Sign and Travel," similar in function and interest rates to bank credit card accounts, for which you can sign up.

WHEN TO PAY CASH AND SAVE: Having said all this, I must add that there are times when you're better off paying cash. The Second Law, "Search constantly for the Point of Mutual Advantage," will help you to identify these situations.

Every establishment which accepts credit cards pays a fee to the credit card company based on monthly volume of sales. For example, an appliance store which sells many thousands of dollars' worth of washers, dryers, and refrigerators to credit card customers each month, may pay 3% or 4% of its credit card sales to the credit card company. The theory is that credit cards make it easier for people to purchase goods and services; the appliance store is sharing the benefits of that ease; and so the store should pay to support the plan. Stores with smaller volumes of sales—say, a bookstore—will have to pay a higher percentage of monthly sales (5% to 8%) in exchange for the convenience of letting their customers "charge it."

In many cases, there is no difference in price, whether you pay with a credit card, a check, or in cash. In these cases it *pays* you to use your credit card. But some businesses are willing to give you a discount if you pay cash. Gas stations, for instance, will often take 4¢ to 10¢ off the price of a gallon of fuel if you pay in cash. (Another way of looking at it is that you pay a few cents more per gallon for the privilege of using your credit card.) In cases where a discount is offered, you save money by paying cash.

Even if a discount is not openly offered, it can't hurt to ask, especially if the item you're buying has a hefty price tag. On the sale of a $400 necklace, the shopowner might have to pay the credit card company as much as $32. He could give you a discount-for-cash of $30 and still come out ahead. Remember this whenever you shop in a place that accepts credit cards.

THE MYSTERIES OF FOREIGN EXCHANGE: "What do I do: change dollars into foreign currency before I leave home, or do it over there?" This question is asked often. There is no completely satisfactory answer.

You should attempt to find out precise exchange

rates both at home and abroad. You should have at least $50 in local currency when your plane touches down in the foreign country. This will allow you to walk right by the long lines at the currency-exchange counters, take a cab, grab a snack, buy a newspaper, and in general remain mobile until you get to a downtown bank. Downtown banks usually offer the best exchange rates, much better than airport exchange counters. But there are differences, even among downtown banks. To understand these differences you must understand how the entire currency-exchange business operates.

Every institution which exchanges currency establishes a "spread," or difference in price, between buying and selling. Here's an example: the Slobovian pazooza is exactly equal to the U.S. dollar in value. You are visiting Slobovia and need pazoozas to pay for your room, meals, and souvenirs. You go to a bank. There you see a bulletin board with the heading "Dollar Rates" and two subheadings, "Buy" and "Sell." Underneath each subheading is an amount. Under "Buy," this amount is SP1.01; under "Sell" it's SP 0.99. What this means is that when you come to get pazoozas, the bank will sell you 0.99 pazoozas for $1. In effect the bank is pocketing 1¢ of your money, because the pazooza is exactly equal to the dollar and you should be getting SP1.00 for US$1.00.

Banks are not in the business of losing money. You need pazoozas, they have pazoozas, so you plunk down $100 and are given 99 pazoozas in exchange. You go out and have a good time (as much as possible) in Slobovia. Just before you are about to board your homeward flight, you notice that you have one pazooza left. Having no use for the Slobovian currency at home, you decide to buy a dollar with that pazooza. You go to the little banklet right there in the air terminal, and you tell them you want to sell a pazooza.

"Sure," they say, "but we buy pazoozas at SP1.01 to US$1.00. You've got to give us that pazooza plus one cent in order to buy a dollar."

"But I only got SP0.99 for every dollar I gave you. How come the dollar is now worth SP1.01?"

"The spread," they answer.

The spread is that 2¢ difference between the buying and selling rates of 0.99 and 1.01. The bank keeps the spread.

The bank may also keep a fee for the transaction. It may be the equivalent of 25¢ or 50¢ or $1, it may be 0.5% or 1% or even 3% of the entire transaction. They may charge you for government revenue stamps, required on banking documents. At the end of all this, the $100 you give them may turn into $93! Wow!

This is why it pays to look into currency exchange, even though it's not always clear exactly what you should do in every case. Many travelers assume that the bank keeps "a buck or so" for its trouble. Watch it. The bank may keep $10 or $15 for its trouble. What you should do is find out what the spread is, find out what the fees are, then pull out your little calculator and go to work. Do the same for several banks, and you'll find the one that gives you back the most pazoozas for your $100. If you're traveling in Slobovia for even a week or two, the difference can easily add up to the price of a luxurious dinner.

How to Get a Passport Cheap

All passports are equal, yes? No.

In 1983 the Passport Office drastically changed the regulations governing passports. For one thing, the price shot up from $10 to $35. For another thing the "execution fee" (what you pay to have the Passport

Office swear you in) went to $7. Finally, the family passport was eliminated. So what used to cost a family $12 now costs about $124, or ten times as much.

So much for the bad news. The good news is that your new passport is good for ten years, twice as long as the old one. Also, you can avoid the execution fee on renewal passports if you follow a few simple procedures. Here's what to do:

The very first time you apply for a passport, find your birth certificate, naturalization papers, or other solid proof of your U.S. citizenship, and go to a passport agency (see below), post office, federal or state court, or probate court. Have with you two copies of a recent photo of yourself, two inches square, good quality, unretouched, bareheaded. You will be asked to fill out the white passport application form. When you've done so, the clerk will ask you to raise your right hand and swear (or affirm) a little oath. Then you pay the $35 passport fee plus the $7 execution fee for each adult. For children under 18, the fee is a flat $20, and the passport is good for five years.

In most cases your passport will be mailed to you, arriving in your mailbox only a few days after you swore the oath. But it's unwise to depend on this. If you can do it, you should apply for a passport a good month in advance of your departure date.

If you can prove (by showing an air ticket, etc.) that you've simply got to have your passport right away, a passport agency will do its best to get it to you right away. This is usually possible.

THE BIG SAVINGS: The big savings comes when you renew your passport. Save the old one! If you've got an old passport, even if it has expired, you can avoid that $7 execution fee. Go to any post office, get a *pink* passport *renewal* form, fill it out, provide the two little photos of yourself as before, and hand over $35 *plus* *your old passport.* You will receive your brand-new passport, and your old one, in the mail a few days later.

At $10 for five years, the old passports cost us $2 per year. At $34 for ten years, the price has gone up to $3.50 per year. But most of the new passports can be read by computers, a welcome development which promises to shorten the Immigration Service lines, the ones you stand in when you reenter the United States.

Any questions? Write to Passport Services, Office of Correspondence, Department of State, 1425 K St. N.W., Washington, DC 20524, or call the nearest passport agency or post office.

There are 13 U.S. Passport Agencies, in Boston, Chicago, Honolulu, Houston, Los Angeles, Miami, New Orleans, New York City, Philadelphia, San Francisco, Seattle, Stamford, Conn., and Washington, D.C.

Do you need a passport? For most of the world, yes. For travel to Canada, Mexico, many Caribbean and Central and South American countries, no. To these places you can use some other weighty document which is proof of identity: a birth certificate or voter registration card is often sufficient (but a driver's license or college ID is not). However, nothing proves your identity as quickly and powerfully as a passport. It makes matters like cashing traveler's checks and checking in for flights very simple.

Must I Learn a Foreign Language?

Not really. During a weekend in Montréal, or a week in Mexico City and Acapulco, you will probably meet mostly those locals who speak English. For a longer trip, a good phrase book helps you open doors, make smiles, win friends, understand what's going on. The series put out by Editions Berlitz (Berlitz Publications) is widely available, inexpensive, and filled with cultural descriptions as well as words and phrases. A good phrase book like this makes a dictionary unnecessary.

It's absolutely true that knowing even a few words and phrases of the local language can make a trip run considerably smoother. Just think of how much use you'll get from the phrases "Where is . . ." "Do you have . . ." "How much does this cost?" and even "What's your name?" You needn't be a linguist or a frantic student to learn them.

Many novel approaches to language-learning have recently been developed, including the one employed in the Bilingual Books series published in Seattle. The format of *French in 10 Minutes a Day* (132 pp., $14.95), for instance, is easy and simple, concentrating on the few very essential phrases you need to know rather than on weighty grammar rules and vocabulary lists.

A phrase book is extremely valuable. But there's simply no substitution for *hearing* and *repeating* the phrases. And in this age of portable cassette players and car stereos, there are plenty of times when you could be learning a bit of the language: driving to work, waiting for the bus, even on the flight or cruise or train trip itself. Any good travel bookstore (see Appendix) or record-and-tape store will have a language section. (Yes! You just never looked for it before.) There will probably be at least one or two sets of records and/or tapes for the language you want, with or without a phrase-and-grammar book. If not, you can ask the bookstore to order it for you; or order it yourself, by mail.

Berlitz Publications has a full list of phrase books, dictionaries, cassettes, and records. Order them through the Traveller's Shopping Service, 600 Grand Ave., Ridgefield, NJ 07657.

Another series that you can order through a bookstore, or directly, is the "Listen and Learn" series put out by Dover Publications, 31 East 2nd St., Mineola, NY 11501 (tel. 516/294-7000). For $14.95 you get three cassettes (90 minutes) of French, German, Italian, Japanese, Spanish, Portuguese, or Russian, plus a manual. For a copy of Dover's *Essential French Grammar* (etc.), add another $2.50 or $2.75, depending on the language you choose. Three-record LP sets cost $15.95, but are available for more languages: all those above, plus Modern Hebrew, Modern Greek, and Swedish. Many of the record sets *include* a copy of the Essential Grammar as well as the manual. The Dover sets may well be the best value for the money.

Language-learning gets even fancier. Any language teacher will tell you that audio-visual aids can help learning, and retention of what is learned. MasterVision, 969 Park Ave., New York, NY 10028, has made up the MasterVision Library of Videocassettes, which includes language-learning programs in German, Spanish, and Italian, with other languages (French, Japanese, Russian) to follow. A 90-minute videocassette costs $69.95, and contains pictures and subtitles to teach you a basic vocabulary of 1,000 words.

Identity Cards That Save You Money

Another thing to do before heading out, whether you travel at home or abroad, is to obtain a student ID card and/or a Youth Hostel card. *Age is no barrier* in many cases. To become a member of the American Youth Hostels, Inc., a person under 18 or over 54 pays $10 a year; one over 18 years of age pays $20 a year; family membership costs $30 annually; and a life membership is $200. With your Youth Hostel Card, you can stay at inexpensive youth hostels all over the world. Buy your hostel membership at any hostel, or contact American

Youth Hostels, Inc., National Headquarters, P.O. Box 37613, Washington, DC 20013-7613 (tel. 202/783-6161); in Canada, contact the Canadian Hosteling Association, 333 River Rd., Place Vanier, Tower A, Vanier City, Ottawa, ON K1L 8H9 (tel. 613/748-5638).

To obtain the International Student Identity Card (ISIC), you must be a full-time high school or university student, and you must send documentary proof of such status such as a letter from the school principal, dean, or registrar, embossed with the official school seal. Many college campuses have an office that issues the ISIC. If yours doesn't, contact the Council on International Educational Exchange (CIEE), 205 East 42nd St., New York, NY 10017 (tel. 212/661-1450), or the CIEE offices in Boston, Seattle, San Francisco, Berkeley, Los Angeles, or San Diego. Note that age is no barrier to obtaining a student card; you can be of any age, but you must be a full-time high school or college student.

With these two cards, a wealth of inexpensive accommodations, flights, meals, and things to do is opened up to you.

What about Visas, Tourist Cards, and Permits?

For foreign countries, there are many items you may want to obtain in advance. When you travel to Third World countries or Eastern Europe, it's often necessary to have a visa or at least a "Tourist Card." Obtaining these permits-to-enter is usually easiest in the U.S. or Canada, with less bureaucratic hassle and fewer payoffs. Think of it this way: the consular officer of Upper Slobovia, sitting in the embassy in Washington or the consulate in New York or Los Angeles, fills requests for Slobovian visas by mail. He's happy to be in North America (most Third World officials are), he likes his job, he wants to appear efficient and modern minded to us, and so he does his best to fulfill your request without any hassle.

Depending on the Third World country you plan to visit, you may be able to obtain visas and Tourist Cards at the border or upon landing in the airport. But consider the position of the Slobovian immigration officer there: probably underpaid, often envious of foreigners—the officer has a lot of incentive to hit you for a bribe. After all, the situation is urgent: your bus or train is about to depart for the interior, or you've just landed and are not about to climb back on a plane rather than pay a small bribe. He's got you. With a visa and/or a Tourist Card already in your pocket, you're in a much stronger position to get through formalities quickly and cheaply.

The advice extends to special-interest permits as well: want to go hunting, or digging in the ruins, or hiking in outlying areas? You'll often need a permit for these activities, and you'll *always* need a permit to import firearms. Get these things in advance, and allow plenty of time for the bureaucracy to churn.

For full information, request the booklet entitled "Visa Requirements of Foreign Countries" from the Bureau of Consular Affairs, CA/PA Room 2807, Department of State, Washington, DC 20520; enclose a stamped, self-addressed business (long) envelope.

COUNTDOWN LISTS

When is the Big Day? Take that date, the date of your departure, and count backward three months. If you plan to leave in mid-June, then think of March 15 as the beginning of your countdown for early preparations.

Planning starts in earnest on April 15, when there

are "60 Days to Takeoff." If you decided on a trip only recently, you can compress all the preparations into this period. But you've missed a whole month of delicious anticipation.

On May 15 begins "30 Days to Takeoff." Things should be running smoothly now. Your mailbox will have offered up all sorts of information, passports, visas, special discount coupons, inoculation forms, maps, and even perhaps hotel reservations and airplane tickets. By this time you know just what to expect at your destination—and you can't wait to get there and try it out!

To make certain that you don't fall behind in your planning, make a schedule for what you're going to do, write it down, take an oath to follow it, and then tell a friend so your friend can check on your progress.

Early Preparations (90 Days)

First of all, get the mail working for you. Send off postcards or notes, or use your telephone and request information.

DOCUMENTS:

☐ Begin applying for visas, if they are required. You'll need a valid passport. *Begin early!* On a trip to Africa, for instance, you may have to mail your passport to one embassy, get it back, mail it to another, get it back, mail it to a third, etc.

HEALTH:

☐ Find out if special precautions (such as inoculations) must be taken for your destination. Contact one or more of the sources listed in this chapter.

☐ Get your International Certificates of Vaccination booklet from the U.S. Public Health Service, a passport agency, or the Superintendent of Documents.

☐ Get information on finding doctors abroad, on medical insurance, and on medical evacuation.

INFORMATION:

☐ Contact city, state, and national chambers of commerce, visitor and convention bureaus, and tourist offices (see Chapter 3 and Appendix).

☐ Find out about special offers and packages from railroads, bus companies, airlines (see Chapters 7, 8, 9, 11, 13, and 14).

☐ Sign up for newsletters (see Chapter 3).

☐ Drop by a travel agency (Chapter 3) and ask some questions about your destination: Will it be crowded? Is it expensive? How long in advance should I make my reservations? Will there be special events, festivals, or performances? You can do this by telephone also.

INSURANCE:

☐ Make a list of the coverage you already have in your homeowner's, automobile, and medical insurance policies, or call your agent and find out. Check the membership contracts of automobile and travel clubs, and credit cards (especially American Express) to see what insurance coverage is provided.

LANGUAGE-LEARNING:

☐ Order cassettes or records, and a phrase book, and set yourself a *regular schedule* in which to learn; even 15 minutes a day is good.

MONEY:

☐ Start looking for places that offer free traveler's checks.

☐ Apply for a credit card.

SHOPPING:

☐ Write to Franzus Company about electrical current, converters, and adapters for your destination.

☐ Shop for very small, lightweight travel appliances you'll need.

60 Days to Takeoff

DOCUMENTS:

☐ Search for the right guidebooks for you and your particular trip (see Chapter 4).

☐ Check the expiration dates on your passport, driver's license, and credit cards. They should extend *well past* the date of your return, or they may not be accepted by foreign officials. Renew if necessary.

☐ Apply for a Youth Hostel Card (remember, age is no barrier) if you like, and an International Student Identity Card.

☐ Apply for an International Driving Permit if you think you'll need one. Ask at a local automobile club.

HEALTH:

☐ Begin your course of inoculations.

☐ Schedule a dental checkup. You don't want a sensitive or aching tooth to ruin your trip. Airplane takeoffs often exacerbate dental weaknesses.

SHOPPING:

☐ Buy the clothing and luggage you'll need (see Chapter 6). *Start wearing any new shoes* to break them in.

30 Days to Takeoff

HEALTH:

☐ Order a supply of any prescription drugs you take regularly. Buy other medical necessaries.

☐ Get the antimalarial pills you need, and begin to take them one or two weeks before departure, according to doctor's orders.

☐ Get a spare pair of glasses, contact lenses, or at least a copy of your prescription.

INSURANCE:

☐ Sign up for any additional coverage you may need, with your insurance agent or a travel agent.

MONEY:

☐ Call a bank and find out the current rate of exchange.

☐ Buy your traveler's checks without fee at a place you've found. You may want to get some denominated in a foreign currency.

PETS:

☐ Arrange for your pets (and houseplants) to be taken care of. Find a house-sitter, pet-sitter, or call kennels. You may have to reserve space for your pet in advance.

One Week Left!

By now all should be going smoothly—except that you're aching to get away! You've got passport, visas, tickets, insurance, clothes, luggage, medicines, glasses, discount coupons, maps, guidebooks. Go over the lists above one more time, just in case.

Now is the time to take care of matters on the home front as well: stopping the newspaper deliveries, having the post office hold your mail, asking a friend to look out for your place.

HEALTH:

☐ You should be taking antimalaria pills by this time, if they are indicated for your destination.

PHOTOGRAPHY:

☐ Check (or have someone check) the batteries in your camera. Decide how many rolls of film you'll need. When you buy them, check the expiration dates. Only buy film with an expiration date that's a year or more in the future.

You did it! Not only are you all ready to go, but you know all about your destination, you know a few words and phrases of the language, you've gotten real bargains on all the necessary travel expenses. More than this, you know *why* you're going. You have realistic expectations, so you're virtually guaranteed of having an enjoyable and rewarding trip.

The actual packing of your bags is going to be an easy matter. Read on.

6

Hold That Bag!

You're about to leave. The date on your ticket is coming up fast.

It's now time to consider carefully what you'll take with you. Taking too little will leave you unprepared. Taking too much will burden you needlessly and add extra expense to your trip.

As with all other aspects of your trip, success here is easy, but you must go about packing with care. Even sophisticated travelers get excited when they're about to head out on a journey. You must get above that excitement and look closely at your real desires and requirements for the trip.

LESS IS MORE

Anyone can see many advantages to traveling light: no need to pay for taxis or porters, no need to break back and shoulders lugging a huge suitcase or two.

There are many more advantages that are not so apparent. Let's "Look Beyond the Obvious."

If you have just one or two small bags, you need not check your bags when you board a plane. The under-seat and overhead storage areas on airplanes provide plenty of room for a moderate amount of luggage these days. So your bags won't be pilfered, damaged, or lost during baggage handling. And you needn't wait in the crowd at the baggage carousel at the end of the flight.

If there is a scarcity of ground transport (say, taxis at an airport), the person who can bypass the baggage claim area will get the last seat on the bus, or one of the few cabs in line.

When you need some personal item during a flight, it will be within reach, not deep in the belly of the plane, inaccessible.

When you've got all of your belongings with you right in the passenger cabin, you can take advantage of fast-breaking situations. I was once flying across the Atlantic to Morocco. My actual destination was Marrakesh, but the flight was heading for Casablanca, where I would have to change planes. But Casablanca was fogbound (as happens frequently), and the plane detoured to . . . Marrakesh! Airline personnel would not open the baggage compartment because this was not the flight's official destination, but they allowed me (and my carry-on shoulder bag) to deplane there. This saved me several hours, and I cashed in the Casablanca-Marrakesh flight coupon for a refund!

Even with those little wheels on it, a big suitcase is a burden. In many places (especially Third World countries) the walkways and sidewalks are not smooth enough for the wheels to operate. And how do you manage all those steps to the Paris Métro with a big bag, even with wheels?

The more you have to carry, the more you have to lose.

It is possible to travel with no more luggage than an airline flight bag or large purse. People who travel this way are not unwashed barbarians. They are the most liberated people on the road.

Until a close friend of mine went on a two-week vacation with three monster suitcases packed like sausages, I thought this dinosaur mode of travel had disappeared from the earth. I was so accustomed to traveling with only one small shoulder bag, I actually thought all those huge suitcases at the airport baggage claim were owned by immigrants moving with large families.

What are the bare essentials? Well, my brother used to put a toothbrush in his pocket and head out to the airport. He didn't even weigh himself down with *money*. Staying with friends, borrowing toothpaste, razors, and soap, wrapping in a towel while a friend took his clothes to the laundromat. . . . It is indeed possible to pack nothing at all. But for most of us this is just a funny story.

You *can* pack lightly. Instead of starting with the checklist (three shirts, four underpants, etc.), do it backward: start with your bag.

SURPRISING NEW LUGGAGE

Rule of thumb: Your bag for a month's travel (or less) in a warmish climate should be small enough to carry on the airplane and stow under the seat, and you should be able to carry it by a shoulder strap for a 20-minute walk without having to put it down (you get to change shoulders, though). The bag itself should be light but strong.

If you must have some more space, *do not* buy a large bag! Buy a second shoulder bag, or a backpack. These days, bags and packs come in such an amazing assortment of styles that you can have whatever you dream of. The best pack is one that converts to a suitcase for hand-carrying: the shoulder straps tuck in here, a carrying handle pops out of there. Yes, such bags exist, and their tidy appearance sets them well apart from the stock image of the ragged, youthful pack-toting vagabond.

THE BIG QUESTION!

It would be impossible to give a useful checklist of what to take, because that depends so much on where you go and what you plan to do when you get there. Going to Acapulco for sun and sea? You can get by with jeans, shirt, and bathing suit. Are you interested in discos? Then you'd better throw in snazzy slacks too.

When you make up your own list, keep these points in mind: Three tops and two pairs of slacks constitute a basic travel wardrobe. Some self-reliant people can actually get along on this minimum. One pair of slacks should be blue jeans, or something similarly informal; the other pair should be more formal. As for the tops, have one shirt or blouse, one jersey or turtleneck, and a T-shirt. The T-shirt is also your undershirt, pajamas, and beach top. Coats and jackets? Take only those you can wear on your back. If cold sets in, use the simple technique of layering—a T-shirt under an overblouse under your all-purpose jacket or coat.

You simply cannot travel heavy and travel cheaply at the same time. It is even possible to travel with no more luggage than an airline flight bag or a large purse.

Women who want something more than this super-basic informality should pack one dress—or skirt and top that looks like a dress—that does not need ironing, two or three blouses, two slacks or skirts, for a total of three interchangeable outfits. Scarves can work wonders dressing up the simplest pants outfit if need be. Take only two pairs of shoes: one very comfy and informal, and one dress-up pair. Take lotions, creams, shampoo, and conditioner in small plastic bottles scrounged for the purpose (big spenders can buy them in variety or drugstores). Instead of curlers, take a single curling iron; it's a bit more work to use the curling iron, but it's lighter and smaller.

This minimum is bound to frighten you: "How will I ever get along for a month on that small wardrobe?" Instead of fear, your actual experience is more likely to yield pleasure. A spartan wardrobe gives you the freedom of not having to worry about clothes, or what to wear. More important, it gives you the truly priceless freedom of easy unencumbered traveling. If you have lots of room in your shoulder bag after it's packed, throw in one more shirt and one more pair of slacks or a skirt. When traveling, you change *people*, not clothes!

As for other items, they depend on climate. You will almost always need a sweater, even in Egypt (where the desert gets very cool at night). The amount of underclothing you take depends directly on the climate. To a hot, dry climate, take very little as it will dry within an hour after you wash it. To a damp, cold climate, take more, because it may take two days to dry.

Do not take clothes that are brand new, especially shoes. Break in clothes before you go, and break in new shoes well. A new shoe not only rubs, it exercises different muscles in your legs. Until those new muscles acquire tone, your legs will be sore. You don't want sore legs on a trip where you will be required to walk half the day—and you walk that much no matter how or where you travel.

If you've forgotten something, or if you find the basic wardrobe much too confining, buy something abroad. It may be cheaper, it may be more expensive, but either way it's nice to buy exotic clothes.

Plan to wash your own clothes. You may not end up washing everything—those blue jeans, for example. But do provide yourself with the capability—they say even President Truman washed out his own underclothes when he traveled. It's quick and convenient, and in some countries it is so expensive to have things laundered that you'd be shocked. For more tips on doing your own laundry, see p. 345.

The absolute minimum number of garments (shirts, trousers, underwear) is two: "wash one, wear one."

THE ANSWER!

What you finally take is up to you. Trust me when I say that you don't really need as much as you think you do. Just so you don't forget some important item, here's a handy checklist of suggested things to take:

Air/seasickness pills
Antidiarrheal medicine
Aspirin
Blouses and tops (3 or 4)
Camera, batteries, film, flashbulbs
Converter and adapter plugs
Credit cards
Documents: trip itinerary, vouchers, receipts,
    reservation slips, etc.
Driver's license
Glasses (contacts), spare
Guidebook
Insurance policies (travelers)
Jacket or suit

Maps
Money (some small bills)
Pants (2 or 3)
Passport
Phrase book
Picnic utensils and condiments
Prescription medicine
Prescription for glasses
Pajamas/nightgown (maybe)
Raincoat
Rubbers or boots (maybe)
Shirts and jerseys (3 or 4)
Shoes (2 pairs)
Stockings/socks (3 or 4 pairs)
Suntan lotion
Sweater
Tickets
Traveler's checks
Underwear (2 to 4 sets)
Vaccination certificates
Visas, Tourist Cards

HOW TO ACTUALLY PACK IT

And now the actual packing. You may want to start
out with a liberal supply of plastic bags—the airtight
seal kind. Fold each garment neatly so it will fit into a
little plastic bag. Force out all the air before locking it,
and the dress or whatever will survive for up to a week
virtually wrinkle-free. One pair of pants with top can
also fit into a little plastic bag. Underwear goes in
another, and so on. Cosmetics, vitamins, camera, and
film all go into a separate plastic bag.

Surrounded by all those neatly sealed baglets,
you're ready to pack your bag or suitcase. Put shoes in
the corners, line the sides with toiletries, then place all

the other clothes upright—like files in a filing cabinet. Not only will they fit into a minimum of space, they'll be easy to identify and pull out without having to rumple up everything else in the bag. If you're using a rucksack or duffle bag, use the outside zipper pockets for documents, paperbacks, and the like (as long as you're taking the bag on the plane).

With any luck, by following these rather simple rules, you'll wind up with everything you need for a comfortable happy trip—and you'll be the character with the smug expression walking jauntily past the baggage carousel.

Your bag, for a month's travel (or less) in a warmish climate, should be small enough to stow under the seat of an airplane, and you should be able to carry it by a shoulder strap for a 20-minute walk without having to put it down.

7

Scouting for Airfares

An airport is a thrilling place. The great planes rise majestically skyward at several hundred miles per hour, defying gravity and leaving the humdrum of hometown life behind.

Every trip by air is an adventure. Only a century ago such an adventure was an impossible dream. Today it's within the reach of virtually everyone, really a dream-come-true. And yet, to live the dream fully you must know what you are doing. The normal air traveler often limits the possibilities of flight by not knowing how to buy it. In many cases the fare for a normal journey could actually pay for two journeys, if the traveler knew how to do it. It's not difficult to get more travel for the same money. You only need to know how. You need a view of the possibilities.

These possibilities have broadened immeasurably today because of airline deregulation. This phenomenon is new. Its full effects are just now being felt. Yet it is already clear how travelers should act in order to reap the benefits of deregulation (and avoid the pitfalls), and how travelers can fly more frequently, and farther, than they ever have done before.

AIR TRAVEL: FACTS AND FIGURES

The world's scheduled airlines carry well over 700 million passengers on domestic flights every year; for international flights, the figure approaches 200 million passengers annually.

The major scheduled U.S. airlines operate more than six million flights per year to and from 500 airports, patronized by 30% of the total adult population of the United States. About half of these 375 million passengers per year are traveling for business, the other half for pleasure; 85% of all passengers are traveling on a special-fare ticket that is cheaper than full fare. Our airlines carry all these people in about 3,200 aircraft, and the average flight is 61% full. In some years (1980, 1986), the airlines do all this without a single fatal accident. Add to this tremendous number of flights those run by the charter and regional carriers, and you have an astounding number of takeoffs and landings which occur every day throughout the country, and only in a fraction of a percentage point is there ever a mishap of any kind.

An Amazing Safety Record

Despite our reactions of horror and dismay at the occasional news of a commercial airliner's crash, the airline industry's safety record is truly amazing. Even in the worst of years, there is only about one fatal accident for every one million departures; in the best of years, there is one fatal accident for every 5 million departures.

To increase your amazement, let me add that the United States has twelve of the fourteen busiest airports in the world. Ranked by total passenger movements, the busiest airport in the world is Chicago's O'Hare, which serves over 50 million passengers per year. Atlanta/Hartsfield, Los Angeles International, and Dallas/Fort Worth are next in line, serving anywhere from 37 to 42.5 million. Then comes London's Heathrow and New York's J.F.K. The next five in line are New York/Newark, Denver/Stapleton, Tokyo/Haneda, San Francisco, and New York/LaGuardia. Miami, Boston, and St. Louis finish the list, with the last of these hosting a "mere" 20 million passengers annually, or only about 38% of bustling O'Hare's traffic.

About 350,000 Americans work for the airlines, helping passengers to fly 335 billion revenue passenger miles each year, and earning operating revenues of $46 billion.

CONQUERING THE FEAR OF FLYING: Okay, you've read the statistics which show that it is far more dangerous to drive to the airport than it is to fly in a plane, but you're still afraid of flying. You can overcome that fear.

Let me say first that fear of flying is understandable. For an intelligent, independent, self-reliant individual, it makes sense to balk at putting oneself into a huge machine and to have that machine hurtle off into space at blinding speed under the control of people whom you may never even have laid eyes on, and have certainly never met, let alone become acquainted with. This is a rational fear.

But that is no consolation when your palms sweat and your heart rate increases, up there in the sky where you can do nothing about it. So you must do something about fear of flying even before you board the plane.

First, take no stimulants (coffee, tea, caffeinated soft drinks, cocoa, chocolate) the day before a flight, or on the day of the flight itself. Also avoid a high-carbohydrate meal just before flight time. You should not board a flight on an empty stomach, however. The meal you have before your flight should be high in protein and low in carbohydrates. Avoid snacks, which are usually carbohydrates. These things set your metabolism zooming, and you don't need it.

Second, take along something more "interactive" than books and magazines. If you like crossword puzzles, take a book of those. If mathematical puzzles and games amuse you, have them with you. You need some pleasurable activity in which you can get "lost."

Third, make an effort to talk with one of your seatmates about flying, even (perhaps especially) about the fear of flying. You'll reassure yourself that the fear is normal, that other people feel it, but that they overcome it for good reasons.

Finally, do this breathing exercise. Inhale using your diaphragm; this sucks your stomach in. Do it to a count of four, then hold your breath for four counts, then exhale for four. Use this breathing exercise for several minutes, several times during a flight, and you will increase the flow of oxygen to your blood. The extra oxygen acts as a natural and foolproof relaxant. The pressurized cabin of an airplane is quite low in oxygen, and getting more is excellent for both mind and body.

YOUR POINT OF VIEW

Here are two ideas you must fix in your mind, along with the Four Laws, when you are thinking about air travel:

Air travel now costs less than ever.
Air travel is a retail commodity.

On the first point: I first crossed the Atlantic in 1966. I paid $305 for a round-trip charter flight between Boston and London. Ten years later, after wild inflation of the dollar, the current dollar price was considerably *lower* (less than $200). In terms of constant dollars, the price was ridiculously low. Jumbo jets, better engines, mass marketing, ingenious scheduling, and ticket sales plans have all reduced the costs of flying. Like telephone service, flying is one of the great bargains of the time. Those with only the standard two-week vacation appreciate fully what a valuable bargain air service is.

The reason we see air travel as "expensive" is that it is often the largest single expense in our travel budget, and it is the first one we have to deal with. Also, the air ticket price represents a single, very evident, large chunk of money. If we added up the cost of hotels, meals, car rentals, and the cost of purchases made on vacation, we might be surprised to find that any one of these categories can be more expensive than the airplane ticket. For instance, you can get a two-week excursion ticket to Europe for about $600, but two weeks of hotels at a moderate $50 per night is $700, and a two-week European car rental can easily cost $650, even for a compact car. But the total cost of a rental car is not easy to see in advance; there is no single chunk of money to look at. You must add up daily charges, mileage estimates, fuel estimates, collision damage waiver, and local taxes, and even then you cannot be sure that the resulting "price" is accurate. Keep this in mind. Air travel is not "the big cost"; it is just one of several big costs, and you can save large amounts on every aspect of your trip.

On the second point: Think of an airplane flight in these terms. The plane costs a lot of money to buy, to store, to maintain. The most efficient and profitable way to use an airplane is to keep it flying as much as possible. When it's flying, it incurs certain expenses: fuel, crew, landing fees, wear and tear. These costs are virtually the same whether the plane is full or empty. If the plane takes off with an empty seat, that empty seat is a symbol of revenue lost forever, because for exactly the same costs the airplane could have made more dollars by finding someone to pay something to fill that seat. Naturally, the airline will want to get as much money as possible for the seat. Two weeks before flight time, chances are good it can get a full fare. But what about two hours before flight time? Or 30 minutes? Chances are now close to zero for getting a full fare, and near zero for getting any money at all. Soon that seat will be airborne, having earned $0. Hence the airlines, travel agents, and consolidators have created a variety of ticket categories and special offers to sell their seats.

The Wave of Deregulation

Deregulation of the airline industry has opened up the marketplace to full-fledged price competition. This is good for you and me because we can benefit from some incredibly low fares—trips at prices that make an airline executive limp with despair. But it's bad because it's confusing. The neat and tidy system of past years is gone, and one can no longer depend on many services once taken for granted. You may have to pay a penalty if you change your reservations or cancel your ticket. You may not be able to check your bags straight through to your destination if you are flying on more than one line—indeed, you may have to buy several tickets rather than just one ticket with several coupons. The friendly airline reservation agent may no longer let you know about flights by other lines. And the check-in clerk may not accept the ticket of another airline in exchange for his own airline's.

But don't let any of this hide the central fact: airfares are lower than they have ever been before, and there are far more opportunities to travel now—

because of deregulation—than there were even last year.

The Secrets of Market Segmentation

In the Introduction to this book I mentioned that travel companies "target specialized markets." This "segmenting" is the hottest thing in travel, as far as the professionals are concerned. What is it all about?

It's basically this: you sell roughly the same commodity (air transportation) to everybody, but you set a different price for each segment of the market. We've all heard of this before. The wealthy couple who want all the luxuries can buy first-class tickets on a jet to Europe for $3,000 or $4,000 apiece. The backpacking student who wants to get there the cheapest possible way can wait around on standby until the last minute, then (if there's a seat left) hand the ticket agent $200 and walk aboard the very same plane. But that's not all there is to segmenting, not by a long shot.

The market today is being broken down into smaller and ever-smaller segments in an attempt to capture customers away from competing airlines (and even trains and buses). At the same time, by carefully setting prices for each segment based on its wants and its needs, an airline company can garner as many dollars as possible for each airline seat.

THE BIG FLAW: Segmentation is marvelous from the customer's point of view, because now you pay only for what you want and need, and not a penny more. You can find a ticket which suits you precisely, at the lowest possible price. There is, however, one enormous flaw. It is this: you may not *know* about that one perfect ticket for you. There are so many airlines, so many flights, so many fares, so much small print, that you may not find that perfect fare, and so you may end up buying more service and freedom than you need, and paying more than you want.

So how is this avoided? Quite simply, by using the Four Laws. Much of the reason why people pay more than necessary for air transportation is because they are still operating with pre-deregulation attitudes. They ask themselves, "Shall I buy a regular-fare ticket, an excursion, or a super-saver?" That's not the question at all.

What you should be asking (remember the Third Law!) is something like this: "I'll bet I haven't even *heard* about the ticket that's best for me. Where do I find out about it?"

The following pages will get you well into the adventure of finding lower and ever-lower fares. You can see by now that the latest up-to-date information is of the greatest importance, so scour the travel publications and newspapers, consult a good travel agent, and use your telephone. I can't predict the special price-war fares that come and go with the seasons, but I can fill you in on the *categories* of air transportation and airfares available to you.

HOW THEY STUFF A PLANE

On the average, only 61 out of every 100 seats on an airplane are occupied at takeoff time; the other 39 seats fly empty. Do the airlines care? Yes and no.

What the airlines care about is not full seats as such. They care about "yield," or how much profit they make from a particular flight. They would rather sell a hundred full fare seats for $750 each than sell two hundred discount seats for $250 each. Besides making more money, they would have fewer people, reservations, meals, and suitcases to deal with.

But they know that they won't fill a plane with full-fare passengers, and so they discount some tickets. The discounting process may start months before flight departure time, and it is possible that someone who bought a discounted ticket a month before the flight may end up paying more than someone who bought a ticket ten days before the flight—or vice-versa! The emphasis for the airlines is always on yield, on how much money a seat can produce at any given time. This gives the whole ticket-selling process the atmosphere of frantic carpet merchants in an oriental bazaar, and gives you fantastic opportunities to get low-priced, high-value tickets.

According to a study done by *USA Today*, American Airlines, with somewhere around 1,600 flights per day, begins the task of filling as many seats as possible almost a year in advance of flight date. On any given day, American's huge computers control an inventory of 150 million seats! About 33,000 fares are changed, on the average, every day, and every change is in the name of yield.

This does not mean that every change is a discount. If seats are selling faster than expected, American's fare experts may actually raise the fare for a few days to see if yield can be increased. But if people stop buying seats when the price rises, they may drop the price to a new low discount level just so seats don't go empty.

The very cheapest seats are the ones you see advertised constantly on television and in the newspapers. Usually very few of these seats are offered, perhaps fewer than a dozen on a plane with several hundred seats. They sell out quickly, and when they're gone, travel agents and airline clerks offer customers the next higher fare.

By all of this high-tech wizardry, the airlines are merely asking, "What's it worth to you?" The answer could be anything from $100 for a deep-discount seat in the rear of the plane, to $1,000 for a plush recliner in first class. The range and variety of prices is truly astounding.

But successfully stuffing a plane is not always handled completely by the airline itself. If the airline feels certain that large blocks of seats on certain flights may go empty, they'll sell those blocks of seats, perhaps a dozen or a hundred at a time, to "consolidators." These consolidators then try to makret the seats as best they can, offering them at very low prices.

This is how they stuff a plane. More detailed information on each marketing method, fare, and point of sale is given below. When an airline fills a plane, however, one thing is certain: that plane will be overbooked if it's humanly possible.

Overbooking Is Everywhere, All the Time

Every scheduled airline overbooks every flight, all the time. This is not callous disregard for passengers' rights and comfort, but an economic necessity. Around 10% to 30% of all passengers with confirmed reservations never show up for the flight, so the airlines figure that if they overbook by about 12% and take 112 reservations for every 100 seats, they'll come out about right. Sometimes there are a few seats empty at takeoff (which then can be filled with standby passengers), sometimes there are a few passengers with confirmed reservations who get "bumped." In either case, there are opportunities for the savvy traveler to get a cheaper flight, a free flight, or even cash. These opportunities come from "denied-boarding coupons" and coupon brokers, explained below. But before we get into the dense thicket of discount fares and deals, let's look at the standard ticket structure. These are the fares that the airlines attempt to sell first.

"Normal" Full Fare Tickets

FIRST CLASS: Very nice, but very pricey. You get to change your mind and your flight for up to a year. But the fare is over twice as much as for an economy flight, which means those little furry booties and that glass of champagne are by no means "free." In effect you are paying hand-made-leather-shoe prices for booties.

BUSINESS CLASS: Each airline has its own name for this service, which offers a few advantages over economy fare for a little bit more money. In effect you get the booties for much less. The valuable part of this fare is the right to unlimited stopovers enroute to your destination, and when returning. This feature is of great value to the business traveler, and may prove the cheapest way for you to fly, as well. One way or round trip.

ECONOMY CLASS: This is the lowest fare that still allows you freedom to change your mind. No advanced-purchase requirements, no charge for cancellation or change, and you can transfer the ticket to another airline. For a small extra fee, you can get a single stopover along the way. One way or round trip.

Apex and Super-Apex Tickets

APEX (Advanced-Purchase Excursion) tickets are the cost-conscious traveler's dependable friend. Costing about 25% less than economy (40% less than business), APEX fares must be booked, and paid for, 21 to 30 days in advance, and you must stay at your destination at least seven but no more than 60 or 90 days, depending on destination. You pay a penalty (usually $50) if you cancel; no stopovers are permitted. Most APEX tickets are transferrable between airlines, though. Super-APEX fares have the same terms as APEX, but they're priced even lower. In effect, they are loss-leaders, which make good advertising. Go after them early, as the seats are few in number and quickly sold. Round trip only.

Super-Low Promotional Fares

These are where the action is. Airlines entering new routes don't price by cost, but by undercutting everybody else. Often the promotional fares will have a fancy advertising name. Most of the time, the airline will tell you right out that their fare is the lowest. The airline certainly does not intend to keep the fare that low after it has built up its clientele. But for the time being, it's a goldmine.

Air travel now costs less than ever.
Air travel is a retail commodity.

The airlines are in fact using all kinds of imaginative gambits to attract customers. All sorts of tricks are employed so that the promotional fare attracts *only* the market segment which the airline wants to attract (retired people, business people who want to take their spouses, students at midwinter break, etc.). Here's an example that you may find unbelievable—but it happened to me, so I know it's true:

I was going to fly to Washington on a business trip. Of course, I looked for the cheapest fare. Talking about my upcoming trip to a friend, she said, "I just saw something about reduced fares to Washington in my company's weekly bulletin. I'll look it up for you."

What she found was this: one of the new post-deregulation airlines was offering a fare of $49 *round trip* to Washington. The normal fare was several hundred dollars; off-peak reduced fares were normally about $130 round trip. All one had to do to get the special fare was to call the airline and ask for the "Q" fare. Why "Q?" You got me?

It worked like a charm. I called, made my reservations, then asked for the "Q" fare.

"You mean the $49 round trip?" the reservation agent asked.

"That's the one," I quickly answered. And that's what I paid, without a hitch. But why?

Well, it seems that this new airline wanted to attract *business* flyers away from a long-established airline which ran the same route. To make business flyers aware of the frequency and quality of its service, the new airline was going to tempt them with unbelievably low fares. Once the business travelers knew that there was an alternative to the established carrier, the new carrier would do away with the "Q" fare and compete on a more normal basis, by offering smaller discounts, free drinks, better schedules, etc. But for the time being, the "Q" fare was a real attention-getter.

But . . . you'd never hear about the "Q" fare unless you worked at one of the companies the new airline had targeted! This fare was *not* offered to the general public, or to other market segments, or even to all business flyers. A few calls were made to a few company travel officers, and these chosen few were informed of the "Q" fare and the way to get it. I was just lucky that I found out about it.

So why did the airline allow me to use it? After all, I didn't work at one of the chosen companies.

Simple: They can't refuse. They can't discriminate on such a basis. How would it look to other business flyers if they said, "Sorry, you don't work for Widget

Industries, so I can't give you that fare"? However, if you haven't heard about the fare, and you don't ask for it, that's not their fault. . . . They're not required to inform you of a fare; they're just required not to refuse you! So it's yours if you know about it.

This is really one of the more exotic examples of super-low promotional fares, but it illustrates how they work, and what market segmenting is all about. Remember, there is a fare that's aimed at *you*. When you find it, you'll get an incredible bargain.

Stick to the Four Laws and you'll turn up such a fare.

Non-Refundable Tickets

As I write this, the airlines are hurting. Competition is stiff, and 90% of all airline passengers are traveling on discount tickets which represent, on the average, only 63% of full, normal fares. One tool which the airlines are using to improve their profits is the non-refundable ticket. This is a super-cheap ticket which resembles greatly a ticket on a charter flight, or even a ticket to a sports event, theater performance, or concert: once you've bought it, it's yours. You can't get a refund from the airline, no matter what. However, you may be allowed to sell it to someone else if you can find a buyer.

The non-refundable ticket is yet another attempt by the airlines to deal with "no-shows," the people who make reservations and then do not use them or cancel them. Certainly the airlines will make money from these tickets, because the law of averages dictates that for every 100 non-refundable tickets sold, a few passengers will not be able to make the flight. It may be illness, it may be a flat tire on the way to the airport, it may be a malfunctioning alarm clock, but whatever the reason, at least a few people are going to miss their flights. And then the airline gets to sell their seats to last-minute or standby passengers, and get paid again for the same seat.

So why would anyone want to buy a non-refundable ticket? Because it's cheap. As with charter flight tickets in earlier years, the non-refundable ticket on a scheduled flight may become the most prominent and available discount ticket of all.

Should you gamble on a non-refundable ticket? Certainly. Back in the heyday of charters, people took the gamble daily, in droves, and 99% of the time they enjoyed great vacations at supremely low prices. Your chance of having a good trip is increased with a scheduled carrier, because you'll avoid the possibility of long delays, which sometimes happen to charter flights. And if you think it's risky, buy flight cancellation insurance from your travel agent. It will add a bit to the cost of your trip, but then you needn't worry about the slings and arrows of outrageous fortune.

Fare Codes Decoded

On every airline ticket, for every flight segment, there is a little box marked "fare basis," and in that little box the agent who writes the ticket puts one or more capital letters, sometimes followed by a number of digits. This is the fare code, and it tells anyone who knows the codes a lot about the fare and the restrictions which apply to the ticket. The letters tell you whether the ticket is full-fare unrestricted, or for night flights only, or for use on weekends only, or for excursions. If a number is part of the fare basis, as in **QLN43**, it may be a reference to an airline rule ("see Rule No. 43"), or to the number of days in advance that you must pay for the ticket, or to the maximum number of days your excursion can last.

The airlines do not use a single, consistent system of fare codes. One airline company may use a certain letter, and another company may use a different one.

But there are general guidelines that will help you to decipher the "fare basis." Here is the airlines' recipe for alphabet soup:

A or **AP:** advanced purchase excursion, usually seen on international tickets.

B or **BE:** an excursion, promotional, or discount economy fare.

C: business class; **CD** is sometimes used for senior citizen fares, **CH** for children's fares.

D: first class excursion.

E or **EX:** excursion, often used in combination with another letter.

F; F1, F2, etc; **FN:** first class; a first class fare temporarily discounted; an off-peak night flight fare.

G: group fare.

H: an excursion, promotional, or discount economy fare; a high season fare.

I or **IT:** inclusive tour fare.

J: business class.

K: off-peak unrestricted economy fare, same as **Y,** but off-peak.

L: low season.

M: an excursion, promotional, or discounted economy fare.

N: a night flight, usually cheaper; often seen as **FN** (first class night fare) or **YN** (economy night fare).

O: "shoulder" season, between high and low seasons.

P: first class; with **A,** as in **AP,** advanced purchase excursion.

Q: an excursion, promotional, or discount economy fare.

R: first class on supersonic Concorde flights.

S: full-fare economy or coach, equivalent to **Y.**

T: not used.

U: "shuttle" flights where reservations are not accepted.

V: off-peak full-fare economy fare.

W: weekend fare.

X: midweek fare.

Y: full-fare economy fare in a peak period, the "standard" class in the airline industry.

Z: not used.

THE "SECRET FARE" TICKET: To illustrate how wild things have gotten in the travel industry, you must know about the "secret fare" ticket. Competition among travel agencies and airlines for good customers has become so fierce that the Air Travel Conference (the industry organization) has considered a proposal to introduce a "secret fare" ticket. On this ticket, the space in which the fare is normally written would be blank, at least on the passenger's copy. (The fare would appear on the coupon sent to the airline's accounting office.) This way, a travel agent could cut the fare drastically, and yet no other passenger or agency would ever know!

How to Get Chosen from a Waiting List

When the travel agent or airline reservation clerk tells you that a flight is full, and that your name has been put on a waiting list, you're disappointed. You want to *go*, you don't want to wonder whether you'll get on the plane or not. There are several things you can do to increase your chances of getting on that plane.

All "waitlists" are not equal, and potential passengers are not necessarily selected from a waitlist in strict order from first to last. This may surprise you, but it's true. When a cancellation comes in, and a name is to be selected from the waitlist, the computer chooses according to one or more of the following "preferences:"

● Single traveler; if only one seat becomes available, the computer will pass over couples and family groups and will look for a single traveler. Ironically, the computer will do the same thing again when a second seat becomes available. So two single travelers will get to fly, but a couple will miss out unless they have had the foresight to tell the reservation clerk to put their names on the waitlist *individually*, not as a party of two.

● Passengers taking several flights or segments on the same airline; if you are waitlisted on one segment, and confirmed on other segments of a multi-segment trip, mention this to the reservation clerk and you may be given preference.

● Frequent flyers; if you are a member of an airline's frequent flyer program, mention it to the reservation clerk at the time your name is put on the waitlist.

● Passengers with emergencies; if this is you, don't fail to mention it to the clerk.

The larger the airplane, the greater the chance that someone will cancel. The greatest chance of cancellation is in the section with the largest number of seats—coach. Fewer cancellations will come in for the smaller business and first-class cabins. Also, cancellations come in more frequently on flights to vacation destinations, less frequently on business flights.

If the waitlist is filled, forget it; chances are virtually non-existent that you will get a confirmed seat. In desperate situations there is one last thing you can do:

go out to the airport well before flight time, let the airline clerk know you are there, and then wait. There may be a last-minute cancellation or a no-show. You will not know until a few minutes before takeoff, but every now and then even an "overbooked" flight takes off with empty seats because of no-shows, and you could be in one of those seats. What you pay for a last-minute seat depends on your nerves. If you can stand the suspense, try to arrange a standby ticket (see below). But for the best chance of getting on the plane, agree to pay the normal fare.

By the way, don't try to increase your chances of flying when you want by "double booking," or making identical reservations on several airlines. The airlines are wise to this practice, and they sometimes cancel one reservation when they see two.

Going "Standby": Pleasures and Perils

The concept of standby travel is a useful one for passengers and airlines alike; if they have an empty seat at the last moment, you get it—at the last moment—at a bargain price. Both are happy.

But with standby you cannot make any reservations, and the hazards may be greater than you realize. I once flew on a major airline to London in October and was assured that I would have no trouble getting a standby seat back to New York. After all, it was off-season; I could fly back midweek; it should be no trouble. However, when it came time for my return I checked with the airline; there were no seats available that day on any airline, and it looked very likely that there would be no seat available for a few days, if the computer was doing its job correctly. Thanks to an ingenious airline reservationist I was able to get onto a flight bound for Washington (for which I had to pay some additional money). From Washington I had to make my own way. I wound up renting a car, which cost a fortune and was exhausting. If I had opted to stay in London, though, I would have had to pay for accommodations, meals, and living expenses for who knows how many days.

Standby is therefore most useful when you've got a cheap or free place to stay at each end of the flight, and can afford to hang around and wait, perhaps even a week, for an available seat.

Another warning is in order over price differentials. Recently, many airlines offered standby fares from various American cities to London. The one-way standby fare from New York, for example, was $250. But because of currency fluctuations, the price for a one-way standby fare from London to New York was $290! Don't ever expect the prices for one-way tickets to be the same in different countries. Rather, ask the airline reservation clerk or your travel agent about prices. Often you can buy a round-trip standby ticket figured at the lower price of the two currencies, even though you cannot make a reservation for the return flight.

There is yet another way to go standby: through a standby operator, a company that acts as a "standby broker" for the airlines, getting prospective passengers to the airport and then directing them to the appropriate flights which have leftover seats. For details, see "Even More Low-Priced Tickets," below, under "Standby Organizers."

Getting "Bumped": Tragedy or Bonanza?

You're standing in line at the airport to get your boarding pass. Though you're a little late, and the place is crowded, with lots of concerned looks on lots of faces, you're not worried because you have a confirmed reservation on your flight. But when your turn comes, the agent looks you in the eye and says,

"I'm sorry, but the plane is overbooked. Would you be willing to volunteer to go on a later flight?" This is it: You've just been "bumped."

You don't have to volunteer, of course, but if no one does, the airline has the right to tell some passengers (usually the late arrivals) that their "confirmed reservation" is not worth the computer screen it's printed on. Maybe you're furious about it, maybe just mildly inconvenienced. As you prepare to do battle, the agent says, "We've booked you on the next available flight, which leaves in less than an hour, and I guarantee that you won't be bumped again." And then the agent hands you a coupon for a free round-trip ticket anywhere the airline flies, good for a year, saying "This is a token of our appreciation for being so understanding." You may think well of the airline for being so good to you, but that is hardly the case. By law, the airline must offer you compensation. You don't have to accept the coupon; you can legally pressure them for cash in an amount that you believe compensates you for the inconvenience caused by the airline's breaking its promise. But many people don't mind the extra hour's wait, and love the idea of a free trip, so they happily take the coupon. This is how one enters the profitable world of "denied-boarding ticket coupons."

You can buy and sell such coupons through a coupon broker, getting cash, or cheap flights, as you wish. For more information, see below under "Even More Low-Priced Tickets," in the section on coupon brokers.

For full current details of your rights in cases of denied boarding, get a copy of the U.S. Department of Transportation's airline consumer booklet, entitled "Fly Rights." It costs $1. Send your request to the Consumer Information Center, Pueblo, CO 81009.

How many people get bumped? Well, in the three-month period of April, May, and June, 1986, *a quarter of a million* Americans didn't get on flights for which they had "confirmed" reservations. Almost 80%, or 200,000 of these passengers, volunteered to give up their seats, and were rewarded with free tickets or cash. But four out of every 10,000 passengers were refused boarding, even though they were unwilling to give up their seats. The airlines may be doing slightly better now, but these numbers give you an idea of the magnitude of the problem.

The World's Best Airports

According to a survey of business travelers, the world's ten most preferred airports are (in alphabetical order) Amsterdam, Atlanta, Dallas/Fort Worth, Frankfurt, London (Heathrow), New York (JFK), Paris (Charles De Gaulle), Singapore, Tampa (International), and Zurich. Amsterdam, Singapore, and Tampa generally got the highest ratings.

HOW TO GET THE MOST OUT OF A TRAVEL AGENT

In Chapter 3, I explained how the travel agency system works. Now that you know this, you can use the knowledge to get yourself dramatically lower fares.

A travel agent can do more than simply find the lowest possible fare in the computer reservation system. By using "creative" ticketing methods, or by rebating part of a large commission, an agent can save you lots of money on virtually any kind of fare, especially on the most expensive ones.

What's Rebating, and Is It Illegal?

Travel agents are required by law to sell tickets on scheduled international airlines at the prices established in the airlines tariff and registered with the government. To sell a seat on an international flight for one penny less is against the law.

Travel agents receive a commission from the airline or cruise ship company for every ticket they write. If they "kick back" some of this commission to you, it is called rebating, and, like selling seats at less than the official fare, it is against the law. Or is it?

On international scheduled airline tickets, price-cutting and rebating are supposedly illegal. A travel agent cannot offer you a rebate, or give you one, or tell someone else to give you one, without breaking the law. (However, you can apparently accept a rebate without breaking the law, provided that you have not asked for it.) But it's all a big joke, because the government knows that rebating and price-cutting of international flights go on all the time (see below under "Air Ticket Consolidators"), with the airlines' help and encouragement, and so the government turns a benign—even an encouraging—eye on the violators. The Department of Transportation and Justice Department see rebating and price-cutting correctly as benefits to passengers, and so they never enforce the law.

On international charter flights and tours, agents can do what they like. And on domestic flights, though it may be against airline regulations, it is not really illegal for you to ask for a rebate and for an agent to give you one. In fact, large corporations and even the United States government ask for—and get—big price cuts and rebates all the time because they buy tickets in large volume. The only rule that the airlines seem to enforce sometimes is the one against advertising of rebates.

This all means that you can go to your friendly travel agent and say, "My kid is going to college on the other side of the country, and for the next four years I'm going to be paying transcontinental airfares for the whole family, in one direction or the other. My kid will be coming home for Thanksgiving, and we'll be going out there every now and then, and also for graduation. Since I'm going to be a steady client of yours buying lots of tickets on the same route, I'd like you to consider rebating half of the commission to me. I'll even make my own reservations each time. You just write the tickets."

An arrangement like this could save you several hundred dollars or more, and is perfectly legal. It's a perfect example of the Second Law, because the Point of Mutual Advantage is where the agent receives your steady business, and you receive tickets at prices lower than you could get from another agent or from the airline. Why didn't you know about it before? Because agents aren't allowed to advertise rebates, and usually they don't want you even to know that a rebate is possible. I might add that no agent is going to smile when you raise the subject of rebates. But business is business, and if you're offering an agent the chance to make good money, the agent should be ready to make it worth your while as well.

Currency-Differential Ticketing

As the dawn brightens over Europe, inconspicuously dressed travelers toting bulging briefcases make their way to airports in Frankfurt, London, Rome, and other important cities. They catch flights to other cities, and make the rounds of the travel agencies, selling their wares. What those bulging briefcases contain, and what these people are selling, are airline tickets.

You might well ask, "Why on earth would a travel agent buy airline tickets from some guy with a brief-case? Travel agents don't buy tickets; they sell tickets." Exactly. They buy cheap tickets from the travelers with the briefcases, and then sell them to agency clients at a hefty markup, and the clients are delighted, because these tickets are priced lower than regular tickets, How? Currency exchange rate fluctuations.

As any traveler knows, currency exchange rates fluctuate daily. But in the air travel industry, ticket prices must be fixed every so often to prevent chaos. For example, government regulations require that airlines file tariffs, with prices, periodically for government approval. Airline advertisements quote prices for various flights, and customers must be able to buy tickets at the advertised prices. Also, airlines often promote travel to certain destinations at certain times of year by offering discounted tickets; but the promotion is only advertised in one city or country, not another. With ticket prices fixed, and currency exchange rates fluctuating, some tickets become cheaper than others.

Here's an example. A British airline decides to offer a fare from London to Paris of £100. The French government approves. The exchange rate between the pound sterling and the French franc is £1 = FFr10 at the time. So any traveler can go to the airline's office or a travel agent in London and buy a ticket to Paris for £100; also, any traveler can go to the airline's office or a travel agent in Paris and buy the same ticket for FFr1,000. The price is equal for both tickets, no matter how you figure it.

But then the French franc weakens, and instead of getting ten francs for one pound, a bank gives you eleven. For a French traveler who has only francs this means nothing, because that ticket to London still costs the same FFR1,000. But to a British traveler, there is now a new possibility. If the traveler buys the ticket in London, it still costs £100. But if that British traveler can get to Paris, and exchanges the same £100 for French francs, the bank will hand over FFr1,100. The British traveler takes FFr1,000, buys that air ticket between London and Paris for FFr1,000, and pockets FFr100 (about £9). So that a £100 ticket actually costs only £91 in Paris, but only if you pay for it in francs. If you ask a Paris travel agent what that ticket costs in pounds, the answer would be "£100."

The mysterious travelers with the bulging briefcases profit from this anomaly. They travel from city to city, from country to country, buying cheaply the tickets their agents' clients want, in places where the local currency has weakened since ticket prices were set. They later sell these tickets to their travel agent friends in countries where the currency has strengthened.

This is all quite legal, and you can do it, too. Though few readers of this book will want to join the crowd of mysterious ticket brokers with bulging briefcases, you can profit from currency exchange fluctuations by keeping an eye out for bargains. Don't assume that all tickets between two points cost the same in every country, and don't assume that paying in one currency is the same as paying in another. A reader of my book, *Israel on $30 and $35 a Day*, once wrote to tell me how he had paid several hundred dollars less for an air ticket from New York to Tel Aviv by buying two separate tickets. He bought a ticket from New York to Paris, and then took advantage of a fall in the franc to buy bargain-priced tickets to and from Tel Aviv, and back to New York.

Some foreign travel agents have taken this one step further, into crime. Several years ago, shady travel agents in some African countries with very weak currencies colluded with ticket brokers to rip off the airlines. The brokers paid for expensive tickets with cheap black-market local currency, then flew to Europe or the United States and submitted numerous unused tickets for refunds. The refunds were based on the expensive official exchange rate, not the black-market rate, and so the brokers pocketed enormous sums of good hard currency at the airlines' expense.

But you needn't lead a life of crime to obtain discounted air tickets. In fact, you need not work hard at all. Just keep the Four Laws in mind, and keep your eyes open for opportunities. If you are traveling abroad, ask your travel agent to look into pricing part or all of the ticket in a foreign currency which has a rate that works to your advantage. Often the easiest way to do this is to price the beginning of the flight (from the U.S. to a foreign country) in U.S. dollars, and the return portion in the currency of the foreign country. The more expensive your ticket, the more important it is for you to take advantage of currency-differential ticketing. And it is not illegal, or even against regulations, although the airlines may not like it because they receive fewer of your dollars.

Discovering "Hidden-City" Ticketing

There is another sort of "creative" ticketing about which you may or may not have heard, called "hidden-city" or "point-beyond" ticketing. This sort of ticket takes advantage of the fact that airfares today are not based completely on total miles traveled. Instead, an airfare is established based on distance, popularity of the destination, location of airline hubs, frequency of flights, and other more technical factors. Thus it is possible to pay as much to fly 300 miles from one provincial American city to another as it is to fly 3,000 miles from coast to coast, or from North America to Europe.

"Hidden-city" ticketing takes advantage of this apparently illogical fact, that flying farther sometimes costs less. Here's an example. You want to fly from New York to Charleston, South Carolina, and the fare is $250. But a promotional flight to Florida costs only $165, and you're allowed to take one stopover! So you designate Charleston as the stopover point, and pay your $165. When you get to Charleston, you simply throw away the Charleston-to-Florida flight coupon of the ticket. If you're flying round-trip, you also throw away the Florida-to-Charleston flight coupon, and fly back to New York. The "hidden-city" term comes from the fact that your real final destination is not the city listed as the final destination or turnaround point on the ticket.

Here's another, more adventurous way to work it. Often there are many discounted promotional fares between the east and west coasts, from New York to Los Angeles, etc. These fares often do not allow stopovers, and usually do not apply to non-stop flights, as those are more desirable, and the airline charges more for the convenience of shorter flight time and only one takeoff and landing. If the promotional fare from New York to Los Angeles is $150, and the lowest fare you can find from New York to Denver is $225, you know what you must do: find a flight that stops over in Denver, and pack all of your things into carry-on luggage. (If you check a bag and your ticket gives your destination as L.A., your bag won't be unloaded at Denver!) When you touch down in Denver, you get off with the Denver-bound passengers, taking all your carry-on luggage with you, and you simply ignore the rest of the flight.

This latter method may present difficulties if you want to return from Denver to New York, because you will have only one flight coupon, from L.A. to New York. It may be that the airlines will accept it with a little convincing; or it may be that there is a cheap promotional flight to L.A., or that you can go standby to L.A.! Or, there may be a promotional or standby fare from Denver to New York.

Hidden-city ticketing is particularly valuable if you have a complicated itinerary to a distant foreign city which involves an expensive ticket. It is often possible for a good travel agent to add one last city to your itinerary and *bring down the price of the entire ticket substantially!* It is perfectly legal if the agent uses as a final destination a city that is not too far from the true destination, and if the agent sticks to the rules and indicates to the airline exactly how the route was constructed. The price drop happens because of anomalies in the supremely complex rules of air travel routing and fare-setting, anomalies that are impossible to eradicate completely. As always, the airline doesn't like it because they receive less money, but if the agent follows all the rules, it's all legal and the airlines don't complain.

A Handy Source of "Creative" Fares

Now you know about the sorts of anomalies and complexities which can yield wonderful bargain fares for agents who know how to do "creative" ticketing. But few agents may have the time or expertise to discover all of the possibilities for these sorts of fares and tickets. Well, they don't have to, because the *Best Fares Discount Bulletin* has already done it for them. This monthly newsletter, available from Best Fares, P.O. Box 171212, Arlington, TX 76003 (tel. 817/261-6114) is compiled by researchers who pore through the airline reservation systems looking for just such unusual fares. The newsletter is a goldmine for agents, which is perhaps why it costs so much ($68 for a one-year subscription). You can order it yourself, but you might find it cheaper to suggest to your travel agent that the Discount Bulletin would be an excellent fare construction tool, and that the agency should subscribe.

THE AIRFARE "BARGAIN BASEMENT"

Everyone knows about bargain basements, those marvelous places in which you can buy brand-new, first-quality goods at ridiculously low prices. But do you know why the prices are so low? Simply because no one has bought these things before. There is nothing wrong with the item you buy in a bargain basement. It's just that someone, somewhere, overstocked it, or ordered too many of it, or had it left over at the end of the season. So they passed it on to a bargain basement to try and at least get a little money for it. You will recall that in the beginning of this chapter I stated that "Air travel is a retail commodity." And so it is.

In an earlier edition of this book, I suggested that travel agencies ought to set up branches in the bargain basements of large department stores, because there is virtually no difference in how these leftover travel products are sold. And now it's happened! Filene's department store in Boston, home of the world-famous Filene's Basement bargain outlet, has a travel agency called the Vacation Outlet. It operates in precisely the same manner as the nearby areas in which you can buy men's, women's and children's clothing and accessories, housewares and hardware, at very low prices. Appropriately, the Vacation Outlet is very near the bargain luggage section.

But you don't have to go all the way to Boston to get bargain airfares, cruises, even full all-expenses-paid tour at bargain-basement rates. In the past few years, numerous channels have been opened up to provide you with access to markdown vacations, cut-rate cruises, and last-minute travel bonanzas. Many travel agencies are involved in offering these bargains, but the most important factor in the market is the consolidator.

Air Ticket Consolidators: Friends or Foes?

In the past several years, a new force has appeared on the airline ticket marketing scene. "Consolidators" are brokerage companies, large or small, that buy blocks of airline seats, usually on international flights, or package tour places, or leisure cruise tickets, or even hotel rooms, at cheap "bulk fare" rates from scheduled airlines, tour operators, cruise lines, and hotel chains, and then resell them at a markup to travel agents and the general public. Known for a long time to budget travelers in London as "bucket shops," the consolidators have largely taken over from the charter flight operators of some years ago. They provide a similar service, but with similar perils.

You cannot buy a bulk fare ticket directly from an airline, and a travel agent won't find the bulk fare price in any computer reservation system. Bulk fare tickets can be bought only through travel agencies which handle them, or from the consolidators themselves.

The service provided by consolidators is to the airlines and to the passengers. The airlines have sophisticated computer techniques for predicting the "load factor" on any flight; the load factor is how full that plane will be when it departs. When the computer tells an airline executive that Flight 001 from New York to Rome will probably take off with 150 empty seats (remember, the average flight is 61% full), the executive calls a consolidator and offers to sell 125 seats at a deep discount. (The airline keeps about 25 seats to sell to its last-minute full-fare customers.) The consolidator pays the airline only a fraction of the full fare for each seat, and then sells as many seats as possible to the public at bargain rates. For instance, if the lowest APEX excursion ticket from New York to Rome costs about $850, an airline might sell that ticket to a consolidator for $300, and the consolidator will then sell it to you for $500 to $650.

A travel agent might get involved by buying a few seats or vacation packages from a consolidator for $450 to $550, and selling them to clients for a slight markup. As I said, air travel is a retail commodity, and the airline ticket business today resembles nothing so much as an oriental bazaar, with furious trading and haggling at all times.

The benefits from consolidators to you, the passenger, are obvious: very cheap tickets and guaranteed reservations on recognized world-class scheduled airlines. You can get such tickets from some travel agencies and travel clubs, or you can buy them through toll-free numbers seen in newspaper and television advertisements. But you must be cautious.

Most consolidators, large and small, are honest and straightforward. But consolidators are not required to be bonded (through many are), and they are not required to put your money into a bank escrow account until after you've returned home safely. When you send off your check or give your credit card number to a consolidator, you must trust that you are doing business with a legitimate firm that can deliver the goods. You have little protection if a consolidator goes out of business while you are still waiting to receive your air ticket, except to stop payment on your check or refuse to pay a credit card charge. And once you have your ticket, you must remember that it is not a full fare ticket. You may be subject to restrictions ("stay more than seven days but no more than 180," "stay over at least one Saturday night," "fly only on Tuesday or Wednesday"). And you may have to pay a hefty fee ($50 to $100) if you want to change your flight dates or itinerary, or if you want to cancel the ticket. In fact, you may not be able to change or cancel the ticket at all. Though there are promises of "guaranteed reservations on scheduled airlines," the consolidator may not let you know which airline and which exact flight you'll be on, or even which exact day you'll depart or the exact price you'll pay, until only a short time before your departure. Furthermore, the airline involved may be well-known and perfectly safe, but it may also have a reputation for surly service and late arrivals. There's work and risk involved in buying a bulk fare ticket, but the savings can be spectacular.

As with any travel product, to avoid scams and rip-offs, ask around, call the Better Business Bureau or the American Society of Travel Agents (see the Appendix of this book for their address), and find out the character of the firm you will be dealing with. Get complete information on restrictions, fees, and penalties, and think it all over before you act. If you buy your bulk fare ticket through a reputable travel agent, and pay with a credit card, you should be fairly well protected from the small chance of loss.

IT'S *NOT* STANDBY!: This procedure is not exactly like "standby" status. In standby status, you have put your name on a waiting list, and you are willing to wait for a certain flight on a certain airline. With a consolidator, you can choose at once from many airlines, cruise lines, and tour operators, but you must choose fast, before others beat you to it (just as in a bargain basement). But, just as in a bargain basement, once you have paid for the goods, they're yours. And once the consolidator receives your payment for a trip, you have a *confirmed* reservation.

Where to Find Deep-Discount Fares

Some of the sources for deep-discount, "bulk" or "consolidator" tickets you may already be familiar with. Others are just now beginning to appear.

NEWSPAPERS: Perhaps you've seen those cryptic advertisements in the travel section of your local newspaper, giving only the name of the consolidator or agency, an address, a telephone number (perhaps toll free), and a list of cities, usually overseas, with fares. And the fares are *low*. This is perhaps the easiest way to get a deep-discount or last-minute ticket, but it is absolutely necessary to find out about the company that you deal with so that you can deal with confidence. Please read the section on "Travel Scams," later in the chapter.

TRAVEL CLUBS: You may also have heard about travel clubs such as Discount Travel International (Narberth, Pa.), Encore Short-Notice Travel (Lanham, Mich.), the Last Minute Travel Club (Allston, Mass.), Moments Notice (New York, N.Y.), Spur of the Moment (Culver City, Calif.), Stand-buys Limited (Southfield, Mich.), Vacations to Go (Houston, Tex.), and Worldwide Discount (Miami Beach, Fla.). Such clubs have been around for a while and are often good sources of information and tickets. Some charge membership fees ($25 to $50 per year), but as the savings on any given trip will probably amount to several times the membership fee, few people find the fee a drawback. One thing you should know about such clubs is that besides deep-discount tickets and last-minute tours and cruises, they will usually try to sell you full-price vacations. The prices on these vacations may be quite good and very competitive, and they may offer the convenience of being able to plan in advance, but you should differentiate between these "normal" flights, tours, and cruises, and the much cheaper "last-minute" deep-discount trips.

A few years ago, the travel clubs were the only easy way you could buy a deep-discount or last-minute ticket. But today there are numerous options, and so you may want to explore the other options before you pay a fee.

NEWSLETTERS: Operating much like a travel club, a discount newsletter lets you know about last-minute and bulk-fare trips, and gives you a number through which you can order. The best example of this is *Arthur Frommer's TRAVEL LETTER* (see Chapter 3), written by the founder of our guidebook series himself, and aimed at a general public, but especially useful for senior citizens, who often have schedules free enough to take advantage of last-minute trip opportunities. A subscription to the letter costs less than a membership in a travel club.

TRAVEL AGENCIES: Many travel agencies have decided that "if you can't lick 'em, join 'em," and have given up the hope of selling a "normal" fare to every customer. They have opened bulk-fare and last-minute desks in their offices, and are selling these deep-discount goods to their customers at a slight markup. The final price you pay can vary from one agency to the next, so you might want to shop around, or at least make several phone calls.

Some new agencies deal only in deep-discount travel, such as the Vacation Outlet in Filene's Basement, mentioned above.

AIRLINE PROGRAMS: In an effort to get in on the profits from last-minute travel, even the airlines themselves have established travel clubs. Eastern, for instance, has a weekenders' club which offers its members special discounted rates on weekend trips which often include flight, hotel, transfers, and some meals. The offer is made only about a week in advance, but Eastern figures that its club members will be ready and willing to get up and go if the price is low enough. In coming years, other airlines will no doubt follow the leader and offer some bulk-fare deals themselves. However, by definition, an airline deal will not be as cheap as what a consolidator can offer, so keep your eyes on other bargain outlets as well.

OUTLETS YET-TO-COME: I don't doubt for a minute that there will be many other people purveying last-minute bargains to the general public, such as automobile clubs, civic organizations, even political and alumni groups. An ingenious method about to begin is the selling of last-minute trips through a cable television network show similar to those home-shopping cable shows. The method will always be the same: watch our television show, or subscribe to our newsletter, or join our travel club, and then call our hotline to find out what's currently offered, or to buy your trip, and act quickly to pin down what you want because the trips will be sold fast. And have your bags packed, because the trip departs in a very short time.

No matter from whom you buy your last-minute vacation or bulk-fare ticket, you must keep two things in mind: Know with whom you are dealing, and whether they're legitimate or not; and try to get as close to the consolidator as you can. The more people that stand between you and the airline, the more people there are to add service charges or profit margins to the price of your ticket.

MAKING YOUR OWN DEALS: Believe it or not, you yourself can go into the last-minute trip and consolidator business. Many tour operators and cruise lines will arrange a last-minute, low-fare deal for you if they have the space and are convinced that you won't buy a ticket otherwise. Some tour operators actually welcome last-minute callers, but the cruise lines have their reputations and their standard fare structures to protect, so they won't encourage callers publicly . . . but they're not stupid, and they'll take the money when it's offered. They may make a stipulation that you not reveal to other passengers the low, low price you paid for equal accommodations.

Of course, many companies refuse to advertise, or even admit, that they make separate, private deals at the last minute. Why should someone sign up to pay full price for a cruise or tour if, by waiting until near departure time, they can get it for half or even a third of the asking price? If this were widely known, the tour operator would have no reservations for six months, and then a rush of applicants one week before departure, creating chaos. So you should think in the spirit of the Four Laws: don't expect to see ads in the papers for discounted tours. But search for the Point of Mutual Advantage; don't take "no" for an answer right away, and you'll contact a tour or cruise operator close to flight time and ask what they can offer. You can even work out an arrangement by which they call you back at a given time (two days before the flight, perhaps) and offer you a confirmed reservation at an agreed price. Why not? It's to their advantage, and yours as well. You may be able to make such arrangements through travel agents, or directly with the operator.

As with any last-minute travel, you must nail down your desired tour swiftly after you make your decision, because they'll go fast. A credit card is the easiest way: just give them your number and the tour is yours. If you pay by check, they may insist on waiting for the check to clear, which takes weeks. You may lose your chance.

You may well ask, "What if I don't get a place?" Here you are, all ready to go, having taken off two weeks' vacation from work, found someone to take care of the cat, stopped the newspaper delivery—and you don't get on the tour. It can happen, of course. The risk is partly what brings the price down so drastically. But you can minimize that risk.

Identify several tour operators who operate to your desired destination. Check out their tour offerings and departure dates *just as though you were planning to go on one of them*. Call and ask about reservations. If a few operators say "Sorry, we're full up," then the chances for getting a last-minute discount may be slim. But if all the operators have place available, you might ask about last-minute prices. Give them your name and telephone number, and say that you're willing to go—at a discount—if they tell you by such and such a time. And remember that the Point of Mutual Advantage is somewhere nearby, a certain date and certain price. It is in the interests of both parties to search for it.

When you know that five flights are leaving for the Caribbean on the same weekend, and that the flights were not full two weeks before departure time, and that five tour companies have your number and know that they can sell a seat to you, you won't worry much. The odds are on your side.

EVEN MORE LOW-PRICED TICKETS

There are still other ways to locate the perfect ticket at the perfect price for you. These include frequent flyer programs (whether you belong or not!), standby organizers, charter flights, coupon brokers, and bartering.

Frequent Flyer Awards Are Great!

In the days of those green or gold trading stamps, thrifty consumers received "free" merchandise for collecting a certain number of stamps. Well, actually, the suitcase or blender or stuffed toy was not really free, because the retail merchant who gave you the stamps had to pay for them—and the merchant passed those costs on to you. But with frequent flyer programs, which have been around since 1981, you are getting a much better deal. Airlines often have unsold seats, and one way they repay you for your loyalty is by giving you freebies such as upgrades to an aircraft's first class section, or even free air tickets. Competition among airlines for loyal customers is fierce, and when you receive a frequent flyer award, you really are getting something of substantial value.

People who know the airline industry all agree: *always* sign up for an airline's frequent flyer program when you take your first flight on that airline (unless you are already a member of the program). It usually costs you nothing at all to do so. And the major programs are so widespread these days that any later flight, or hotel stay, or car rental, or some other travel service, may bring you "points" on a program you've signed up for. In addition, the airlines periodically offer special deals on air tickets or even package vacations to their frequent flyer program members. If you're not a member, you'll never find the special offer in your mailbox.

When you've accumulated a good number of points in your frequent flyer "account," you're free to redeem them for a coupon good for a flight, or hotel stay, or some other award. Often you can take the flight on another airline, if that airline is a partner in the same frequent flyer program. The coupon you receive for your award is truly valuable.

In fact, a coupon is so valuable that there is a lively trade in frequent flyer mileage certificates just as there is in denied-boarding coupons (see below). Trading frequent flyer awards is a lot riskier, however. It is strictly against airline regulations, but most of the time the airlines never discover that the "relative" to whom you have "given" a coupon is not a relative at all. In most cases, airline personnel do not ask for identification when you check in for a domestic flight anyway, so who's to know you got your ticket with a "grey-market" coupon?

There are some travelers who fly so much that they will never, ever use up all of the mileage points in their frequent flyer accounts. These travelers are the ones who sell their mileage certificates. For instance, a business executive who flies to Europe every week or two might sell a certificate good for a first-class round-trip flight between New York and London. Such a ticket costs almost $4,000 if bought through normal channels. The broker pays the traveler about $1,400. The broker then turns around and sells the coupon to a travel agent or corporate travel manager for about $1,800, and the agent or travel manager exchanges the coupon for a first-class, round-trip ticket between New York and London, which can be sold to a customer for about $2,400. So everyone pockets big profits (or savings), but the airline loses a $4,000 sale.

You don't have to go through a broker to buy or sell a denied-boarding coupon or frequent flyer award. You can simply advertise that you want to buy or sell such a coupon in a classified advertisement in a newspaper. In the big metropolitan papers, there is usually a heading such as "Travel" or "Tickets," and that's the place to look, or to place your ad.

Note that this is a good way to turn even a low-value "companion" coupon into cash. Some frequent flyer awards state that if you buy a full-fare ticket at a normal price, you have the right to bring a companion along for a very reduced rate, or even for free. Your problem, then, is to find someone willing to go on the same plane with you, and looking for a bargain. Besides checking in together, you needn't know the person at all or do anything more with them; and even the joint check-in may be unnecessary in some cases.

Standby Organizers

Besides the ticket consolidators described above, there is another sort of operator who offers a valuable service. This is the standby organizer, a broker who signs up lots of prospective travelers, gets them to the airport, and then directs them to airlines that have leftover seats just before departure. With this sort of operator you normally pay a fee, or at least a deposit on your ticket price. The operator tells you when you must arrive at the airport, and promises to try to get you a seat to a general destination.

It goes like this. You see an ad in the newspaper travel section for super-cheap fares to Europe. You call the operator, and are told to send in $20 or $25, and then to be at the airport on Tuesday evening, ready to go. When you show up, the operator may tell you that you can choose among Paris, Stockholm, or Zurich. Some operators will promise only to get you to "Europe," while others will call you only if things look good for the particular destination city you want. If you must choose, you make your pick, and then wait to see if there is a seat. If there is (and the operator would not have called you to come if there were not a good chance of a seat), you go. If not, you can try the next available flight, that evening or the next day, and you'll have priority over any other standby customer arriving later. If the operator finds you a seat to "Europe" (say, to Rome), and it's just not anywhere near where you want to go, then you can refuse to fly, but you lose your deposit.

The standby operator system is crude, but it provides about the cheapest fares going, on the world-class scheduled carriers.

All about Charters

Once the low-fare stars of the air travel industry, charter flights are not as much in evidence these days. The reasons for this obscurity are obvious. Now there are so many different ways to get cheap flights, that filling an entire plane for one special charter trip seems cumbersome and old fashioned.

But charter flights are still around, and they are better than ever. Actually, to call them "charter" flights at all is not accurate in most cases. Operators of charter flights run so many flights, usually on a regular weekly schedule, that they resemble the scheduled airlines in most ways. The big difference between a charter company and a scheduled airline is that the charter operator does not own or lease its own airplanes and airport services. Instead, it rents—"charters"—them, usually from a "supplemental carrier," an airline that does not run scheduled flights. Sometimes, charter operators rent their planes and services from the big scheduled airlines. And a charter ticket entitles you only to a certain flight on a certain day at a certain time. If you miss that flight, you've lost your money . . . period! Flexibility is nil, except that you are usually allowed to sell the ticket to someone else before the flight, if you can find a buyer.

But who are these supplemental carriers? Today there are only a handful of independent American airlines in the charter business, including Tower Air, American Trans Air, and Rich International. They have good, safe planes and expert crews. Their meals are catered by the same companies that cater to the scheduled airlines. They use the same terminal facilities at the airport; in fact, they usually rent departure and arrival gates from the major scheduled airlines.

The European charter airlines are just as good, and perhaps better. In most cases, European charter airlines are wholly-owned subsidiary companies of each country's national flag carrier. For instance, KLM owns and operates Martinair; British Airways has its British Airtours; Lufthansa has Condor; Swissair provides the same high-quality service on its Balair charter planes; and Air Charter International is almost the same as its parent, Air France. A few other charter airlines are independent companies not owned by the national carriers. These include LTU (West Germany), Spantax (Spain), and Minerve (France).

Why would world-class national airlines bother to set up charter airlines to compete with their regular scheduled flights? There are several reasons.

First of all, charter flights have one-class seating. Every seat is coach. On some charter airlines, notably the European ones, seating is much more cramped than on a scheduled airline; on the American charters, seating is about equal to what you'd expect in coach class on a scheduled airline.

Second, tickets on a charter flight are usually non-refundable, doing away with the airlines' pernicious problem of "no-shows," people who make reservations but then never show up for the flight.

Third, charters are not bound to strict schedules as are the scheduled airlines. This means that it is perfectly legal for a charter flight to announce a delay in departure of four, six, or even 12 or more hours (scheduled flights and arriving flights have runway priority over charter departures). Though such long delays are unusual, they are permissible, and should be anticipated. In addition, a charter company has the right to cancel a flight entirely, even at the last moment. Cancellations, when they occur, are usually made because a flight was insufficiently booked. In many cases, the charter company will help you to find another flight, perhaps on another charter. Also, you should consider buying trip cancellation insurance, which usually costs about 5% of the cost of the trip. If the charter is cancelled, or if there is illness or a death in the family and you cannot take the trip as scheduled, the insurance may cover your loss. Read the cancellation insurance policy carefully before you buy, as not all foreseeable situations are insured.

In any case, and most importantly, you should know what you are buying. The charter operator will give you, or mail you, a "Tour Participant Contract" which spells out all of the rules. The contract may be in small print on the last page of a brochure or booklet. Read it! You will discover, for instance, that the charter operator has the right to cancel the flight within a certain period before the flight, and that a departure delay of even 48 hours may not go against the terms of the contract. Know what you're getting. Charter flights are marvelous bargains, but you must not expect things that were never promised to you.

WHEN A CHARTER GOES BANKRUPT . . .: Every now and then a news report circulates, bemoaning the fate of several hundred people stranded in some distant city because their charter tour company went bankrupt. In some cases other airlines will help them to fly home (usually on a standby or reduced-fare basis). But sometimes they're just out in the cold. If they want to get home, they have to buy a regular one-way ticket, the most expensive kind of ticket there is.

This does not happen frequently at all, especially considering the thousands of charters that operate each year. Even so, you'll want to protect yourself from such a fate. You can, easily.

When you sign up for a charter, whether you do it on your own or through a travel agent, make sure that your money (check or credit card payment) goes *not* to the charter company, but into that company's *escrow account* in a bank. Each charter company is supposed to open an escrow account at a reputable bank, and to keep all funds relating to each particular charter flight in that account *until after the flight has successfully returned*. When the flight returns, the bank releases the funds to the company—not before.

Even having your money in the escrow account is not completely foolproof (what is?), because enforcement of the escrow law is not perfect, and things can go wrong. But most of the time the escrow payment protects you very well.

HAVE YOU HEARD ABOUT *JAXFAX*?: Where do you ferret out the dates, departure cities, and prices for charter transportation? The most obvious way is to consult the Sunday travel section of your local newspaper, or if you live in a small town, the Sunday travel section of the nearest large-city newspaper. Any major charter program will certainly be advertised.

A fare more comprehensive source of information is the monthly *JaxFax*, magazine of the air chartering industry, published from 280 Tokeneke Rd., Darien, CT 06820 (tel. 203/655-8746). Travel agents all over the nation subscribe to *JaxFax* for its listings of all charters scheduled to depart this country in the next six months. Subscription price is $12 a year, but you don't have to subscribe. Simply visit a nearby travel agency and ask courteously whether you may peruse their current copy of *JaxFax* on the premises. Since the same travel agent can then book you aboard that charter and earn a commission, he or she will usually be happy to oblige.

Free Money from Coupon Brokers

As of this writing there is a brisk trade in buying and selling the coupons. In fact, you may be approached by a coupon broker the moment you turn away from the airline check-in counter. The broker quotes you a price, and you agree. You open your hand and the broker places several crisp $100 bills in it. Wow!

The broker was there all the time, hiding behind a newspaper, or dark glasses, or a soft-drink machine. Brokers know the flights that are frequently oversold, and they know all of the other brokers. The first broker to arrive at the beleaguered check-in counter takes a scrap of paper and jots down the names of all the other brokers as they arrive on the scene. The first one there gets first crack at the coupons, the second arrival gets second try, and so on.

Coupon brokerage is a darkish corner of the air transport industry. Is it legal? Let me shine some light on it.

Though the airlines don't like the practice, it is not, as of this writing, illegal for you to sell a coupon, and it is probably not illegal for brokers to buy and sell them. And there's big profit in it for everybody . . . except the airlines. They figure that they lose money, because the coupon was supposed to be used by you for an extra, unplanned trip. Instead, it is sold to a traveler who has already planned a trip, and who would buy a regular ticket from the airline, except that by buying a coupon, that traveler can get the flight cheaper.

Some savvy travelers actually set themselves up to get bumped just to earn the coupons. They buy tickets on flights which they think will be oversold, and then are first to speak up when the call goes out for volunteers. There are even stories of people able to work their way around the country on coupons, paying out nothing for flights.

What does all this mean to you? It means that you should be prepared in several very important ways. First, be prepared to ask yourself, "Shall I volunteer to get 'bumped'?" On some flights, you will definitely not want to, but on others, when you've got a little extra time, why not? You'll probably be airborne within an hour or two in any case, and you could have a coupon for a free round-trip flight in your pocket. Second, if you are approached by a broker, maybe you should not accept the broker's first offer. If the coupon is worth $100 to someone, why not $200? Do a little haggling. If the broker refuses, you can always just accept his first offer.

Whether you get a free flight or free money, you're well off either way. By the way, this whole coupon game is good in the United States on domestic airlines which must abide by Department of Transportation regulations regarding bumping. However, the Department of Transportation's rules for international flights are different; and in foreign countries, with other laws, none of this may be possible.

Should I sign up for a tour? Of course you should. Often there is no cheaper way to get airfare and accommodations, even if you make all the arrangements yourself. And remember, you can usually buy air only or even toss out the land package and still save money.

Tickets Without Cash or Credit

Believe it or not, you can obtain air tickets (and even cruises and tours) for absolutely no money—through barter. Barter is when two people exchange *goods or services*, not money, and it's very big in the travel industry.

What's the advantage? Basically, both barterers are passing on discounts to each other. If you make or sell something, or have valuable services (musician, doctor, lawyer, accountant, carpenter, plumber, electrician, etc.) you can barter. Here's how it works:

You are a professional who would gladly trade, say, six hours of working time in exchange for a ticket to Hawaii. So you contact a barter broker, or join a barter club, and look for an airline person or travel agent who needs your services (they will be looking for you!). If the ticket is valued at $300 and you charge $50 per hour for your time, you simply do six hours' work for the person who provides the ticket.

The person who provides the ticket is happy because the ticket was a bonus, or a special low fare not generally available. In effect you both get first-quality goods at discount rates.

Note that you must pay all applicable taxes on barter transactions as though you were buying for cash. The aim of barter is not to avoid taxes. Rather, it is to exchange business discounts with others.

How do you find out about barter? Simple. Look in the Yellow Pages under "Barter & Trade Exchanges." Contact one of the organizations listed, and follow the Four Laws.

Air Courier Flights

The fastest way to get important documents and materials from one point to another is to get on a plane with them and fly there. In a matter of hours, you can be anywhere in the world.

Let's say you found 50 businesses that would pay $35 a pound for such a sure-fire courier service. If you filled your suitcases to the 44-lb. international baggage limit, you could earn $1,540—plenty for your air ticket and other expenses, with a hefty profit left over.

This is exactly the way air courier companies work. By utilizing the checked baggage allowance of an actual passenger as freight transportation, these firms provide a valuable service to businesses, and make a good profit.

But who is the air courier, the person who actually flies from New York to Los Angeles or London with a suitcase full of papers? It could easily be you.

Here's how: If you live in or near New York, Los Angeles, Miami, or one of several other large business cities, you contact an air courier company (see below, or look in the *Yellow Pages* under "Air Courier Services"), obtain an application, fill it out, and receive approval. You then coordinate flight dates with the courier company, and pay a fee which ranges from insubstantial to several hundred dollars—but always less than half of what you'd pay even for a bargain-priced air ticket to the same destination. You pack a small carry-on bag and head out to the airport.

At the airport, you meet an agent of the courier company, who has already checked-in several sacks or boxes of documents and materials. The agent gives you your ticket and a "manifest," or list of the contents of the checked baggage, and you board your flight.

When you arrive, another courier company agent meets you, takes the manifest, retrieves the baggage, bids you goodbye, and you're free of your courier obligation. If your flight is abroad, the manifest becomes a customs declaration, but its accuracy (and any duties) are the responsibility of the air courier company. On the return flight, you do the same thing again.

The advantages? Air travel to many exciting cities, both in North America and overseas, for a mere fraction of the lowest available airfares.

The disadvantages? You can only travel with carry-on luggage, no matter where you're going or for how long. And the courier company has the right to "bump" you from your flight at the last moment; the ticket, though it's in your name, is actually the property of the courier company.

Is this illegal? Not at all. Many reputable firms send their time-sensitive documents and materials by air courier services, and there is no hanky-panky with drugs or other illegal substances. This is a business, not a racket.

The main air courier cities are New York, Los Angeles, and Miami. With the advent of Federal Express, facsimile transmission, and electronic mail, air courier opportunities may not last for decades, so grab them while you can. Write to one or more of these companies, requesting information and application forms; enclose a stamped, self-addressed business-size envelope:

Air Facilities, 3100 N.W. 72nd Ave., Suite 111, Miami, FL 33122 (tel. 305/477-8300).

Graf Airfreight, 5811 Willoughby Ave., Hollywood, CA 90038 (tel. 213/461-1547).

Halbart Express, 147-05 17th Street, Jamaica, NY 11434 (tel. 718/656-8189).

Now Voyager Freelance Courier, 71 Varick St., New York, NY 10013 (tel. 212/431-1616).

TNT Skypak, 400 Post Ave., Westbury, NY 11590; or 845 Cowan Rd., Burlingame, CA 94010.

WHY YOU SHOULD TAKE A TOUR

The perennial question: Should I sign up for a tour? Of course you should. Often, there is no cheaper way to get airfare and accommodations, even if you make all the arrangements yourself.

And remember, you can often purchase the air travel only and still save an incredible amount over the regular fares by doing so. Even if you can't purchase air only, you can always toss out the land package (hotels and meals) that you've paid for, make your own accommodations and meals arrangements, and still save money. Here's why. Most of the land packages are negotiated at incredibly low prices, so that even if you add the cost of the land package into your overall airfare you'll still be paying less than if you took a regular airfare (or sometimes even a discounted airfare). So don't look down your nose at the package tour; if you have limited time, often you can't beat it for value.

If you do buy the whole package, look carefully at what you do in fact get for your money. Read the brochure carefully, including all the fine print. Ask friends if they've taken a tour with the outfit you're thinking of traveling with. You might even go so far as to check with the hotel of your choice about what kind of room you can expect. If you're promised beachfront accommodations, make sure that you're not going to be staying at a hotel miles from the beach with just a glimpse of the sea off in the distance. These things can happen. Also, ask what kind of food will be served at mealtime. You don't want dried up veal chops and other American fare. And remember, many of the sightseeing offerings, nightlife packages, and other little bonuses may *seem* to be included in the price. Often they're not. Make sure.

If you still don't get satisfactory treatment, then you can inform your Better Business Bureau and the consumer department of the U.S. Tour Operators Association, 211 East 51st St., Suite 12-B, New York, NY 10022 (tel. 212/944-5727). Better to make sure you'll have a good trip before you go!

Package Tour Quality Checklist

When you compare tours, tour operating companies, itineraries, and prices, here are some things to look carefully at:

● Quality of hotels: Ask a knowledgeable travel agent, or buy a guidebook and see how they describe the hotel(s) you'll be staying in. It may not matter to you that your hotel is budget class, with spartan furnishings and few services. But if it is such a hotel, the tour had better be quite cheap.

● Hotel location: Is your hotel near where you want to be? The museums? The beach? Can you walk from your hotel to interesting sights, restaurants, and nightspots, or must you take a bus or taxi everywhere? Hotels in inconvenient locations are cheaper, and some tour operators use them because it allows them to advertise a lower price.

● Precise itinerary: This means not just the number of days and nights, but the days and nights you'll be spending where you want to be. A tour to Israel that spends two days in fascinating Jerusalem and the same amount of time in Beersheba, a nice but fairly boring town, is no bargain. Find one that spends four nights in Jerusalem, with a day-trip to Beersheba.

● Meals included: How many, and what quality? If the brochure says only "breakfast included," that could mean soggy toast and watery coffee. But if it says "a lavish buffet breakfast," you've got a better chance of good food. If in doubt, ask the tour operator very specifically about sample menus. Pick a day, and a hotel, and ask what they might be serving. Are lunch and dinner "table d'hôte," a set menu with no choice allowed? Or can you choose from the hotel or restaurant's regular menu as you like? If the tour operator says, "You can order anything on the menu and it's included," is it completely included? Often on tours you are allowed to choose as you like from the menu, but the most delicious items are subject to a surcharge.

● Sightseeing included: Beware of the tour to Istanbul for which the brochure states, "We'll go to the Blue Mosque, and Sancta Sophia, and Topkapi Palace, and the Cistern Basilica, and then visit the Grand Bazaar for a afternoon of shopping. The operative word here is "visit," and to "go to" the Blue Mosque, etc., may mean only that your bus swings by so that you can take a photo through the bus window! It may be that the only place you actually get out of the bus and visit is the Grand Bazaar. Find out how many buildings and sites you will actually tour; pick a favorite attraction and ask specifically how long the tour spends there and what you see, and then compare the answers from several tour groups. Also, check whether sightseeing admissions, guides, and other costs are included in the tour price.

● Special events and entertainment activities included: A tour with a welcome cocktail party, theme party, concert evening, and other activities offers you more than one which states, "the evening is yours to enjoy as you like," unless you specifically want lots of time on your own.

● "Optional" activities: You can be certain that any side-trip, special event, or performance listed as "optional" in a tour brochure is going to cost you more. "Optional" actually means "you pay more for this."

● Size of tour group: Many groups fill a normal tour bus, about 45 people. If you have more than this, the group is unwieldy. It takes quite a while to get 45 passengers on and off a bus, through an airport, etc., so a tour with smaller groups (18 to 25 people) is definitely a better-quality tour.

● Guides: If a tour can boast that a company guide will accompany you every step of the way, that's a real advantage. Many companies have only one representative in a destination city. The representative meets you on arrival, settles you in your hotel, and then turns you over to local guides. This may work all right, but it is definitely better to have a single person available every step of the way. You can get to know such a guide (and the guide can get to know you and your needs), and service may be considerably better.

HOW TO AVOID TRAVEL SCAMS

"Free trips!" "Flights to Hawaii, only $39!" "You may already have won!" How is one to know when confronted with a travel scam? How can you tell when the offer that sounds too good to be true is indeed false? There are so many desirable and truly stupendous legitimate travel values available today, that it's easy for the rip-off deals to hide among them. Though there's no foolproof way for everyone to avoid dishonest travel promotions all of the time, you can do a great deal to protect yourself. Let me tell you right up front: most scams are perpetrated by "telemarketing," that is, by a scam operator calling victims "cold." Beware, beware when you answer the phone and someone you never heard of tries to sell you the bargain of your life!

The first and easiest thing you can do is to book your travel through a travel agent, and to pay with a credit card, in person. A travel agent must accept some responsibility for the arrangements made, and if there is anything questionable or unsure about a particular arrangement, reservation, tour, or company, the agent must let you know. And if you pay by credit card in person, you can refuse payment to the credit card company if you do not receive the services for which you've arranged.

I hasten to add a warning: one of the most pernicious travel scams is one (described below) that involves a request, by telephone, for your credit card number. *Never* reveal your credit card number to anyone you don't know who calls you and asks for it. Give your credit card number only when you initiate the call and are sure of the legitimacy of the firm that you are calling, or can otherwise confirm the identity of the person and the company who will make use of your number.

Your second line of defense, after the travel agent and the credit card, is to know something about how travel scams operate. I'll describe some of the classic scams below, so that you can recognize them when you see them. But keep in mind that travel scams try very hard to look like legitimate bargain offers, and you should not pass up a legitimate offer just out of suspicion. Rather, *check it out*. I'll explain how to do that a bit later on.

The Classic Travel Scams Revealed

The *modus operandi* of scam operators changes all the time, but one thing is always the same: scam operators try as hard as they can to make their scams look like legitimate bargains. As the dishonest deals are discovered, their perpetrators move on to different areas of business and change their tactics. But they are always around. One estimate of travel scam operators says that it takes a month for them to buy a mailing list, mail out postcards or flyers or make lots of telephone calls; another month to garner responses, credit card numbers, and checks; and a third month to cash in, close down, and disappear. Watch out for these:

THE MYSTERY CALLER: The worst of the travel scams is the mysterious caller who identifies him or herself as a travel agent or tour operator or sweepstakes official. The caller tells you that you have won or been selected to receive a free trip, or flight, or cruise, or vacation, etc. If you say that you don't remember entering a contest, or giving out your name, they'll say, "Oh, lots of people forget. It happens all the time." Then they'll tell you that although the trip is free, you must pay the taxes, or they must confirm your identity, etc., and so they must ask you just to give them your credit card number. Also, you must tell them your number right now, or the prize will be granted to the runner-up. Don't fall for it!

If you think there's a chance that the offer is legitimate, ask them to send you written materials. Don't listen if they say that there's no time. Express Mail services can ship documents anywhere in the United States overnight, so if time is short, and the offer is legitimate, they can send documents to you by Express Mail, or Federal Express, or United Parcel Service, or some other courier service. Once you've received printed materials explaining the offer completely, and once you've checked to see that such a company actually exists at the address and telephone number given, and once you've called a travel agent or

Better Business Bureau to inquire about the legitimacy of the company and its offers, then you can accept or refuse the offer as you like. If the offer gives specific information about travel service providers (airlines, hotels, tour companies), call them to make sure that they are indeed participating in the offer.

A variation on the Mystery Caller is to get you to do the calling. It's the scam described below under "Too Good to Be True."

THE BOGUS VOUCHER: You are offered a voucher good for an incredibly cheap flight, or a stay in a hotel, or another travel service. Just send in $30 or $40 or $60, and the voucher is yours. You send in a check. That may be the end of it; you may never hear from the company. Or, you send your check, and receive the voucher, but when you get to the airport for your flight, or arrive at the hotel, they've never heard of the company, or the special offer, and they won't honor the voucher. You've lost your money.

The beauties of this scam, as far as its perpetrators are concerned, are several. First, the amount of money is small, and most people won't go to great lengths to recover $30 or even $60. Second, vouchers are indeed an accepted practice in the travel industry, and so the deal looks as though it could be legitimate. Third, there's a time lapse between when you pay for the voucher, and when you actually use it, which gives the scam artists time to disappear.

A recent development in the travel industry may help to reduce the number of voucher scams. These are travel vouchers issued by the big credit card companies such as VISA and MasterCard. Such vouchers are underwritten by an issuing bank, and bear the credit card company's logo and details of validity, so you can put more trust in their value.

TO GOOD TO BE TRUE: There are some companies, perhaps established even four or five years, that put out extremely deceptive advertisements. One such scam runs like this: you receive a postcard saying that you have been "selected" (how? they never say) to receive one of several "vacation packages." No prices or details are given, but you are asked to call the company, perhaps on a particular day, for more details. When you call, a company agent asks your choice of destination, and tells you that the trip will be for so many days and nights. Next comes payment. The agent may say that the vacation is free, but that you must pay a "service charge;" or perhaps the agent will say that the "vacation package" is yours for an extremely low price. In either case, you must pay the price or fee at once to "pin the offer down," or to "meet the deadline," or that acceptance of the offer is "first come, first served," though you can take your "vacation" later. The agent will usually ask for your credit card number. Several days or weeks later you may receive a voucher in the mail, good for your "vacation." You are instructed to mail this voucher to another company, which will accept it and make your reservations. What you discover sooner or later is that both companies are part of the same operation; that the "vacation" does not include transportation, or meals, but only a reservation at a sleazy motel somewhere. When you ask for a refund, an agent may say that the "service charge" is not refundable, or that it will take some time, or that "the check is in the mail."

Is this whole process illegal? Well, yes and no. They'll give you your five nights in the sleazy motel if you want them! To prove that it's a case of deceptive advertising is difficult, expensive, and time-consuming. A company may undertake these shady practices, come under investigation by state or federal officials, and then stop the advertising for a while, just long enough so that the investigations are dropped. When officials have turned their attention to the next scam, the shady operators start up again, perhaps in another state. All they need is a mailing list, some postcards, a telephone, and a compliant sleazy motel or two.

How can you protect yourself? First, no travel agent would have done business with such a company. But even without an agent, be suspicious of any offer which does not give you full details of the offer, in large print or small print, before requiring payment. As for the "urgency" of the matter, you can still take advantage of an urgent offer by asking them to rush full printed details of the offer to you. Or simply get the company's telephone number, hang up, call a travel agent or Better Business Bureau and ask about the deal, and then call the company back if you're satisfied that it's legitimate. No honest company would tell you that you should not do this, or that "there's not enough time."

HALF REAL, HALF FAKE: Another scam involves a company that provides a legitimate service to you at a legitimate price, but also demands that you purchase another service, and this other service turns out to be a scam. For instance, you might get a call or a note in the mail saying that you can fly down to some sunny vacation spot on a well-known airline, and stay in a well-known hotel. The company actually does book the flight for you, and all goes according to plan . . . until you arrive at your hotel. The reservation clerk does not have your reservation, and the hotel does not know the travel company that supposedly made your reservation, or sent payment, or that gave you a "voucher good for your stay at the hotel." The fact that the airline part of the deal was legitimate throws you off balance. You assume that it is not the travel company's fault but the hotel's fault, and so you join battle with the hotel, a process that will get you nowhere, as the hotel is completely ignorant of the whole scam, and entirely blameless.

FALSE ADVERTISING: With so many fantastic and legitimate travel bargains available these days, many very respectable, world-class companies have begun to write their advertisements in misleading ways. For instance, one company just publishes a list of incredibly low fares to Europe along with the company name and telephone number. When you call and inquire, you discover that the fare is for off season, on Tuesday only, standby! This is all right, but they should give some indication in the ad that there are lots of restrictions, or that it's a standby proposition.

A variation of this is to advertise, just before the busy summer tourist season, airfares or tour package prices that will be applicable only in the late fall. Readers of the ads get excited about the prices, only to call and find out they'll have to fly in November! In classic bait-and-switch style, the company will then try to convince them to fly in summer, at a much higher price.

Another classic ploy is the ad which states "Vacations starting at $200, complete." The catchword here is "starting at," of course. That means that there are two seats on the plane (perhaps just one!) at that price. It's a loss leader, and your chance of getting a decent vacation at that price are virtually nil. This sort of ad is willfully and knowingly misleading, but it is used by many of our most "respected" companies.

How to Protect Yourself

At a time when travelers have never had it better, it's a shame that unscrupulous promoters and out-and-out crooks bilk innocent vacationers of their hard-earned money. But it is precisely because travelers have it so good, with so many excellent bargains available, that the crooks succeed. Look upon the time spent in checking out your vacation bargain as time well invested in your own happiness and security. And watch out for the attitude which whispers to you, "Oh, don't worry. This is vacation! This is supposed to be fun!" Don't let romantic dreams of the perfect, incredibly cheap vacation fill your mind until *after* you are sure that the dream will come true. Once you're sure, dream on!

But first, confirm information, offers, and legitimacy from several sources. Call your local Better Business Bureau, or, if they have no information, call Directory Assistance for some large city (New York, Chicago, Los Angeles, Houston) and ask for the number of that city's Better Business Bureau. Then call that Bureau and ask your questions. Travel scams are usually nationwide, and often concentrated in big cities, and the problem may show up in a big city first.

You can also call travel industry organizations such as the U.S. Tour Operators Association (USTOA), and the American Society of Travel Agents (ASTA). Their addresses are listed in the Appendix to this book.

Finally, you can call your state Attorney General's office. The office staff will be among the first to hear that people have been defrauded, and they can also give you good advice on ways to confirm a company's legitimacy.

YOU CAN BEAT JET-LAG!

Jet-lag is one of the banes of the modern traveler. On a short vacation, it's disappointing to find yourself sleeping through the best part of an otherwise exciting day in a distant city or resort.

Until recently, it seemed as though jet-lag was just

one of the tradeoffs we had to give for the convenience of fast air travel. But the Argonne National Laboratory, 9700 South Cass Ave., Argonne, IL 60439, has found a way to beat jet-lag. Here's the secret:

Jet-lag happens when your body's "clock" receives confusing "signals" on a trip, such as long naps at midday, cocktails for breakfast, and breakfast at suppertime. Until it sorts out these signals and realizes that it is in a new and different time environment, your "clock" will try to put you to sleep when it always has, which is your hometime bedtime. It does this even if your hometime bedtime is the same as teatime in London. Instead of dozing over your tea and biscuits, do this:

"Reset" your body's clock by giving it certain new signals. Start four days before you leave.

On the fourth day before you leave, eat a hearty high-protein breakfast and lunch. If you drink coffee, do it *only* between 3 and 5 p.m. Then, for dinner eat mostly carbohydrates—pasta, crêpes, potatoes, and other starches, sweet desserts if you like. This will stimulate your body to sleep.

On the third day before you leave, eat very sparingly: salads, light soups, unbuttered toast, fruit. Keep the total of calories and carbohydrates way down. Again, don't drink coffee except between 3 and 5 p.m.

On the second day before you leave, repeat what you did on the fourth day before: big breakfast and lunch (have steak and eggs if you like!), coffee only between 3 and 5 p.m., and a carbohydrate supper.

On the day before you leave, repeat the fasting of the third day before: salads, light soups, fruit. If you want coffee or any other caffeinated beverage, drink it according to which way you'll be flying. If you're headed west (toward Hawaii or Japan, for example), drink it in the morning. Headed east (toward Europe) drink it only between 6 and 11 p.m.

Now for the flight itself. Don't drink alcoholic beverages during the flight (sorry, that's the rule!). With their quick conversion to carbohydrates, they alter the delicate signals you've been sending to your body's clock for four days; and in the thin air of an airplane cabin, they affect you even more than when you drink on the ground. So no drinks.

Sleep as much as you can, until it's breakfast-time *at your destination point*. Don't sleep any longer than this. When people are eating breakfast where you're going, wake up and do the same. Have a nice big protein-rich breakfast, and drink coffee or tea if you like. For the rest of the day, stay alert and active, have meals according to the normal schedule at your destination, and forget about jet-lag! Remember to follow the same procedure on your return flight.

8

Solving Your Transportation Needs

The Third Law, "Look Beyond the Obvious," is especially applicable to ground transportation. Most of us have long-standing habits and thought patterns regarding surface travel. Many times these habits and thoughts have very little to do with today's realities in the realm of travel. By observing the Four Laws, and Third Law in particular, we can increase our enjoyment of travel while lowering the costs considerably.

In this chapter, I'll show you how to save surprising amounts of money when you rent a car, drive your own car, take a train (at home or abroad, commuter or long distance), ride the bus, or board a ship. Your attitude at first will probably be, "I know all about those things. He has nothing to tell me." Well, read carefully. I bet you'll change your mind.

SURPRISING FACTS ON *REAL* COSTS

In many situations, we assume that going by private car is the least expensive way to go. And often we assume that renting a car is expensive. Well, there are many times when these thoughts are correct. But you will be surprised at some of the figures and facts given below, and they will change your outlook.

Wow! That Much?

The American Automobile Association, 811 Gatehouse Rd., Falls Church, VA 22047 (tel. 703/222-6701), calculates that it costs over $178 per day for the average American family of four to take a summer vacation by private car. This figure includes driving costs, meals, and lodging. The price for two people without children might well be over $100 a day.

It costs over 30¢ per mile to own and operate a compact car in America, and this doesn't even include tolls and parking fees: $1.20 every four miles, $12 every 40 miles. To drive from New York to Los Angeles (3,000 miles), the actual cost is $900 *just for the car,* not for hotels, meals, tolls, parking, and incidentals. And you can get a flight from New York to L.A. for about $250.

However, most Americans already own cars. They would not buy a car specifically to drive from New York to L.A. Therefore, when they plan a driving trip, they aren't starting from scratch. They are already paying almost $10 per day just to *own* the car (purchase price, insurance, license plates, depreciation, financing, etc.). The additional cost to *operate* the car is thus only about 10¢ or 20¢ per mile (fuel, oil, maintenance, tires). At 15¢ or 20¢ a mile, for two people riding together, that New York–L.A. trip looks a lot more reasonable: $450 or $600.

But think again: add to that cost the $80 or more per day necessary for lodgings and meals, and a week's trip across country will cost $850 to $1,000. The $80 figure includes budget accommodations, but no frills such as cocktails before dinner or admission to attractions along the way. If you do the drive in a week, there's no time for attractions. And you have to drive back too.

Rental cars are also very expensive, particularly abroad. Several years ago I rented a car in England. I knew that in the car rental business they handed out 10% discounts all the time, so I offered to rent the car for a week, rather than just two days, if they gave me the "10% commercial discount." (I planned to rent it for a week in any case.) I got the discount, and my total cost for the car was still $60 a day—and that's in England, where you can't drive very far before you hit water. I rented the very cheapest car. Gas costs $3 per gallon in England.

Keep these points in mind:

> Four or more people sharing a car is budget travel. One or two people sharing a car is luxury travel.

> Figure car expenses realistically and completely. Here are items you must include:

>> Fuel, at 5¢ to 10¢ per mile (40 mpg to 20 mpg)
>> Oil, tires, maintenance, wear-and-tear, insurance, etc.
>> Parking and tolls
>> Highway food and lodging costs

For a rental car, you must figure:

>> Daily or weekly rental charge
>> Mileage charge (this and fuel are the highest charges!)

Full insurance charge

Taxes (often very high; 20% to 33% is not unusual abroad)

Fuel

Parking and tolls

Pickup and delivery charges (if you use these services)

Stamp taxes, "document fees," or "execution fees"

REAL-LIFE EXAMPLE: Not too long ago, my wife and I took a trip to France. We did all the right things: we wrote to friends in Paris and asked them to look at local rental rates. We asked, "Could you arrange something for us in advance that would be cheaper? Or would it be cheaper for us to rent right at the airport than to reserve in advance?" The answer was that arranging a rental from North America, before leaving home, was the most cost-effective way.

So we did that. We shopped the car rental companies. We asked about special deals, unlimited mileage, insurance, etc. The company we finally chose offered unlimited mileage on a week-long rental of a car somewhat larger than a compact. The daily cost was moderate, the Collision Damage Waiver high as usual. Part of the total rental bill was to be paid in dollars, the other part in francs. We added all of this up, and the total came to about $275. Fair enough.

We forgot gas and tax.

Fuel for the car ("you must use premium, or your insurance is void") cost an astounding amount by American standards. And the tax on the total rental bill, including the Collision Damage Waiver, was 33.33%! Also, we chose in a few instances to drive on France's excellent high-speed toll roads. The cost was about twice or three times the toll on an American turnpike.

The total, absolute, final cost of our car rental was $450, or almost *twice* our original estimate!

It was worth it. The car was great, and France is spectacular, but I wish we had done a little more planning and questioning so as to avoid "payment shock."

Here's another, even more astounding example to demonstrate the dangers of hidden rental car costs, and the shady methods by which some companies operate.

My cousin flew out to the Southwest for a vacation. She rented the cheapest car from the company with the lowest price. The rental price for a week with unlimited mileage was $67. She kept the car for ten days. What was her total cost? It was $270. How can that possibly be?

The Collision Damage Waiver was $10 a day, so the minimum price for a ten-day rental immediately became $167. But here's the stinger: the charge for each extra day after that first week's rental was $32 per day! Three extra days would have cost $96, so of course my cousin simply signed up for two weeks' rental, at $134. So now we're at $234. Finally, the company used the "empty tank" basis to figure gas usage, and charged my cousin $18 for gas which they had gotten for free (see below under "Fiddling with Fuel Costs"). So now we're at $252, and after she had added in her own costs for fuel, and tax on the rental, the total for my cousin's rental was $270, or *four times* the advertised "weekly rental" price! Beware, beware of these car rental people and the way they do business!

HIDDEN SAVINGS ON CAR RENTALS

You may think that the car rental companies' rates are ironclad. Really they're not. In fact, all sorts of

deals are possible—discounts for longer rentals, unlimited mileage or a certain number of free miles, free
return delivery ("rent here, leave there"). The amount
is limited only by demand, and by your ingenuity. This
sort of thing goes on all the time wherever a company
is stuck with a surplus of cars. If you don't believe it,
stand near a rental counter in an airport sometime.
You may be astounded to find that the rental company
does not have ironclad rates at all. Instead, each
person who shows up at the counter will get a rate
based on his *expectations* and previous arrangements.
I saw a man come up to a rental counter with an open
magazine in his hand. "Look at the price they're
giving on the West coast," he said, and showed the
clerk an advertisement for that company's cars. "But
that's a different market," the clerk answered, "and
we have a different rate structure here." Clutching his
magazine and smiling, the potential customer replied,
"Well, a car is a car, and if you can do it there I'll bet
you can do it here." A minute later the clerk was on
the phone to a supervisor, checking the inventory of
available cars and getting permission to work out a
special deal: the low price, or a price one dollar higher
than the low price, or a fancier car for the standard-car
price, or free miles.

Not too long ago, I read in *Business Week* of a
similar incident. In this account, a traveler called the
toll-free number of a major car rental firm, and reserved a car at an airport in a distant city—Denver, to
be precise. He asked for the "corporate rate," and was
told that this was a "discounted" $210 per week.

When he got to Stapleton International Airport, he
asked prices at a few of the other car rental counters in
the airport, and discovered that they were offering
rates of $169 to $179 per week for the same car. But
wait! He then asked the clerk of his original, major
company what the current rate for a week's rental

was. She replied, "Well, sir, since you don't have a reservation, I have a car here for $129 per week." Believe it. It happens. And can you imagine how much this fellow would have saved by picking up the courtesy phones for a few of the off-airport rental companies and compared their prices?

If you want to reserve in advance, and also to do a little shopping once you get to the airport, avoid giving your credit card number to the car rental reservations agent. Say that you just don't have your card in hand at the moment, but that you'll have it when you get to your destination. This way you can easily cancel your reservation if you find a better deal.

RETURN VS. PICKUP: In my long travel experience, I have discovered yet another angle on the car rental business. It's this: although the people at the rental car pickup desks may say cars are in short supply, the people over in the departures lobby, where cars are returned, know that lots of cars are available. You can learn many interesting things by having a chat with the return desk clerks. For instance, they might say, "We're flooded with big cars now, but small ones are in short supply." Thus, if you want to rent a big, comfortable car, go over to the rental pickup desk and ask for a subcompact.

"Oh, gee," the clerk will say, "we don't have any. Why not rent a larger car?"

"Well, I really can't afford a big car," you answer.

After some jockeying for position over their price and your budget, you get the car you wanted at a substantial discount because "they didn't have the car you wanted."

Where and What to Rent

No matter what car rental company you choose to rent from you will always save money away from the airport—sometimes as much as 50% off the major-company rate if you go to one of the "other" companies. Obviously, rental offices at airports have very high overheads and a captive audience. The business traveler can afford to rent there; the well-heeled character and the tired lazy traveler will want to fall into a car as they get off the plane—but smart travelers will want to rent from the offices away from the airport. By "away from the airport" I don't mean in Timbuctoo. The difference is this: with the top firms, you get off your plane, wander down the concourse, and come to a row of car rental counters. A charming clerk will wait on you right away. With the lower-priced (but still nationally known) rental companies, you find the row of car rental counters, and then look for a special telephone which connects to a rental counter *near* the airport. A charming clerk will answer the phone and will send a free shuttle bus to pick you up. The difference is just this: with the less-expensive companies, you ride for ten minutes before you're actually face to face with the charming clerk. And when you return the car, you take the same shuttle bus back to the airport.

You may think that the car rental
companies' rates are ironclad.
They're not.
In fact, all sorts of deals are possible.

Automatic 10% Discount

Virtually every major car rental company grants a 10% discount on its normal daily rates. It grants this discount to huge masses of people. You probably already qualify.

The company you work for, the large organization you are associated with, your automobile or travel club, has probably already secured an agreement for the 10% discount. Remember, *everybody* gets this one. Everybody except the unsuspecting soul who doesn't know about it. Even if you think you don't "qualify" for it through your company or auto club, ask for it. Like the 1% traveler's check fee, this is an easy giveaway.

The universal 10% discount does not apply on special rates such as weekend packages, however. Those rates are already substantially discounted from the normal rates. The 10% discount usually applies *only* to the normal daily rates.

Don't Pay Again—You've Already Paid!

Competition among car rental companies is fierce these days, and everyone wants to make the rates look good. One of the devices for this is to charge a reasonable daily rate with unlimited mileage. This is great, as the mileage rate used to be *the biggest amount* of a car rental.

In the old days the mileage rate looked small to the renter ("What? Only 20¢ a mile? That's nothing!"), but it added up. After two days of moderate driving (250 miles per day), you'd owe the rental company $100 *just for mileage*. People got wise to this, and so the progressive rental companies began to offer unlimited mileage, included in the daily rate. But now there's a new trick.

It's with the insurance. It used to be that you'd receive full collision coverage as part of the rental fee. If there was a deductible amount (that is, an amount for which you were still responsible) it was $100 or so. Thus if you bashed a tail-light, you'd have to pay for one tail-light out of your own pocket. If you bent a fender badly, the insurance would pay for most of it, but you'd still have to pay the first $100. You could avoid even this $100 liability by purchasing a "Collision Damage Waiver" for a dollar or two extra per day. With the Waiver, you were not liable for *anything* that might happen to the car under normal conditions.

The insurance provisions are still much the same, but the figures are radically different. If you rent a car today without buying the Collision Damage Waiver, you may be responsible for $750 or $1,000 or even more if there's damage to the car during the period of your rental. Obviously, no one wants to take such a chance, so you purchase the Collision Damage Waiver. But wait! It now costs $7 or more *per day*. So that attractive daily unlimited-mileage rate of $26 is now up to $33 or more. What a difference!

The sad thing is that so many people are already covered . . . by their own auto insurance! In most cases when you rent a car your own private auto insurance provisions *transfer automatically* to the rental car. Thus if you have $15,000 of collision coverage with a $200 deductible on your own private car, and your car's current value is at least equal to that of the rental car, you're covered the same way on the rental car. In the event of an accident, you pay only the $200, your own insurance company pays the next $550 or $800, or whatever, up to where the car rental insurance company takes over. If you don't carry enough collision insurance on your own car and you plan to rent cars several times in an insurance period, it may be worthwhile to take out some collision coverage; it may end up being cheaper than Collision Damage Waivers at $7 per day.

So do these two things: inquire about the cost of a Collision Damage Waiver *whenever* you contact a car rental company; inquire for each class of car you may rent, because the cost often goes up along with the size and luxury of the car. Also, contact your automobile insurance agent and ask what coverage you may already have that would be applicable during a car rental.

As this edition goes to press, there are several new and welcome developments in the murky field of Collision Damage Waivers. First of all, American Express announced that holders of its Gold and Platinum charge cards would automatically be insured against collision damage at no cost when they paid for rental cars using these cards. This is a fine solution to the Collision Damage Waiver ripoff, but be sure to look into other insurance matters. Collision damage is only one peril. What about vandalism and auto theft? Be sure you're protected against these as well.

Another welcome development is the offering of a collision damage insurance policy to travelers renting cars. The policy is sold through travel agents, and is issued by Travel Guard International of Stevens Point, Wisconsin. Thirty days of coverage for repairs up to $25,000 costs about $19. This compares to Collision Damage Waiver charges of $7 to $10 a day ($210 to $300 a month!) levied by the car rental companies. What a difference!

The other hidden expense in car rentals is the Personal Injury insurance. Most people with health or travel insurance are already covered. Thus it makes little sense to purchase additional coverage from the car rental company. If you are injured, only one company will pay the bill in any case; you'll never be paid twice. So in most cases you needn't pay for this.

For a full list of major car rental companies, see the Appendix, "Car Rental Guide," at the back of this book.

Special Savings Abroad

Besides comparison-shopping among the rental companies, you should know that rental cars are cheaper in some countries than in others. Of course, if you are only visiting one country this has little relevance, but if you are going on an extensive trip through several European countries you should stop and think and discover where you will be better off renting the car.

As of this writing, here is the order of countries for rental costs in Europe, from Spain (the cheapest) to Italy (the most expensive). Following each name is that country's tax rate for V.A.T. (Value-Added Tax), the European super-sales tax, which contributes much to the cost of renting a car:

Spain (12%)
Luxembourg (12%)
Portugal (16%)
West Germany (14%)
Holland (20%)
Great Britain (15%)
Belgium (25%)
Switzerland (none)
Denmark (22%)
Greece (18%)
Austria (21.2% to 33.32%)
Ireland (10%)
France (33.33%)
Italy (18%)

Norway, Sweden, and Finland top all the other countries of Europe in rental car costs. If you plan to rent a car in France for more than two or three weeks, lease it instead. You'll save hundreds of dollars. Usually, the same companies which rent cars can arrange a lease.

Different countries obviously also have different types of cars available and also varying gas prices. In Europe gas is often double the U.S. price; therefore you are much better off with a small car that gets good gas mileage. Remember, you don't have to sacrifice too much in space and comfort to obtain this savings. In Britain, for example, you may regard their subcompact model as too small and too uncomfortable. Opt instead for a compact like the Ford Escort, and you'll get space, comfort, and almost comparable mileage.

Discounts and Special Promotions

All car rental companies have busy periods and slack periods: their busiest time is Monday noon through Thursday noon when traveling business people require their services and will pay highly for them. Slack periods are Thursday noon to Monday, and therefore most companies offer special end-of-the-week packages that grant substantial discounts off the daily rates. The package may demand a two- or three-day minimum rental; it may offer some free mileage. Even if the package does not include any free mileage, it will still represent a substantial savings depending on the distance you travel.

No matter what car rental company you choose to rent from, you will usually save money by renting away from the airport.

Certain destinations generate more and greater discounts than others. A very popular destination and the resultant competition for business will give rise to all kinds of special promotions—fly/drive packages, no drop-off charges, etc. Florida is a prime example. Here you'll pay a fraction of what you'd pay in New York for a car rental. Sleuth out such special deals from newspapers, airlines, tour operators, the media, friends, and take advantage of them. Don't wait until you get to your destination and hope to obtain a discounted car. Always figure out which package/deal is better for you. Find out what the daily rate plus mileage charge is and what, let's say, the weekend package charge is and what it gives you. Compare the prices based on how far you intend to drive and choose accordingly.

In general, try to avoid renting on a daily basis unless you're only going a very short distance. One of the highest costs of any daily car rental bill is the mileage charge, which may be as high as 20¢ or 30¢ per mile. If you travel 500 miles in a three-day rental, you'll pay a whopping $100 to $150 in addition to the daily rate which, let's say, is $40. That's $220 to $270 plus insurance, sales tax, and of course, fuel costs. If you do anticipate driving long distances your best value-for-money are the unlimited-mileage weekly packages. Rent for one, two, or three weeks and you'll pay a flat sum and avoid those high mileage charges.

In any case, it's best to *overestimate* the rental period. There is no penalty for bringing a car back early. But if you decide you want to keep it for a day or two longer, you're required to notify the rental company by phone, and this may entail considerable hassle and long-distance expense. So if you plan a week's rental, have them make out the contract for eight, nine, or even ten days. This is the advice of Reader Tom Glow, of San Antonio, Texas.

Sometimes you can even get an additional discount if you book in advance. For example, I recently rented a car for a week from Hertz at the Heathrow airport. Because I knew my schedule, and had planned far enough ahead to book three weeks in advance, I received a 50% discount off the regular unlimited-mileage weekly package. Instead of paying $350 I paid $175.

Do shop around for car rentals. Read the advertisements and use your telephone. Most of the major outfits have toll-free numbers and by calling you can accurately compute the costs and determine which is the most cost-effective deal for you. Remember, deals vary from company to company.

Budget, Thrifty, Econo-Car, etc.

That brings me to another point. We all know the advantages of the two giants, Hertz and Avis—new cars, good service, instant substitution of another car if yours breaks down. In short, all the advantages you'd expect an international network of offices to automatically deliver. But you pay for that. Next time you consider renting a car, check the prices of the "other" firms: Budget, Thrifty, Dollar, Econo-Car, and other similar companies, both here and abroad.

Their company policies demand that they keep their prices below those of the big companies. That is, if Hertz charges $32 a day, Dollar will charge $29 a day. If Hertz comes down to $29, Dollar will drop to $26. If you want to check the rates in the city or area you intend to visit, go to any travel agent and ask to see their copy of *Ground Transportation Services*. Compare the rates and then follow up with phone calls on the companies' toll-free numbers (see the AT&T *Toll-Free 800 Directory* under "Automobile Rental and Leasing") just to make sure that you have up-to-the-minute information on prices, discounts, etc.

The Locals

Besides Hertz and Avis and the budget car rental companies, there are always a number of smaller, local companies that rent cars at much lower rates. Although you may find their location inconvenient, their cars perhaps a little older, their services not so extensive, their rates may still appeal to you. Compute the overall costs and choose accordingly. Some of these small local firms will in fact pick you up and ferry you back to the airport for free. The tourist offices can usually provide you with details about the local car rental companies. And many auto dealerships and garages, both at home and abroad, will rent you a car.

Rent a Wreck

Some rental firms offer older-model cars for use in restricted areas, at greatly reduced charges. It would be easy to be misled by their innovative, but less-than-appealing names: Rent-A-Wreck, Ugly Duckling, etc., but the truth is that the cars are usually maintained in excellent shape. While they don't have that new-car shine, they're probably better looking than that second car you bought for the kids. Most are between two and five years old, and all firms pay for road service, should you need it. Insurance is provided by almost all firms, some at a slight additional fee, and most will accept major credit cards. On the minus side, there's almost always a restriction on the driving radius, there are *no* one-way rentals, none has facilities at airports, and few provide airport transportation. Also, not all are open seven days a week around the clock, which means you must pick up and return cars during specified office hours. Still, if your holiday is centered on one city and environs, the savings in rental will more than offset any airport taxis and other small inconveniences.

If you're ready for the risks and potential hazards, then you can rent a car for much less than from the "airport" companies. Most of these companies are locally owned and operated. To find them, go to the library and check the Yellow Pages for your destination city, or else contact the local tourist offices and convention bureaus.

Fiddling with Fuel Costs

Car rental companies fiddle with fuel cost as much as they do with the collision damage waiver, and you must watch them just as closely on this.

THE "FULL TANK" BASIS: The matter of fuel used to be easy. Car rental companies figured everything on a "full tank" basis. A rental car was delivered to you with a full tank of gas, and you were expected to return it with a full tank of gas, or else pay for the rental company to fill the tank. Smart travelers always return their rental car with a full tank of gas, knowing that the car rental company would otherwise fill the tank from one of their own pumps, with gas priced 30% or 40% above the prevailing cost per gallon. Or if the company didn't actually fill the tank, they would estimate the amount of gas needed to fill the tank, and would charge you accordingly. Of course, their estimates were always high, in their favor, and the price per gallon also unconscionably high. Thus, if your car actually needed $5 of gas to be full, you might end up paying the rental company $10 or even $12; so smart renters always topped off the tank before returning the car.

THE "EMPTY TANK" BASIS: These days, the matter of gas is not always so easy, as some companies operate on an "empty tank" basis. In theory, this means that the rental company hands over a car with no gas in it, and you return a car with no gas in it, buying and paying for any and all gas you use.

Of course, this is impossible. The company is not going to siphon all the gas out of each car returned after a rental. The "empty tank" basis is an ill-disguised method to cheat you out of a few more dollars.

Using the "empty tank" method, the car rental company hands over a car with only part of a tank of gas. If the tank is half full, they will estimate it at two-thirds or even three-quarters. They will then calculate the number of gallons in three-fourths of a tank, and will charge you an impossibly high price per gallon for it. So they've got your money even before you set foot in the car!

As you drive away, the agent will tell you (or it will be written into the rental contract in tiny print) that "you've already paid for any gas in the car, so return the car with an empty tank." Of course, it's impossible to return a car with an empty tank, and inconvenient even to plan so that you return with a small amount of gas. Chances are that you'll return the car with about a half-tank of gas. And so the cycle begins again, with the company charging the *next* renter for the gas you put in the car! In effect, you pay an extremely high price for gas, and you pay it twice.

AVOIDING THE RIP-OFFS: How can you avoid gas tank rip-offs? If the company uses the "full tank" basis, simply be sure to return the car with a full tank.

If you suspect that the company may use the "empty tank" basis, ask about the company's policy on gas early in the contract writing if the agent doesn't specifically mention it. If the agent says, "We charge you for what's in the car right now, and then you return the car with an empty tank," you'll know you're confronted with the "empty tank" basis.

Stop everything right there and tell the agent that you want to verify the amount of gas. Go to the car, look at the fuel gauge, and insist that you be charged only for the reading. Don't let the agent give you stories, like "Oh, we set the gauges low so that people don't run out of gas." Be sure the estimate on the contract and the needle on the fuel gauge agree.

Then bargain over price. They don't want to waste time doing this, and if you insist that $1.75 is far too much for a gallon of gas, they must come down or lose your business. Pretty soon they'll get bored by your resistance and bring the price of a gallon down to something reasonable. If they don't, then take your argument one step further.

Tell the agent that you want only a gallon of gas in the car, and that they should remove any "extra" gas from the car, or furnish you with a car that has only one gallon in it. Or simply insist that since the company policy is that a tank is empty when the car is rented, the gas in there is no responsibility of yours. They can siphon it out, or they can let you have it for free.

A compromise position is that you will bring the car back with exactly as much gas as when you began your trip, and then they should charge you nothing at all for gas. Or you can insist that they use the same estimating method and same gas prices when you return the car, and should *reimburse you* for any gas left in the tank at the time of return.

Fight for your rights! The "empty tank" basis is not a legitimate way to do business; it is nothing but a cheat, and you must not let yourself be cheated. An agent will not feel good about defending such a policy and will probably give in to your demands if you persist. Remember the First Law, and obey it. If all else fails, ask yourself truly, "Do I want to do business with a company that has set out to cheat me even before I've sat in the driver's seat?"

DRIVEAWAYS

In North America you can cut the costs of driving by signing up for a "driveaway," a private car entrusted by its owner to a firm which finds drivers to take the car to a certain destination. Often the car's owner is flying to his destination, but wants his car there as well. You must be over 21 (occasionally over 25), and have a driver's license and references (easy to arrange). Foreign visitors need an International Drivers Permit. You call a driveaway firm after finding their number in the phone book or classified ad (usually under "Driveaways" or "Automobile Transport and Driveaway Companies;" in AT&T's *Toll-Free 800 Directory*, look under "Automobile Transporting and Driveaway Service"), ask if there is a car going to your destination, sign a contract, pay a deposit, and you're on your way with a full tank of gas. After that, fuel costs are negotiable, and may be your responsibility; repairs are the owner's. On average you'll be expected to clock around 400 miles a day. You must deliver the car according to the schedule stated in the contract, although a phone call to the owner contributes to good rapport, and often yields concessions: "All right, stop in New Orleans for a day. Enjoy yourself." By the way, try to locate a car for your return journey at the same time as you reserve a car for the outbound trip.

A CAR FOR FREE (ALMOST)

You're going to California for several months and you'd like to have a car so you can get around L.A. Why not buy a used car, use it, and sell it at the end of the month? Of course, it's a gamble: How do I find a good car? What if it breaks down? How can I be sure I'll sell it again? Luck is involved, but with clear thinking and a bit of luck, it'll work out fine.

Consider this: used cars are priced according to year, mileage, and general condition. If you buy a used car for $1,000 put several thousand miles on it in a month or two, and don't get in any bad accidents *the car has lost no value whatsoever!* You can sell it for what you paid, perhaps more. The year hasn't changed, the condition has not changed noticeably, and a few thousand miles more means nothing—it's the ten-thousands figure that counts. With luck and skill, you can have a car for a month for absolutely nothing; though in most cases you'll be out of pocket for gas, insurance, license and title fees, and sales tax.

There are many garages, body shop, new- and used-car dealerships which specialize in fixing up used cars for resale. If the mechanics at some such place have worked on a car, they know its condition. You may be able to get a commitment from them (legal or informal) to repurchase the car from you at a specified price. After all, they know the car. They don't have to spend a lot of time examining and testing it. Your month of use is not going to change the car's condition very much.

Even if they won't commit themselves, chances are good that they'll help you out. If you buy the car for $1,000 and sell it back for $900, they pocket $100 for virtually no work. They will probably want to take the car and use it to produce another $100.

RIDES FOR FREE

In many countries, hitchhiking is the generally accepted means of transport. Sometimes the ride is understood to be free of charge, sometimes you will be expected to pay (perhaps the equivalent of bus fare), sometimes it is proper to offer payment, though the driver may refuse to accept it.

Don't dismiss hitching outright as antisocial and unsafe. Instead, ask around and get information on safety and local hitching customs. For example, in the U.S. there is no nationwide law against hitchhiking. Individual cities and states make their own laws. Almost anywhere, women must be much more careful than men. Also, be aware that "the thumb" is not a universally accepted signal that you want a ride. In many countries you are expected to flag down a vehicle with your hand, or wait at a gas station, roadside restaurant, or crossroads.

Prearranged rides, though usually more expensive than hitchhiking, are generally safer and more convenient. You can meet and talk with the driver and other passengers before you leave, and agree on sharing charges.

Rides are available almost everywhere, throughout the world, wherever travelers go. Bulletin boards in colleges, youth hostels, cafés, Ys, and inexpensive hotels are excellent places to search for the ride you want, or to post your own notice asking for riders to share expenses if you have the car. Some large American cities even have "ride centers," agents-for-profit who match up rides and riders for a small fee. For information leads, call the biggest college or university in the area. Many colleges operate formal ride services, and if they don't, they'll know who does.

SECRETS OF TRAIN TRAVEL

Sometimes going by train is less expensive than going by other means, sometimes it's not. For a single person, the train is cheaper than going by car, more comfortable than going by bus, and sometimes more restful and convenient than going by plane. And in Europe, the train is usually far cheaper than the plane for short or medium-length journeys.

Plane or Train?

Using the train to advantage takes careful thinking. As trains run from city center to city center, one doesn't pay for airport buses, downtown parking, and so forth. The fastest trains on some routes can rival the plane time, depending on the location of stations and airports. For instance, I used to take the night train between Istanbul and Ankara. I took a cheap public ferry to the station in Istanbul, got the train at 8 p.m., had a good dinner in the dining car, and went to bed in a private sleeping compartment at 11 p.m. At 6 a.m. the next morning I awoke to find the pastel colors of the Anatolian plateau rolling by my window. I washed and shaved in my compartment, wandered down to the dining car, finished breakfast as we entered the suburbs of Ankara, and alighted from the train at 7 a.m., fresh, shaved, breakfasted, and ready for the day.

To get right to the center of Ankara by 7 a.m. by plane, I would have had to go the night before; the alternative would be to have gotten up at 3 or 4 a.m. to get to the air terminal to catch the (expensive) airport bus so that I could catch the 6 a.m. flight. I'd touch down after 8:30 a.m., and by the time I was in the airport bus and headed into town it would be 9. The airport is 32 miles outside Ankara, and it would be 10 a.m. before I reached the center of the city. All this hassle cost twice as much as the train trip. The point is this: the plane trip took half the time, but not at the *right* time. And it cost double.

Using the train to best advantage is possible at home as well. Some routes are the ideal distance for a train trip: four hours or less for a daytime trip, eight hours or more for an overnight. When you compare the train with the plane, remember to add in all the costs of getting to and from the airport, plus the time this may take. We've all gone through that frustrating experience of spending three hours traveling to and from the airports for a 45-minute flight. By the way, in a fog a 45-minute flight can turn into an all-day wait. Trains run in fog.

A Rolling Hotel

The same advantage is yours in other countries. Even if a sleeping compartment is very expensive (as in most of Europe), you can still get a decent night's sleep on a train. Underneath the seat cushion of every European compartment seat is a strap. Pull on that strap and your seat will "recline" just a bit; do the same thing to the strap under the seat across from yours, and you have a sort of bed. Pick an empty compartment if possible, and there is your "private" sleeping car.

The trick here is to choose a milk-run train, the slowest you can find. Often no one will be on it, you'll have plenty of time to sleep, and you'll end up with a private or almost-private compartment.

To take the ultimate advantage of this form of accommodation, buy a EurailPass before you leave home and you can sleep on the train any night you choose. See Paris on Tuesday, and when you get tired, wander down to the Gare de Lyon and get the 9 p.m. to Marseilles. Have a night's rest, and awaken at 8:10 a.m. as the train pulls into Marseilles. Tour Marseilles on Wednesday, and at 10:53 p.m. catch the train back to Paris, arriving at 8:28 a.m. Thursday is thus another Paris day. It may be a bit disorienting, but you get your accommodation almost for free.

I say "almost," because the train back to Paris is an "all-couchette" train, on which you must pay a supplement for your couchette. The couchette is a shelf-like bed, somewhat more comfortable than pulling two seats together. You are given a pillow and a paper blanket of sorts.

European stations are marvels for the traveler who sleeps on trains. In France, Switzerland, and many other countries, major-city stations have private pay cubicles for washing up, shaving, even bathing. Rental electric razors—sterilized automatically between uses—hang on the wall, and buzz into action when you drop a coin in the slot. After a shave, drop in another coin and get a spritz of cologne! Vending machines sell toothbrushes and paste, soap, moist towelettes, combs, and shoe polish. You may even find a very simple lodging with cot-equipped cubicles so you can have a snooze, or even a full night's rest.

Discount Fares

Every railroad has special discount fares for certain classes of passengers. Children, senior citizens, families traveling together, military personnel in uniform, students—in a few countries the list is even longer. But even if you don't fit one of these categories, you may be able to save money. Often during the "off-season" you'll find all kinds of specials available.

EURAILPASS: Undoubtedly one of the best bargains in

rail travel, the EurailPass is superb if you intend to crisscross the continent for an extended time.

This pass is good for *unlimited* first-class rail travel throughout all of Europe (other than the British Isles) for a specified amount of time. The best value goes to the traveler on a two-month vacation or longer. Those under the age of 26 can purchase a Eurail Youthpass, entitling them to unlimited second-class transportation for two months.

In some cases the EurailPass is good also on lake steamers, post buses, and ferries. Always inquire—the answer can only be "No." You must purchase the ticket outside Europe. Write or visit the nearest European railway office in any major city in North America, see a travel agent, or contact Forsyth Travel Library (see the Appendix under "Travel Bookstores").

OTHER CONTINENTAL PASSES: Similar continental passes are offered to foreign visitors in the United States by Amtrak. The USA Railpass is sold only outside North America to nonresidents of the U.S. and Canada. It's good for unlimited rail travel on all Amtrak lines, but does not include sleeping car accommodations. A traveler must begin using it 90 days after it's issued.

THE NATIONAL PASSES: Most countries throughout the world sell special passes for travel throughout their railroad networks. These can represent huge savings. Some of them also give you other advantages. For example, the French National Railroads France Vacances pass throws in a one-day car rental, a four-day Parisian Métro pass, round-trip transportation between airport and air terminal in Paris, and a museum pass. There are also special reductions for families and senior citizens. A similar unlimited-mileage Britrail

Pass is available for travel throughout England, Scotland, and Wales. It must be purchased outside Britain. The Swiss railways offer some excellent deals. Some countries offer special coupons that reflect discounts. Find out about them from the Tourist Offices well *before you leave*.

Did You Know There Are Rail Package Tours?

In many countries it is possible to buy a package tour of transportation-and-hotel based on a train ticket and a budget lodging. Since the tour company is not chartering one particular vehicle (as with airplanes), but rather is utilizing a continuous system (the railroads and ferries), you can often set your own departure and return dates. Once I bought a "tour" from London to Paris and back, which gave me reduced-price train and ferry tickets, three nights at a budget hotel in Paris, and I was allowed to "break" my tour for a four-day side trip to Geneva after I had stayed the three nights in Paris. I tailored the trip exactly to my needs, and got it at a discount price. If I subtracted the normal train fares from the tour price, the hotel in Paris ended up costing about $3 per night.

More and more railroads are operating their own tour agencies, putting together such packages in conjunction with hotels, resorts, and rental car agencies, in order to entice you into taking the train. Even if you can't speak the language, write down your itinerary, look up the word for "tour," "package," or "discount trip," and present the paper to a travel agent or railroad clerk.

In North America, Amtrak and VIA Rail Canada operate many tours (Amtrak runs close to 200) of all kinds. Although railfare is often additional, the accommodations packages can be great bargains and other special arrangements such as car rental discounts may also be available. For information, write for Amtrak's Travel Planner, P.O. Box 7717, Itasca, IL 60143.

Do-It-Yourself Tours

Remember that on most rail journeys, you can hop off and on trains at will, breaking your trip whenever and wherever you like. So if you plan to see Europe from London to Vienna, buy a round-trip ticket London-Vienna-London, and stop in Brussels, Cologne, Bonn, Frankfurt, and Linz along the way—a distinct bonus of rail over air travel.

How to Save Money Every Day

On heavily traveled commuter lines anywhere in the world, and these include some intercity ones, you can save money by riding when the crush of commuters doesn't—which is exactly what you want to do in any case. Ask about "peak" and "off-peak," or similarly named fares. If you make a round trip in a day, or within a certain number of days, you may get a discount.

Always ask about special discounted ticket booklets for subways, metros, undergrounds, etc.

Special Hints on Riding the European Rails

European trains are of two kinds: magnificent and awful. The magnificents provide superb, rapid service and can be recognized by the fact that they carry names as well as numbers—the famous *Simplon-Orient Express* and the *Golden Arrow,* for instance. They normally run overnight, stop only in the largest cities, and cut hours from your travel time. Thus the Intercity Express makes the trip from Munich to Frankfurt in 3 hours and 45 minutes. A lesser train traveling exactly the same route takes two hours longer. If you always schedule your trips and your connections for the sleek named-trains, traveling in Europe can be a cinch.

On these named expresses, you will also quickly learn that you can pay as much as 33% to 50% more for the privilege of riding first class and getting an inch or two extra seat padding. It follows that you should always travel second class on a major European express; a second-class ticket will purchase a perfectly comfortable, well-padded seat. Second class should be trusted only on the expresses though; elsewhere you could find yourself sitting on a very uncomfortable wooden bench in a veritable rattletrap. By sticking to second class on the expresses, train transportation costs become very reasonable.

SCHEDULES: If you're planning a grand rail tour of Europe including Britain, you might want to get hold of the latest copy of the Thomas Cook Continental Timetable of European railroads. This comprehensive 500-page timetable details all of Europe's passenger rail services with great accuracy. It is available from Forsyth Travel Library and several other travel book-stores (see the Appendix) for less than $20. The Thomas Cook Overseas Timetable (400+ pages) covers rail services in the rest of the world.

GOING BY BUS

Buses go everywhere. The modern emphasis on good roads has fostered spiderwebs of bus routes in virtually every country.

All else being equal, bus travel is not the most preferable way to go. Seats are cramped, conveniences are limited; you may have to put up with music, excessive heating or air conditioning. On trains you may have a café or restaurant, and you can walk around; train seats are larger and roomier than bus seats. But generally the train costs 20% more than the bus, travels more slowly, and may not go where you want to go.

Special Passes

You can save money on bus tickets by asking about tour or excursion prices, round-trip or frequent-user discounts, or unlimited-mileage passes. The unlimited-mileage passes often come in several fashions, and you may qualify for extra discounts if you're a foreign tourist and purchase the tickets outside the country in which you will use them.

There's no doubt about it—bus travel can be extremely cheap. In Turkey, for instance, you can catch a big comfortable new Mercedes-Benz coach, perhaps equipped with television and stereo, at almost any time of the day, going virtually anywhere in the country, and the cost will be only about 1¢ per mile.

Bus Packages

From "The Historic East" to the "Old West Heritage," there's a bus package tour to suit almost every taste—and size of pocketbook. If you think you'd like to take a bus tour, it will pay to shop around for the best value. Here are some of the questions to keep in mind when choosing a bus package tour: Do you know exactly what services (meals, accommodations, etc.) are included in the tour price? Does the tour offer special features you'd be able to take advantage of? For example, can you join the tour later, or leave it early and get a refund for the unused portion of the trip? How large a group does the tour include? Is there enough free time for you to do some exploring on your own, or is the tour overly regimented for your taste? Is smoking permitted in the motorcoach? Is the tour operator a member of the U.S. Tour Operators Association? USTOA members must carry liability insurance covering their tours and must maintain a bond or other security to reimburse purchasers or depositors in case of the member's bankruptcy or insolvency.

Jitney Cabs

A jitney cab is a taxi shared by several travelers who may not know one another but who band together and split the cost of a given trip. The taxi may be an ancient Chrysler limousine, a shiny new seven-passenger Mercedes, a minibus, or just a car. The ride may be from First Street to Fifth Street, from downtown to the suburbs, from city to city, or even country to country.

Jitney cabs can afford to run where buses can't, for a jitney can run profitably on a handful of people where a bus would need several dozen. Jitneys are almost always faster than buses, more direct, and often more comfortable. They usually cost a bit more than the bus.

In the Middle East, *jitneys* are especially popular. Called *dolmush* (Turkey), *sherut* (Israel), *servis* (Egypt and other Arab countries), they are operated by hundreds of little private agencies, and they travel virtually everywhere, even to and from Europe!

In Mexico, they're called *peseros*; look for jitneys in many other countries. Hotel clerks know what they are (if they exist), who runs them, and which agencies operate to which destinations. Often, a jitney heading out on a long trip will be willing to swing by your hotel and pick you up.

Jitney drivers in foreign countries may try to rip you off on the fare. Confirm the fare with a hotel clerk, policeman, or ideally with several other passengers.

BY MOTORCYCLE, MOPED, BICYCLE

You can rent, lease, or buy a two-wheeled conveyance if you use some ingenuity. Al fresco travel has its own rewards and drawbacks, however. It is cheaper than a car, more fun and adventurous at times. But it's also exhausting, wet, hot in the sun, uncomfortable, and more dangerous. Theft is more of a problem—theft of your things, your vehicle, or parts of your vehicle. Traveling by bicycle shares some of the characteristics of motorcycle travel, but over long distances cyclists usually travel in groups on organized tours, which is safer, more convenient, and more fun. Guidebooks to bicycle trips abound on bookstore shelves, and several organizations sponsor bicycle trips in various parts of the world.

Bicycles and mopeds are, of course, ideal for hopping around cities and can sometimes be rented very cheaply. Depending on the size and power a moped can get as many as 150 miles to the gallon. But mopeds can be dangerous. Be careful.

GOING BY SHIP

So much for the major forms of ground transportation. We come now to the subject of sea transportation. If you're looking for a cost-effective way of getting to a particular destination (cruises are another matter) then you're not going to find it on the high seas. Even before the fuel crisis, shipline after shipline announced that they were ceasing to operate particular vessels, and the process has continued. The New York Harbor piers are eerily quiet these days. Some attempts have been made to encourage folk to travel by sea, but they're few and far between. For example, British Airways has a special arrangement with Cunard whereby you can fly one way and return aboard the *Queen Elizabeth II* or vice versa. Costs are high, although many people still say that you should experience such a crossing at least once in a lifetime.

Freighters

For the most part, you can forget about these too. With the exception of occasional ships leaving from Norfolk or Newport News, Virginia, the average freighter charges very little less than the average passenger liner. And even if you save some money, you'll nearly double your travel time (most freighters take from eight to ten days to cross the Atlantic) and you'll place yourself at the mercy of erratic and sporadic sailing schedules (some passengers wait a week in New York for their freighter to finally leave).

This is not to say that freighter travel isn't a unique and satisfying experience.

For information about freighter travel write to the following organizations:

Ford's Freighter Travel Guide, 19448 Londelius Blvd., Northridge, CA 91324 (tel. 818/701-7414); **Pearl's Freighter Trips,** 175 Great Neck Rd., Suite 306, Great Neck, NY 11021 (tel. 516/487-8385).

9

I Need a Room . . .

HOW IT ALL BEGAN

The English word *inn* is over a thousand years old. At first it meant just *house,* abode, lodging—a place to come in from the elements and rest. By the year 1400 an inn was also a place where travelers could put up for the night and get something to eat. An inn fulfilled the traveler's basic needs. If there were no inn, the traveler would have to ask at a house for hospitality. By the early 1800s inns were coming to be known as *taverns*. The interesting people who passed through town often put up at the local inn, and any local person bored with hometown life could drop by the inn and find out about the rest of the country or the rest of the world over a hot meal or a cold drink.

The *public house,* that is, the house built for anyone to use, was becoming a social center along with the church and the manor. It had already—several centuries ago—strayed from its role as a provider of the bare essentials for travelers.

About this time the *hotel* appeared on the scene. Borrowed from French, *hotel* had originally been *hostel,* the French equivalent of the English inn. But by the late 1700s and early 1800s, a *hôtel* in French was a grand and imposing building, a rich man's city mansion or the city hall. Taken into English, it signified a large and particularly sumptuous inn.

In 1766 one English traveler by the name of Tobias Smollett was already exclaiming, "The expence of living at an hotel is enormous!" Another traveler mocked the pretentiousness of the word: "Groping your way to the inn—I beg pardon—*hotel*. . . ." This progress from simple lodging to sumptuous luxury is still going on.

From its beginning as a social center, the hotel has advanced to become a temporary office and corporate headquarters, housing for a convention (the modern equivalent of a tradesmen's fair), and quarters for mass travel—what in medieval or Renaissance times would have been a festival. It has little to do with mere washing, changing, and sleeping anymore, except that all of us have to do that on a daily basis to remain healthy and happy.

Luckily for us all, the urge to travel and the basic needs have not changed—and the means to fulfill them are still at hand. You can still knock on the door of a private home and find clean lodgings for the night; you can still come across simple, basic accommodations for which an honest price is charged, and which will not leave you exclaiming, like Smollett, "The expence of living at an hotel is enormous!" This applies to every single country in the world.

Later in this chapter I'll discuss the various kinds of inexpensive lodgings available and how and where you can find them, but first here are some tips on how you can enjoy the wonderful facilities of the luxury hotel or resort at bargain prices.

LUXURY HOTELS AT BARGAIN PRICES

For a number of years, U.S. tax laws encouraged the construction of luxury hotels. Great towers rose in every city from coast to coast, built not so much because they would provide needed lodging for luxury travelers, but because it made good business sense to take advantage of tax incentives.

Now our country is oversupplied with luxury hotel rooms in many cities. While this may be bad news for the hotel chains, it is wonderful news for us, the traveling public. It means that competition for luxury hotel rooms is brisk, and reductions in unrealistically high "rack rates" (a hotel's equivalent of "list price") are easy to find.

Do you doubt me?

Look at the number of hotel chains that have joined the airlines' frequent traveler programs, offering free nights or "mileage points" in return for your business. Look at hotels in cities with airports which offer special "standby" rates (up to 50% discount) to travelers who ask for a room only after 7 p.m. Look at the annual hotel occupancy rate in the U.S. of 60%, with more and more hotels opening up all the time.

The average cost of a room, single or double, luxury or budget, full-price or discount, is about $70 these days. So when a hotel tries to charge you $200, there had better be some very good reasons. In many cases, those reasons don't exist, and you can easily get a big reduction.

What Makes a Good Hotel?

When people judge a hotel, they look for convenience of location: clean, attractive, comfortable rooms of good size, with climate control that can be set accurately by the guest. They like good lights for reading, comfortable beds, television sets that work properly, and no excessive noise.

What people do not like are long lines at check-in and check-out, high hotel prices for laundry and dry cleaning, lots of staff who expect lots of tips, and outrageous surcharges for telephone service (see Chapter 13 under "A Fortune for a Phone Call!").

Hotel Market Segmentation

As with the airline industry, the hotel industry has begun to offer different services to the different segments of the traveling public. Addressing the desires of travelers as mentioned above, hotel firms are now opening all sorts of new types of hotels, including these:

ALL-SUITE HOTELS: These are popular because travelers get a bedroom, kitchenette, living room, dining nook, and bathroom for the normal price of a luxury hotel room. The living room is always equipped with a couch that folds out to make a comfortable bed, and the dining area can also serve as a work area for business executives.

These small suites are especially popular with traveling families, and with people relocating to a new city who need a place to stay for a few weeks until they find permanent lodgings. In fact, one company, Quality International's Quality Suites-Residency, aims at travelers wanting to rent by the week. Besides the popular Embassy Suites and Guest Quarters Suite Hotels, the Sheraton Corporation is building Sheraton Suites, and Hilton Hotels is developing Hilton Suites. There will no doubt be several other companies as well. Rates for all-suite hotels may be anywhere from $70 to $180.

"COURTYARD" HOTELS: These are very comfortable, even luxurious hotels which rent rooms at prices that are moderate compared to those of the standard luxury hotels. Marriott was among the first companies to embrace the concept of providing travelers, especially business travelers, with a large, luxurious room, use of a restaurant and lounge, meeting rooms and a swimming pool, at a moderate price. The way they do this is to cut out the expensive frills that are only used by conventions: the ballroom, the health club, the three restaurants and three bars, the nightclub, the downtown location. Courtyard hotels have excellent locations, but are not perhaps right in the very center of town.

Doubletree Hotels has its "(Compri) Hotels," with an interesting twist. Guests pay one moderate price, and receive room, breakfast and snacks, drinks, and use of the swimming pool, all included. (The name "[Compri]" comes from the French word *compris*, meaning "included.") The (Compri) hotel does not have a restaurant as such, just a small cafeteria line from which sandwiches, snacks, full breakfasts, and drinks (both hard and soft) are available, all included in the price. Instead of a lobby, there's a large, comfortable, multi-purpose lounge that serves as a conversation area and library, conference room, snack bar, and workplace.

Hilton is developing "courtyard" properties under the name of Hil-Crest by Hilton. But whatever the company, "courtyard" hotels normally charge between $45 and $85 for a room.

BED-AND-BREAKFAST: North America has had its "tourist homes" and "guesthouses" ever since the invention of the automobile. But the recent popularity of bed-and-breakfast houses was brought back from

Europe by North American travelers who got to know and love them over there.

Bed-and-breakfast in America has evolved into something different than in Europe. We now look upon a B&B not as a comfy low-budget lodging (with the emphasis on low budget), but as moderately-priced or even high-priced lodging where we can find warmth, quaintness, and a sense of community. These qualities are completely lacking from the normal highway motel, which may charge a good deal less for a room.

In many tourist areas, bed-and-breakfast houses are being built from scratch, or old buildings are being gutted and rebuilt to accommodate B&B guests. In effect, the B&B is evolving into a sort of small, cozy hotel.

OFFBEAT DESIGNS: There are hotels that look like small, posh, antique villages, in which each building in the village is actually filled with hotel rooms (mostly small suites). There are brand-new hotels built to resemble ante-bellum southern mansions, complete with screened porch and comfy rocking chairs. There are capsule hotels (described below). And there is a bewildering assortment of budget motels, from "budget-budget" to "luxury budget." But more of those a bit later.

A HOTEL DIRECTORY: The American Hotel & Motel Association, the lodging industry's trade association, publishes an annual directory of its member hotel companies. All of the major hotel chains in this country, and many of the smaller ones, plus numerous foreign chains, are members of the AH&MA. The 500-page directory does not list the services provided by each hotel, but it does list each member hotel company, its head office address, telephone number, and

principal officers; and the name, location, and number
of rooms at each of the company's properties. For a
copy of the directory, send $29.50 to the American
Hotel & Motel Association, 1201 New York Ave. NW,
Washington, DC 20005 (tel. 202/223-6872). To avoid
delay, it's a good idea to call them first and confirm
that the directory's price is still the same.

What about Reservations?

When thinking about making hotel reservations, all
of us think about calling some toll-free telephone
number, asking price and availability, and then reserving a room for a particular date. We see no problem in
this. That's because the problems are hidden.

THE SECRETS OF TOLL-FREE NUMBERS: In most
cases, the toll-free number you call for reservations is
not the hotel, of course. It may not even be the hotel
company. It is probably a separate company, or at
least a separate department of the hotel company, with
the duty of arranging reservations. It has another duty
as well: to maximize profits. It performs this duty by
charging as much for a hotel room as possible.

If the toll-free line is connected to an independent
reservation company, that company gets paid for each
and every reservation it makes. Like a travel agent, it
may even garner a percentage of the entire hotel bill.
This is true from the big luxury hotels all the way
down to the bed-and-breakfast reservation services.

I have a friend who runs a B&B in a small Vermont
town, and she normally charges $30 per night for two
people; but if the reservation comes through the B&B
toll-free service, she charges $35. That extra $5 covers
the commission she must pay to the B&B service. So
much for "toll free!" Instead of spending $1 or $2 on a

direct call to the B&B, lots of people spend $5 to call "toll free."

It is not always true that by following the Third Law and calling the hotel directly you will get cheaper rates. But it is sometimes true, and I'll mention more about this a little later in this chapter. For now, keep in mind that when you deal with a toll-free reservation line, you are putting another broker, another middleman, into the process of making a reservation, because all the toll-free service does is pass the information on to the hotel. Because the toll-free number seems to make reservations easier for you, the hotel gets more reservations. So a toll-free reservation service actually helps the hotel, and the reservation service company itself, more than it helps you.

"CONFIRMED" RESERVATIONS DISAPPEAR: Once your reservation is confirmed, you're all set, right? Unfortunately, no.

It may shock you to learn that hotels can and do play cavalier with "confirmed," even pre-paid reservations. Many a guest arrives at the hotel, reservation slip in hand, only to learn that a convention or business meeting or wedding or family reunion has filled the hotel entirely, and they must go elsewhere. Usually the hotel will have made you another reservation in a nearby hotel "for similar accommodations at a similar price." This may be all right. But what if you had your heart set on staying at that famous country inn, or right next to your company's branch office, or right on the beach, and the "alternate accommodation" does not meet that requirement? You're stuck.

Although the hotel can and will seize your deposit if you do not arrive, or if you cancel too close to arrival time, the hotel can and does slip out of its responsibilities by offering to provide "equivalent accommodations."

What about if you prepay, sending a check or giving your credit card number? Most hotels have a policy of not holding reservations after 6 p.m. unless they have a credit card number to "guarantee" payment for the room. You arrive at midnight, only to find that the comfy room you've been dreaming about all through your tiring journey is occupied, and so are all of the hotel's other rooms. How can this be? Isn't it guaranteed?

In theory, yes. In practice, no. Hotels will re-sell a room, even one guaranteed by a deposit or credit card, after a certain time (often 11:45 p.m. or midnight). Luckily for you, this is usually easy to avoid. Simply call the hotel around 6 p.m., or whenever you can, and tell them your situation and your plans. Let them know that the flight is delayed, or that the car broke down, or that the bridge is out. If you keep them aware that you will indeed be arriving to claim the room, they will keep it open. But your guarantee of payment alone may not do it.

What about Traveling with Pets?

Many hotels, motels, inns, and bed-and-breakfast houses do not accept pets, as any pet-lover knows. But there are certain hotels that do, and if you plan your trip in advance, you can enjoy it with your pet.

The following hotel chains will often welcome pets, and have facilities for them: Days Inn, Econo Lodges of America, Econo-Travel Motor Hotels, Holiday Inns, Howard Johnson Hotels, La Quinta Motor Inns, Motel 6, Quality Inns, Ramada Inns, and Sheraton Hotels and Inns.

A 65-page booklet listing many American hotels which welcome pets is published by the Gaines Dog Care Center. Called "Touring With Towser," it's available for $1.50 from this address: Touring With Towser, Gaines, P.O. Box 8177, Kankakee, IL 60902.

How Hotels Set Prices

Wherever you stay, you should understand how these establishments put prices on their rooms, and how you can get the lowest possible prices.

The leading fiction among travelers is that hotels have set prices for their rooms. Sure, there are the so-called rack rates, the prices printed up in brochures and charged to the unsuspecting traveler who comes in off the street and says "I want a room." But in fact, hotel managers are working in a volatile marketplace, which resembles nothing so much as an Oriental bazaar. A big festival or event will fill the city and all its hotels with visitors, and the managers can charge the high "rack rates," plus perhaps a "special supplement," plus a hefty service charge. However, when off-season comes, the weather is unpleasant, and there's nothing going on, hotels will rent out rooms for next to nothing.

Does this sound familiar? In Chapter 7 we saw how the airlines targeted special segments of the travel market. Well, hotels are doing the same thing because they too are purveyors of a retail service. The big difference is that there is no well-organized "bargain basement" for hotel rooms as there is for airplane seats, tour places, and cruise berths. Or is there?

A service called ENCORE, operated by American Leisure Industries, Inc., 4501 Forbes Blvd., Lanham, MD 20706 (tel. toll free 800/638-0930), says you can get your second night at 2,000 participating hotels *free* if you're an ENCORE member. The club also provides special rates on tours and cruises, discounts on car rentals, guaranteed lowest airfare, a magazine, etc. How can they offer such a thing as free nights in top hotels?

Simple. Because at various times, it is to the Mutual Advantage of hoteliers and patrons to do business at a lower price. The ENCORE plan may help you to get the feel for how this works. But I contend that by following the Four Laws you can end up with similar results. It may help to recall the example which I described in the Introduction to this book. Then read the following guidelines carefully.

The Myth of High Prices

A top marketing consultant to the hotel industry was quoted in *Travel Weekly* as saying, "There's nobody that doesn't discount." And an important marketing study quoted in the same industry publication showed that price-conscious hotel guests included *most top-level corporate officers*. These people are not "cheap." Far from it. They realize that renting a hotel room is doing business. To do business, the hotel charges—and the customer pays—what the market will bear. And this market price varies from city to city, day to day, and season to season.

Some discount periods are so self-evident that they have been institutionalized: the weekend package, the off-season rate, the long-term discount, the group rate. These discounts are large and readily available; I'll mention them a little later on. Right now I want to show you how to get the best possible price on the best accommodations.

INSIDE A HOTEL MANAGER'S MIND: The manager is interested in far more than getting the highest price for a room. The success of a hotel is judged on the amount of money it receives for its room rentals, certainly. But the real point of pride is the *occupancy rate*. When hotel managers get together to compare notes, the one who can boast of the highest occupancy rate is looked upon as the top manager: he's the one with the most customers; he's the one who is the best businessman. The average occupancy rate worldwide is 70%.

It's assumed that prices have not been slashed to a point "inconsistent with the hotel's dignity," which means to a point where the hotel loses money. But if lots of rooms are filled on lots of nights (the gauge is the number of "bed-nights") for a decent price, the manager is in heaven.

Besides bringing in money from room rentals, the manager can assume that all those guests will spend more money (and thus render him more profit) in the hotel's restaurants and bars, in the gift shop, at the parking garage, and on room service.

WHERE *YOU* FIT IN: Now let's bring you into the picture. You would like to stay at the fine hotel operated by this particular manager. Like any traveler, you want to know what a room costs.

Like most travelers, you assume that there is pretty much one price. You call the hotel's toll-free telephone number and ask the price of a room. What does the reservation clerk say? The answer to your question is another question: "For what dates, please?" That should be your first hint that not all room rates are the same.

Are you coming on a weekend? As part of a large group? In the off-season? At a slack time? Then you will be quoted a moderate rate. Are you coming for the Olympics, or a Presidential Inauguration, or the World Series? Then the rate will be very high. Where now are those solid "rack rates" you thought were so firm? Which one is the rack rate?

When you give the dates you expect to stay, and tell the clerk how many people will be staying, you may be asked if you want a Standard, Superior, or Deluxe room. Again, no simple, solid rate! Perhaps, you want to know all three prices. Finally, then, you will be told a price.

What do you think of it? Too high for you? Then say

so! To most people, it never occurs to say, "Well, that's a bit more than I wanted to spend. Do you have any discount plans for those dates?" What do you suppose those top corporate executives say when first quoted a rate? They're businesspeople. Whether they're going for business or pleasure, they'll ask, "Do you have a commercial rate?" "Commercial rate" is something of a buzzword in the hotel industry. It allows a hotel to grant a discount and still to retain its dignity and high-class image. It is absolutely certain that if you do not ask about discounts, the clerk will not tell you about them.

If a good business type still thinks a price is a bit too high, he'll say, "I can get just as nice a room at the Ritz for $50 less, but I want to stay with you. How about $50 less?"

If the response from the reservation clerk is "I'm sorry, but that's the price," an executive's response may well be this: "Give me my price, and I'll pay you right away, up front." The clerk may give in to that, or call the supervisor or assistant manager. The hotel wants your business, and (remember the Fourth Law) if you commit yourself, they'll go a long way to accommodate you. After all, this is business.

MONEY-SAVING STRATAGEMS: If you don't get what you want over the phone, don't be disappointed. For one thing, the reservation clerk is a minor official in the hotel structure. In fact, if the number you are calling is toll free, the clerk may not even work for the hotel, but for an independent reservation service. As we saw from the example in the Introduction to this book, it sometimes pays to call the hotel directly, bypassing the toll-free number. But nothing fills you in on the true situation of the hotel rooms market as much as being on the spot.

You may have just arrived after an exhausting flight

or a long drive. Treat yourself to a convenient hotel, and do your hotel research in the morning if you're too tired to do it right away.

To accomplish getting a room for less on arrival, do this: find out the state of the rooms market. Ask an airline clerk, "Things pretty quiet in Boston these days, not so many visitors?" Ask a tourist information officer, "What's the hotel situation here in Vienna? Lots of rooms available?" Ask a taxi driver, "How's business? Lots of visitors in town?"

If you have time, drop in at a nice hotel and ask a front-desk clerk. They always know how things are. You might say, "You seem pretty busy. Are there other hotels in town with more empty rooms?" The clerk will be *very happy* to tell you about how the competition has lots of rooms available. I did this in Acapulco. By asking at one hotel, I discovered a neighboring hotel that was only 50% filled. The manager could hardly look his colleagues in the eye; he was desperate for customers, and ready to do business. I got a luxurious room right on the beach for a very reasonable price.

Once you know that the room situation is not tight, you're ready to find the Point of Mutual Advantage.

FINDING THAT ALL-IMPORTANT *POINT:* When you've found a good hotel that you like, discuss business, following the Fourth Law.

As with any business relationship, there are matters of etiquette to be observed. You must show confidence, which comes with knowing that this is a matter which should benefit both sides. And you must also be willing to let the hotel "do you a favor." A matter of pride is concerned here, and if you help the hotel to look as though the discount was *their* idea, you'll get surprising results.

So after you've asked the price, and they've quoted

one, just suggest some alternatives. Remember, they won't tell you about discounts unless you ask. To suggest an alternative while you are both standing there only takes five seconds. The worst that can happen is that they'll say, "I'm sorry, but we're quite full right now, and we're not authorized to make special arrangements."

More likely they'll say, "Sure, why not?" They'll "do you a favor." Once this happens to you (and it will), you'll wonder why you never tried it before.

You don't believe that hotels are ready to hand out all sorts of discounts, virtually at the drop of a suitcase? A college professor wrote to say that "the Sheraton corporation offers a 25% discount, at participating hotels and inns worldwide, on room reservations in any but their minimum category, to students and faculty members. All registered students and bona fide faculty members are eligible; they need not be on school business. Reservations should be requested at the discount rate as far in advance as possible. I have found that the further in advance you request the discount, the better your chance of getting it. Appropriate school identification is to be presented upon request, but I have only been asked for it once."

Now, he is a qualified faculty member. But does it *really* matter if you are, or aren't? Isn't this the Fourth Law in operation? If you ask for a similar discount well in advance, and mention some big organization, might they not give it to you?

Here's more proof, from another reader of this book: "Prior to my sister's wedding, a room was reserved for the newlyweds at an airport Holiday Inn in preparation for their honeymoon departure. Only the normal procedures were followed, and the price was $95. But upon hearing this, I called the same hotel and asked about honeymoon packages. They offered this: a deluxe room, Jacuzzi, free champagne, buffet breakfast, and free transfer to the airport . . . for $72! Needless to say, the reservation was swiftly altered.''

As this reader notes, the airport hotel was no doubt attempting to attract the "honeymoon segment," people using the airport to depart on honeymoons. But no hotel I know would *require* that this be your "first" honeymoon. Why not your second, or third? Do you need any better reason for a second honeymoon than free champagne and a discount on a deluxe room? Would they really mind if you requested it? Of course not.

Remember that these discounts are not "gifts" or "privileges" granted to some and not others. They are business tactics, which help the hotel to find the Point of Mutual Advantage. By availing yourself of discounts you are doing legitimate business with the hotel; you are not depriving them of anything. Rather, you are doing just what they want you to do: buying their services. And if you "allow" them to "give" you a discount, you're making a business deal look like a favor. They love it!

Here are some more business strategies you can use:

1. Ask (again) about a "commercial" or "corporate" rate. Remember, this is a buzzword. It has nothing to do with commerce in many cases. But it sounds better to the hotel people than "discount," and it allows the hotel to look "proper" while granting you a discount. Ask about honeymoon and weekend packages, discounts for members of large organizations, etc. As demonstrated by the letter quoted above, most people don't get these discounts merely because they don't ask for them.

2. Suggest an alternative price: "Well, I was

actually looking for something in the range of $85." Don't go too low or the hotel will lose "pride." But by countering with a reasonable figure, you let the hotel know that you are ready to do business. They can have your business (which, if their occupancy rate is low, they badly want) provided they meet, or at least come near, your price.

3. Accept their price, but suggest that they allow you to stay *two* nights for the price of one. If they're not busy, they lose nothing. You will only use a little water, and electricity, and a set of towels; and you might patronize their restaurants, bars, or parking garage. Or offer to pay their price for two nights if you can stay free the third night. When staying a week, offer to pay for five nights and get the last two free.

4. Offer to pay in cash if they grant a 5% discount. Any hotel must pay a credit card company between 4% and 8% of any credit card transaction.

5. If you're traveling with family or friends, ask for permission to have others share your double room at no extra charge. If you would prefer two rooms, offer to pay the normal *single-room* price for each double room. Or get a deluxe room or suite for the normal price of a standard double room.

6. Agree to pay the room price they quote, but ask for some free services: free parking, free use of recreational facilities, etc. Concentrate on services that the hotel provides anyway, and that cost them nothing extra to provide. The parking lot and the tennis court will cost them the same to maintain whether you use them or not. They will readily grant you

these, but may hesitate if you ask for commodities—meals, drinks, etc.—rather than services.

If you're not on the same wavelength, and their price is not what you want, try someplace else. In fact, now's the time to ask if they know of another hotel nearby, which is not so full. Again, they will be more than happy to tell you of their rival's low occupancy rate. Besides getting valuable information for you, this question also sends a signal to them: I'd love to do business with *you,* but you'd better take the opportunity quickly or I'll be gone.

These strategies work anywhere in the world when hotels are not heavily booked. Try one—or more. You'll see.

Here now are details on some of the more common, garden-variety discounts.

Weekend Packages

As with car rentals, hotel discounts and special offers coincide with the weekly and the yearly business cycle. For example, during the week, city hotels are fully occupied with out-of-town businesspeople. When they go home on weekends the rooms are empty, and to fill the gap between Thursday and Monday most major hotels offer weekend packages, which are one of the best bargains around.

How do you find out about such packages? Write or call the appropriate Convention and Tourist Bureau and ask them. In New York, for example, the Convention and Tourist Bureau will send you a free brochure listing all the weekend and other packages offered by the major hotels. If you already have a destination chosen and a hotel picked out, call the hotel and ask what they have available.

By the way, at resorts you'll often find the reverse is true. For example, during the winter ski resorts fill up on weekends with skiing fanatics, so you'll find resorts offering special reduced mid-week packages including reduced lift tickets, etc.

Off-Season Discounts

On a yearly cycle, you'll find hotels and resorts offering fantastic bargains during their off-season. Off-season varies according to your destination. Here are the dates that airlines consider low season for ten European countries: September 15 to May 14 for Austria, England, France, Italy, Spain, Sweden, and Yugoslavia; from September 15 to May 30 for Czechoslovakia; from September 1 to May 14 for Ireland; and from November 1 to March 31 for Portugal.

If you choose to go just at the end of the on-season or just before it begins, you can enjoy everything the destination has to offer at a substantial reduction in price.

Package Tours

This is yet another way of enjoying a full-facility establishment at a substantially discounted rate. In fact these tours are a boon to the traveler who has a limited amount of vacation time.

The tour packager relies on volume to obtain massive discounts off hotel accommodation prices. On any tour you will most likely have the choice of several hotels ranging from standard to deluxe. For the deluxe accommodations you'll pay a supplement, but you'll still be staying at the hotel at a rate that you could never command as an independent traveler unless you were taking advantage of the weekend package or something similar.

If you do choose to take a package, check that the

tour operator is a member of the U.S. Tour Operators Association before you make your reservation, and ask your friends and acquaintances if they have ever traveled with the company. Note their opinions and experiences. Also, you may want to check with the Better Business Bureau about the company's complaint record. Then read the brochures very carefully. Look at what you get on your tour for the price. What you actually get and what it may seem to say that you get may be two very different things. Be alert.

Even after all these caveats, on a one-week or two-week vacation you'll rarely beat the value, whether you go to Austria on a ski package or to Mexico or the Caribbean on a sun package. You might say the package tour is our somewhat telescoped modern version of the Grand Tour.

THE LOWEST PRICES OF ALL

In North American cities, the place to look for an inexpensive room is most often in a motel on the outskirts. In many (but not all) cases, this means you must have a car, because public transport to the center is either slow, or infrequent, or nonexistent.

Downtown hotels have largely become the preserve of expense-account travelers, conventioneers, and the wealthy. Of course, the convenience of staying right downtown is apparent: you get more time to see the sights as they're right outside, you needn't worry about traffic jams, or parking (after that first time when you arrive), you can head back to your room for a forgotten guidebook or a quick nap very easily. With a motel on the outskirts, about the only advantage is price. But with the average double room in a decent downtown hotel costing $100 to $150 or even more per night, a motel room at $55 to $75 looks very good indeed—you can stay twice as long for the same price. Here are some tips:

- Look for "clusters" of motels, often near major highway intersections; if one or two are full, or expensive, you can check others nearby.
- Figure your commuting costs into the motel price when comparing that price with a downtown hotel's; if you must drive ten miles, cross a toll bridge, and park in a pay lot, this may add substantially to the cost of your motel stay.

Budget Motel Chains

Anyone who drives the major highways of North America is familiar with the budget motel chains. Located at the outskirts of cities or airports, clustered at major Interstate Highway junctions, these places offer clean and comfortable, if simple, accommodations at low prices ranging from $20 to $50 per room.

In the last few years, the budget motel business has been booming. Lots of the largest hotel companies have gotten into the act, and the number and variety of budget motels has grown by huge amounts. There's now a "budget" motel for every taste.

The lowest priced of the budget motels charge as little as $20 or $25 for a room. Days Inn, Econo-Lodge, McSleep, and Motel 6 are some of these truly budget chains. In these places you get a comfortable bed, modern tile bath with shower, wall-to-wall carpeting, and perhaps a television. Some motels even have swimming pools, and all have the little conveniences such as ice machines and vending machines. They do not have restaurants or cocktail lounges, though these services are usually found very nearby.

In the so-called moderate-budget range of motels are

companies like Super 8 Motels. These have all the services of the low-budget places, plus televisions and more furniture in the rooms, perhaps coin laundries, a swimming pool, and other little services.

Many of the newest entrants into the budget motel sweepstakes are at the upper end of the budget price spectrum. The so-called luxury-budget motels are being built and operated under names such as Hampton Inns (a Holiday Inn affiliate), Country Inns (by Radisson Hotels), Fairfield Inns (Marriott), Rodeway Inns (Ramada), Comfort Inns and Comfort Suites (Quality Inns), La Quinta Motor Inns. More comforts, better locations, swimming pools, and more spacious grounds are some of the bonuses here. In addition, many of these motels have guest rooms entered from an interior hallway. The hallway is reached only by passing through the lobby. This is an excellent security feature.

For a complete list of all these motel companies, and locations of the motels, write to the American Hotel & Motel Association and order a copy of its Directory (see above).

Residence Hotels

These are older, plainer hotels, found in virtually every American city, which cater mostly to long-term residents. They often have a few rooms for "transients," or travelers who want to rent a room by the day. The rates can be quite reasonable, and the locations are often all right, though not excellent. The rooms themselves may be old-fashioned, perhaps even a bit dowdy, but otherwise perfectly presentable.

However, reader A. Fast of Nanuet, N.Y., has written to me with a warning. He notes that the room in a residence hotel that is offered to you for rent by the day may not be the same room that would be offered for a week or more. The hotel charges more (and profits more) from daily rentals, so the room rented by the day should be nicer, with more modern touches and conveniences. The room rented by the week may be older, less presentable, and less comfortable. So it's a good idea to determine exactly which room you get for which rate.

SPECIAL INEXPENSIVE LODGINGS

Now let's turn to the inexpensive lodgings that I was talking about in the introduction to this chapter. How can you find these inexpensive lodgings? Specific information is helpful, because even from earliest times one house or another in a village or town was usually designated as the inn or hospitality house. (Perhaps it had an extra room, or its occupants wanted to earn a bit of money in exchange for the service.) But much more important than specific directions or recommendations is an *awareness* of how lodging places operate, and why.

The basic difference between an old-style inn and a new-style inn and a new-style hotel is this: the inn was a building which *came to be used* as a lodging for travelers, whereas the hotel was a building that was *designed to be used* by travelers. Therefore the hotel was—from the very beginning—supposed to be a very profitable business enterprise. It was designed and built to accommodate and to please those who would and could pay more.

This ancient difference is still evident today. A Hilton or Sheraton was *built* for the business traveler. A guesthouse, tourist home, bed-and-breakfast, or dormitory was *built to do something else:* house a family, or students at school. Only *incidentally* is it a lodging for travelers, and therein lies the difference. It is not equipped with all of the luxury facilities that are designed and built into a hotel; it would be very

---

When you see a roadside guesthouse, don't succumb to that weird twentieth-century trauma by which normal people are filled with terror and their courage flees them when confronted by the prospect of an unstandardized product.

---

expensive to convert it; and the proprietors are not interested in converting it into luxury accommodations.

Many variations on these themes exist, and in fact some inns have become exclusive, expensive, and very fancy, while some hotels and motels may offer very good rates. But in general, you can save money by directing your efforts to finding accommodations in a building that was not built primarily to house travelers.

Stay with "Friends"

You can find rooms in private homes virtually everywhere, because the urge to take in travelers and earn a little extra money from surplus space is universal. In the U.S., "tourist homes" were the places our thrifty grandparents and great-grandparents stayed when they had no friends or relatives in town. Many of today's American tourist homes, guesthouses, and bed-and-breakfast places survive from that time, and show their Victorian-era origins.

You've passed them on the road and along the main street in a small town: signs that say "Guests," or "Overnight Guests," or "Murphy's Tourist Home." With the advent of the modern motel and the ulcer-making schedule, most travelers did just that—pass these places by in favor of standardized accommodations where they could just pull off the highway at any time of the day or night, without reservations, and find a private room with bath and toilet. No lady of the house to get out of bed if you arrived at midnight, no walking down the hall to the bathroom, no questions asked, no pleasantries to make, no proprieties—except payment—to be observed. No surprises, no variety, no human contact, please! I've got miles to cover.

How do you tell a good guesthouse or tourist home? You look at it . . . and no self-respecting guesthouse owner will ever refuse to show you the room.

Surprisingly, many guesthouses didn't close, but have continued in operation through the "motel decades," and they continue today. Travel through any small New England town and you're sure to spot one or two guesthouses. While the fancy "country inn" a block away is charging $145 per night, the lady who runs the guesthouse will ask $40 or $50 for two, and will offer authentic warmth in the bargain.

How do you locate a good guesthouse or tourist home? By asking at a local chamber of commerce, tourist information booth, or room-finding service. The latter are very popular in European towns and cities (often located in central train stations) where hundreds of rooms in dozens of houses can benefit from a central clearing office for room requests. In small resort towns throughout the world, people with rooms to rent for the night, for the week, or longer, will meet incoming trains, buses, and ferry boats (Greek islands, for example). They may have a handful of cards printed with the name, phone number, address, and directions to the house; or they may just ask, "Need a room?"

Or you may simply drive past a tourist home in a small town that displays a sign out front. *Stop your car and look!* Don't succumb to that weird twentieth-century trauma by which normal people are filled with terror, and their courage flees them, when confronted by the prospect of an unstandardized product. As for dealing with the guesthouse or tourist home owner, that person is in the lodging business just like the hotelier and motel owner, but on a more modest scale.

How do you tell a good guesthouse or tourist home? You look at it. As it is not a standardized product, you're not expected to register and pay up until you've inspected the facilities—the owner will *expect* that you want to examine the room, the beds, the bath—and learn the price. This only takes a few minutes, and no self-respecting guesthouse owner will ever refuse to show you the room. If you decide to take the room—fine. If you don't take it, the owner will figure it's not what you wanted, and he'll wait for the next ring. As for you, head down the road and perhaps the next tourist home will have that double bed, or garden view, or extra cot for the baby that you'd really like to have.

The Bed-and-Breakfast Movement in North America

In recent years North Americans have been opening their homes to travelers. The increase in hotel prices and a new familiarity with lodgings in the rest of the world have led many people to consider renting rooms to travelers. The modern tactic for making it work is the bed-and-breakfast association. These private clearinghouses take reservations, set rates, provide directions. Bed-and-breakfast associations have sprung up in every major American city recently, and more are being organized every day. Entrepreneurs are compiling nationwide lists of bed-and-breakfast leagues, and travel writers are producing guidebooks which deal exclusively with bed-and-breakfasts, or which include information about certain houses and leagues.

In any city, a riffle through the phone book (stopping at logical places: "Bed and Breakfast," "Guesthouse Accommodation," "Lodging Bureau") will often produce the desired number. If not, a call to the Tourist Bureau or Convention and Visitors' Bureau (every city of any size has one of these, under a similar name) will get you the information you want.

What about accommodations? What's the room like? The officer at the bed-and-breakfast association will describe a room or rooms to you, tell you about its location, and quote the price. Associations try to aim for a fairly high standard: private bath, television, air conditioning, etc. But any room that is neat and reasonably commodious is usually accepted for booking, and the traveler pays only for what he gets. A plainish room comes at a lower price. With the room comes a fairly full breakfast, perhaps not bacon-eggs-cereal-home-fries-juice-porridge, but more than just rolls and coffee. You can find out about the breakfast when you find out about the room that goes with it. After you've sampled it, you can register compliments or complaints with the association too. Most B&Bs would much rather have their association receive the former than the latter.

Pensions and Other Special Accommodations

Besides tourist homes and bed-and-breakfasts, many other types of accommodation provide the simple, traditional services of the age-old inn at lower rates than the large luxury modern hotels.

In many European countries, some families do more than take in transient visitors and give them breakfast—they feed them as well. The classic *pension* (France) or *pensione* (Italy) is one or more large apartments with several rooms let to guests by the week or month. Meals are family style, and are included with the room in the weekly price. Sometimes you can make arrangements for breakfast and dinner only, at a slightly lower price. This is probably what you want, as you'll want to try some restaurants, and you won't want to traipse all the way back to your pension every day for lunch.

If you choose to go just at the end of the on-season or just before it begins, you can enjoy everything the destination has to offer at a substantial reduction in price.

How do you locate a pension? Through a lodging service such as exists in many cities, through a guidebook, or through another pension. If you have the name of one pension, you can find all the others. Pension owners keep track of one another.

Different countries have different types of moderately priced accommodations where travelers have been lodging down through the centuries. In England

and Switzerland, you'll find small country inns as well as bed-and-breakfast places and pensions; in Denmark they're called *kros*, while in Japan they're known as *minshuku* (private homes) or *ryokans* (moderately priced inns). In Spain the *paradores* are a good value; in Portugal the *estalagems* and *pensoes* are similar.

Ask the tourist offices about such accommodations. Not only will you get good value for money, you'll also really savor the local flavor.

LESS ORTHODOX ACCOMMODATIONS

For trips of a different nature, one can take advantage of various less orthodox accommodations. Because of the splendid benefits in some of these plans, you may just want to alter your travel plans and make them fit the accommodations, rather than vice-versa.

Home-Swapping and Time-Sharing

Home-swapping and time-sharing are twin concepts with many of the same benefits and disadvantages. Both of them involve a hefty commitment: you've got to be willing to let someone live in your home with your things while you're away, or you've got to be willing to pay a substantial sum for the right to share a place and its furnishings with others. If you are willing to do these things, read on.

Both home-swapping and time-sharing have a crucial element: location. If you live in Timbuktoo it's going to be very difficult to find someone who wants to swap homes with you. With an apartment in Manhattan or San Francisco, you can write your home-swapping ticket anywhere in the world, however. The same goes for time-sharing. If you buy one or two weeks in a condominium at Lake Mudbath, you can expect to swap only with those who have time-sharing condos in Blackfly Woods or Revolting Sands, whereas a week's time-sharing rights in Acapulco or Vail will open the door to a swap anywhere you like. *Someone has got to want your place before any sort of a swap will work.*

A Hilton or Sheraton was *built* for the business traveler. A guesthouse, tourist home, bed-and-breakfast, or dormitory was *built to do something else*: house a family, or students at school. Only incidentally is it a lodging for travelers, and therein lies the difference.

Assuming that you have rights in a desirable location, you can go about the business of making connections. This can be done through classified ads in publications you know and enjoy, which is a good way to contact like-minded people. *The New York Review of Books*, for example, has a column of classifieds for house-swapping, which is frequently consulted by academics and literati. The advantage here is not only that like-minded people will be trustworthy (though there's never any guarantee), but also that they will want to go where you live and vice-versa. Look in the back pages of magazines and newspapers you receive to see if there are possibilities for home swaps. Also try through organizations and clubs you've joined. Perhaps a foreign branch will scout leads for you, or post notices.

HOME-EXCHANGE ORGANIZATIONS: Though I think it best that you make arrangements on your own, you can get help if necessary. Home-exchange organizations are businesses that publish directories or maintain databases to help get prospective home-swappers together. These companies do not guarantee that they will find you someone, or that the house you go to will be exactly what you want, or that your own home will be well taken care of. You must make sure of these things on your own. However, the home-exchange organizations do provide valuable contacts. Here are some of the more active ones:

Educator's Vacation Alternatives, 317 Piedmont Rd., Santa Barbara, CA 93105 (tel. 805/698-2947).

Exchange Network, P.O. Box 752, Ocean Springs, MS 39564 (tel. toll free 800/562-6529).

Global Home Exchange Service, P.O. Box 2015, South Burlington, VT 05401-2015 (tel. 802/985-3825).

Hideaways International, P.O. Box 1459, Concord, MA 01742 (tel. 617/369-0252 or toll free 800/843-4433).

Holiday Exchanges, P.O. Box 5294, Ventura, CA 93003 (tel. 805/642-4879).

Home Exchange International, 185 Park Row, Suite 14D, New York, NY 10038 (tel. 212/349-5340), or 22458 Ventura Blvd., Suite E., Woodland Hills, CA 91364-1581 (tel. 818/992-8990).

International Home Exchange Service, P.O. Box 3975, San Francisco, CA 94119 (tel. 415/382-0300).

InterService Home Exchange, P.O. Box 87, Glen Echo, MD 20812 (tel. 301/299-7442).

Loan-a-Home, 2 Park Lane 6E, Mount Vernon, NY 10552 (tel. 914/664-7640).

Vacation Exchange Club, 12006 111th Avenue, Suite 12, Youngstown, AZ 85363 (tel. 602/972-2186).

WorldWide Exchange, P.O. Box 1563, San Leandro, CA 94577 (tel. 415/521-7890).

If you're apprehensive about swapping homes, *Your Place and Mine*, by Cindy Gum (available for $5.95 from Gum Publications, 15195 El Camino Grande, Suite 100, Saratoga, CA 95070, tel. 408/395-1617), will help you organize such exchanges and avoid most of the pitfalls.

A book that covers the subject of home (and car) exchanges in detail is *Frommer's Swap & Go: Home Exchanging Made Easy*, by Albert C. and Verna E. Beerbower. Besides exchanges, the $10.95 book includes lots of other travel tips as well. Ask for it in any bookstore, or order it using the handy form at the back of this book.

TIME-SHARING ORGANIZATIONS: Before you buy your time-sharing property, you should inquire about exchange plans and possibilities. Are you in the very early stages of considering time-sharing? Then write for information to the organizations that operate the most widespread exchange plans: **Interval International,** P.O. Box 4301920 (6262 Sunset, Penthouse 1), Miami, FL 33143 (tel. 305/666-1861 or toll free 800/828-8200); **Resort Condominiums International,** P.O. Box 80229, Indianapolis, IN 42680 (tel. 317/876-8899 or toll free 800/338-7777 or 800/428-6169; in Canada, call toll free 800/265-1391). By the way, you should know that your annual time-sharing swap may cost you upward of $80 because you must pay a membership fee in the exchange organization, and then pay a fee for their arrangement of the swap. This cost is above and beyond any normal maintenance fees you must pay on your time-sharing property.

"Self-Catering" Accommodations

"Self-catering" is the British term for housekeeping accommodations. Renting a cottage, villa, or kitchen-equipped room is very popular with the British, who have a vast network of rental cottages, brokers, information sources, and customers. The reason is simple. Renting accommodations without service (no bellhops, chambermaids, desk clerks, janitors, or elevator operators to pay) is good profit for the renter and good-value housing for the traveler.

In general, you can save money by directing your efforts to finding accommodations in a building that was *not* built *primarily* to house travelers.

Self-catering accommodations exist throughout the world. The advantages are that you get lots of space to yourself, the chance to save money by cooking your own meals, and as a bonus, your accommodations are frequently charming and offer a unique way of experiencing the country and its people. The disadvantages: rentals tend to be long-term only, at least a week, probably a fortnight (two weeks), preferably a month or more. Also, you are effectively tied down to the immediate surroundings of your rental cottage—you've got to come "home" each night. In England, however, with so much beauty and so many sights of interest within such a small space, this is hardly a disadvantage.

In North America, rental cottages and housekeeping or "efficiency" rooms in hotels, motels, and country inns are also widely available. In years to come, these lodgings will become even more important as hotel prices continue to rise. Sources of information, and clearinghouses for rentals, will expand and amplify, making it easier to rent quickly, at long distance. For now, here are some tips on finding the self-catering accommodation you want, where and when you want it:

Sit down and decide what you want:

> Exact arrival and departure dates
> Amount you want to pay
> General location
> Number of rooms
> Number of beds
> Walking distance to transport, markets, beach

Get source materials. Many mazagines and newspapers carry self-catering rental advertisements in their classified ads. The more local the publication and distribution, the more local the ads. But in any internationally distributed magazine or newspaper you can find ads for properties in many parts of the world. Also write to the tourist authorities (as outlined in Chapter 3; see "Travel Resources," Appendix 1: "Tourist Offices Worldwide," for addresses) and ask them for tips on finding self-catering accommodations.

Write to the agent or owner for the specifics. Send your list of requirements and a self-addressed envelope, stamped if you're sending it to a place in your own country, or with an IRC (International Reply Coupon, sold at all post offices) if you're sending it abroad. Ask for photos, which you should return to the agent or owner after you've looked at them. Arranging for a flat or villa can take time, especially if you must do it through the international mails—it may take you a month just to write and to receive a reply.

Also, the most popular periods will be booked in advance, so get your bid in as early as possible.

Don't let your imagination run away with you. By all means, dream about how much fun you'll have, the walks you'll take, the beaches you'll comb, the country markets and small-town shops you'll get to know.

While the fancy "country inn" a block away is charging $145 a night, the lady who runs the guesthouse will ask $40 or $50 for two, and will offer authentic warmth in the bargain.

But don't expect your rental home to be exactly what you imagined it to be. It's not supposed to conform to your dream, it's only supposed to be as advertised. Am I being a killjoy? Well, the biggest disappointment renters face is when their quaint Elizabethan thatched cottage in Shakespeare Country turns out to be a tile-roofed guesthouse in a suburb of Stratford-upon-Avon. The picture showed the front of the house, but not the roof? Then don't imagine a thatched roof. The picture showed the outside, which was quaint and cozy, but not the inside? Perhaps the interior is all spiffy-modern, white walls and streamlined furniture, which happens to be the owner's conception of the Good Life. When selecting a rental place, *be conscious of what you don't know*, to avoid disappointment. What you want is expectations and dreams based on what you do know; the rest is adventure, and unless you actively set yourself up for disappointment, you're sure to enjoy the adventure. Keep an open mind until you can "feel" the place and try it on for size.

The savings? Two people who plan to dine out a lot are not the best candidates for big savings when it comes to self-catering rentals. Families are the big savers. But if a couple nibbles breakfast in the kitchen, prepares most lunches as picnics, and cooks the occasional dinner—or more—at home, they will still save substantially over the cost of equivalent standardized lodgings and meals. You must compare prices on a weekly or monthly basis. If you'd expect to spend $40 or $50 per night on room and breakfast, plus about $20 or $30 daily for lunch and dinner—and these prices are *not high* in many North American tourist areas, nor in Europe—then your weekly costs would be $420 to $560. You can spend the same amount, but dine more elegantly in more expensive restaurants, by cutting lodging costs with a self-catering rental, or you can spend a smaller total amount by getting a rental and cooking at least some meals for yourself.

VACATION RENTAL ORGANIZATIONS: Self-catering accommodations can be anything from a castle to a travel trailer. In England, for example, one firm will rent you a fixed-base trailer at bargain rates. Contact them for specifications and prices: **Hoseasons Holidays Ltd.,** Sunway House, 89 Bridge Rd., Oulton Broad, Lowestoft, Suffolk NR32 3LT, England (tel. 0502/501515).

Stateside firms which arrange vacation rentals in Europe include **Villas International,** 71 W. 23rd St., New York, NY 10010 (tel. toll free 800/221-2260, or 212/929-7585). They list over 20,000 European and Caribbean rentals.

Another is **At Home Abroad,** 405 East 56th St., Suite 6H, New York, NY 10022 (tel. 212/421-9165).

If you don't want to be bothered with organizations, listings, application forms, etc., many self-catering guidebooks are available.

University Accommodations

The crush of visitors to certain cities at certain times of year produces an abundant crop of nonstandard accommodations. Local officials, attempting to deal with the influx of people, look all over for the essentials: rooms, beds, simple meals. University housing, often empty for weeks or months at a time, is a perfect candidate to be converted to temporary transient housing. The university makes a few dollars on its buildings, and you get a cheap, simple, clean, safe place to stay.

Availability of dorm rooms is very changeable. The only way to be sure that dorm rooms exist in a given city at a given time is to call or write. You may have to reserve in advance, though few places will hold you to this if you look respectable, appear on their doorstep, and they have a room free.

Use the telephone book, or if you're looking in another state or country, go to the library and use their resources. Or better yet, consult the CIEE's *Where to Stay USA,* available in book stores, by mail order (see the last pages of this book), or from CIEE, 205 East 42nd St., New York, NY 10017.

THE REALLY CHEAP OPTIONS

Youth Hostels

You have to be willing to accept sexually segregated dormitory accommodations to stay in a youth hostel, because that's what most of them have: girls' dorms and boys' dorms. You may have to help with the chores of keeping the hostel tidy. You may find that you can't enter the hostel before 5 p.m., and must leave it by 10 a.m. the next morning, even if you're staying several days. And you may find a three-night maximum stay regulation in busy seasons.

What you get in return is a clean, friendly place to stay at the lowest possible price. Inexpensive but nourishing meals may be available as a bonus; there may be simple cooking facilities so you can prepare your own food. A youth hostel is about the best place in the world to ask questions, scan notice-boards, and pick up the most current information on budget travel.

In some Third World countries, youth hostels are

Self-catering accommodations exist throughout the world. The advantages are that you get lots of space to yourself, the chance to save money by cooking your own meals, and as a bonus your accommodations are frequently charming and offer a unique way of experiencing the country and its people.

---

pretty much of a disappointment. Find out the situation first before planning a hosteling trip to such a place.

Membership is currently $10 for under 18s and over-60s, $20 for adults. For more information and for directories of youth hostels in North America and abroad, write the American Youth Hostels National

Office, P.O. Box 37613, Washington, DC 20013-7613. Also be aware that the Youth Hostels Association offers some very low-cost tours in the United States and abroad (for example, a bicycle tour through China). Programs are outlined in their *Highroad to Adventure* booklet, available from the address above.

YMCAs and YWCAs

Part of the purpose of the Ys is to provide basic, decent accommodations: you can't host a business meeting or hold a convention at a Y. A few are unsuitable, but in general the Ys provide decent if spartan rooms (mostly singles) for a very low price, throughout much of the world.

In Hartford, the YWCA is a modern high-rise, much like a good hotel with its cafeteria, rooms-with-bath, which have a fine view of the state capitol, and sports facilities. In Jerusalem the YMCA is a mammoth pseudo-Oriental palace with many rooms, indoor pool, cafeteria, game and sports rooms, even lectures and entertainment. In Montréal the YMCA and YWCA both have superb downtown locations plus comfortable, though unglamorous, facilities.

A Y room may have a television set, or even a private bathroom. Often you have a choice, and you needn't pay for these if you don't want them. In general, YMCAs accept both men and women as guests, while YWCAs accept women only. The main problem with Ys is that the rooms offer such value-for-money that they're often booked solid by residents. If you write ahead, though, you can usually get a room.

Want more information? Contact the YMCA, 356 West 34th St., New York, NY 10001 (tel. 212/760-5850); same address for the YWCA.

Camping

Anyplace to which large numbers of people can drive will have camping facilities.

University housing, often empty for weeks or months at a time, is a perfect candidate to be converted to temporary transient housing. The university makes a few dollars on its buildings, and you get a cheap, simple, clean, safe place to stay.

You must think of camping as more than roughing it with a nylon tent and a backpack. Modern tents that pop open in a few minutes, sleeping bags and pads of space-age materials, highly organized camping areas equipped with showers, laundromats, shops, sports grounds, even restaurants and entertainment—all these make camping much easier and more comfortable than your traditional idea of life in the wilderness.

The very easiest camping of all is in a well-equipped van. No tent to set up, no weather to worry about. Often one can just pull off the road or park near a beach, and the cost of an overnight stay is nearly nothing.

In many countries you can rent camper vans, large campers, or trailers. They are not cheap, though, and you should add up all costs very carefully before arranging a rental.

The U.S. National Park Service system offers unique and spectacular settings for camping trips. You can get an overview of the possibilities throughout the

U.S. by sending for the *Guide and Map for National Parks* to the U.S. Department of the Interior, National Park Service, Washington, DC 20240. You can even reserve ahead in at least seven national parks through any Ticketron agency.

For private campgrounds *Woodall's* is a comprehensive directory with listings of campgrounds in the U.S. and Canada; experienced campers swear by it.

For some idea of costs, ask a travel agent or contact the Recreation Vehicle Industry Association, P.O. Box 2999, Reston, VA 22090 (tel. 703/620-6003). Oftentimes, buying a used camper is a much better idea, as used campers retain a high proportion of their value from year to year. As with a car, if you sell the van in the same year you buy it, and if you haven't run it into the ground, you may recover the purchase price completely.

Once-in-a-while camping is a possibility for serendipitous travelers who may find their funds running

WAVE OF THE FUTURE?

The Japanese, so skillful at miniaturization and making exquisite, small things, have turned their attention to hotels. In Tokyo now the lodgings with the highest occupancy rates (70% to 80% during the week) are "capsule hotels." Each tiny capsule, only large enough to lie down in, is equipped with a television, radio, clock, and lamp. The shower is down the hall.

Space is minimal, but so is the price: about $25 a night—in expensive Tokyo! Come to think of it, if all you want to do is go to bed, watch a little TV or read, wake up when the alarm goes off, shower, and depart, why pay $200? But is the rest of the world ready for the capsule hotel?

low or are in a place where accommodations are hard to find. If you've had the foresight to stow a small tent and air mattresses in the car (along with your picnic supplies), you can have that fail-safe option for a night or two.

In some countries, camping has become as convenient as staying in a motel. Israel, for example, has a system of established campsites where you rent a tent (already pitched) and cots just as you would a motel room.

Taking it one stage further, there are now companies offering camping tours, most often through Europe. The price of the tour usually includes meals, transportation, and equipment. It makes an ideal trip for the young at heart or solo traveler who is visiting Europe for the first time. Check with your travel agent, and keep camping in mind while gathering information on your destination.

10

Savvy Dining

Good cuisine, all by itself, provides ample reason for embarking on a journey. Who could drive through Louisiana without having gumbo, or spend time in Québec and not try tourtière?

The cuisines of France and Italy, though copied throughout the world, are finest on their home turf. And what about rock lobster in New England, key lime pie in Florida, and just about anything in California?

Before we set out on some adventurous trip to a new area, we know what to expect in terms of sights: Westminster Abbey, the Dome of the Rock, the Empire State Building. The greatest adventure of all may come when we discover the local foods. For example, this happens to everyone who visits Turkey for the first time. Everyone knows about the splendors of Topkapi Palace, but few people have heard of *ayse kadin fasulye*, the savory string beans cooked with amb and tomatoes. "I never imagined they had such good food here!" is a typical response. Similarly, everyone wants to see the pyramids in Cairo. But do they know they will discover the heavenly dessert called *ummu-ali*?

You'll spend an hour or two at the pyramids, but dozens of hours at Egyptian dining tables. You look at the pyramids, but you also look at nicely prepared dishes; then you enjoy their aroma and flavor, something that most of us would not want to do with a pyramid.

Dining well does not necessarily mean dining expensively. Though it can be bliss to unfurl a snowy linen napkin in the hushed atmosphere of an elegant restaurant, who has not enjoyed a delicious tuck-in at a neighborhood bistro in Paris, a trattoria in Rome, a café in Harvard Square, a tiny lokanta in Istanbul?

FOUR RULES FOR DINING WELL

Food has other important functions on a journey. If you eat well, you feel well. And if you eat wisely, you'll get the most possible enjoyment from your trip without spending more than you wanted to.

Four rules are helpful guides to dining well without wasting valuable travel resources:

1. Eat well to stay healthy. Sickness and distress are not only unpleasant, they are expensive. They rob you of vacation time and vacation money.
2. Dine according to the customs of the country. If you do this, you will eat better, and more, and you will spend the same—or less—than a local person does for food.
3. Remember that lunch is cheaper than dinner.
4. Plan ahead to prepare at least some of your meals yourself.

Eat Well to Stay Healthy

Some people think this simply means not starving yourself. Not only must you eat enough, many times you will find you must eat more because of your increased level of activity. Get enough food. Also, have regular meals. And choose those foods that will give you the greatest nutritional value for the money. Don't order a soft drink with your sandwich, order milk. Milk is virtually a complete food, whereas soda is a mixture of water, sugar, flavor, and caffeine. Often a glass of milk costs *less* than a glass of soda.

KNOW YOUR NUTRITION: If you know nothing about nutrition, learn something before you go away, so that you can make intelligent decisions. One can easily drop into a hamburger stand and spend $5 or $6 on foods of questionable value: "milkshakes" which contain little milk, but lots of sugar, salt, and chemicals; fried side orders (french fries, fried onion rings), which pound-for-pound are more expensive than filet mignon; sodas, cookies, and sweet desserts. But a hamburger stand is not necessarily a "junk food" dispensary, though it is a "fast food" one. Look at what's in the normal chain-restaurant hamburger: bread, beef, tomato, lettuce, pickled cucumber. Add a salad, and you have a decently balanced light meal. It's not "health food," but it is basically quite nutritious. And the cost for this balanced mini-meal? About $4. Have a hamburger or cheeseburger, salad, and milk. Look upon the french fries and milkshakes as rather perilous forms of entertainment, but not as valuable foods.

Your knowledge of nutrition will come in handier abroad, where the standard hamburger may not be available. Faced with a Turkish breakfast table, what would you see? Hard-boiled eggs (perhaps nature's most perfect food), black olives, salty white cheese (the salt helps retain your fluids in the hot, dry summer), bread and jam, *su boreği* (a flaky pastry filled with cheese and herbs), fruit juices, and a cauldron of *sicak süt* (warm milk with sugar). Protein, carbohydrates, edible oils, vitamins—they're all here, just take your pick. You won't find bacon in a Moslem country. Bacon, like french fries, is an entertainment, not a food. This brings us to the second rule:

Copy Local Dining Habits

Dine according to the customs of the country. This means that you must not only eat *what* the locals eat, but eat it *when* and *where* they eat it. A good example: orange juice at breakfast. Countries without the bounty of Florida and California have not developed the custom of having orange juice at breakfast all year long. If you order it specially, it will cost like the dickens. You may pass a fresh juice stand on the street, and it may be citrus season—in that case orange juice makes sense. Or keep an eye out for neighborhood greengrocers—where you can buy oranges or other high-Vitamin C fruits for a pick-me-up snack. If the local people show no signs of scurvy, they're getting their Vitamin C daily, and you can too, at the same affordable prices they're paying.

Butter is another example. Few countries look upon butter as a necessary table condiment. Having butter on the table morning, noon, and night would seem to them like our having a bowl of whipped cream always in sight. You can get butter anywhere. You will pay dearly for it.

You'll be surprised at how much you can save not only by eating what local people do, but also *where* they eat. In most countries of southern Europe (Italy, France, Spain), for example, you'll notice that restaurants do not include coffee on their special three-course tourist menu (it's rarely on the menu at all). It is customary there to drink coffee at a separate bar/café rather than in a restaurant that serves food. And that means not only after-dinner but also breakfast coffee. So head for a bar/café for delicious morning-fresh rolls and breakfast coffee to start your day in a most enjoyable, very European manner.

Dine according to the customs of the country. This means that you must not only eat *what* the locals eat, but also eat it *when* and *where* they eat it.

You'll save considerably. Even here in the United States, working people will drop into a deli for coffee and a roll, croissant, bagel, etc.; such a breakfast may cost $1.25, but a comparable one will cost you at least twice as much at your hotel. Similarly, in Britain, the working folk go to the pubs for lunch, and it's here that you'll find the best food values and most authentic local snacks and dishes as well as the jovial company of the "locals." As a general rule, avoid hotel dining, especially for lunch and breakfast. A hotel coffeeshop will often charge double the price of a similar establishment two blocks from the hotel.

FOLLOW THE RHYTHM: Also, get used to the *rhythm* of eating in a foreign country. In England, big breakfast, light pub lunch, light snacks at teatime, late moderate supper. In Mexico, light breakfast, large late lunch, light supper. To find out the customs of the country, ask about them. Everyone likes to talk about food, dining, local delicacies, and habits. They'll give you rapturous discourses on dishes their mothers used to make, on a favorite local chef's specialties, on the richness of the country's produce.

COMMUNICATE YOUR WILLINGNESS TO EXPERIMENT: Local people will assume you want your own sort of food. You must get around this. In Cairo's better hotels one finds almost exclusively Western food (at Western prices). The Western food is prepared by Eastern chefs who don't care for it and never eat it. This Western food is at best mediocre, at worst godawful. In a local Cairo restaurant you can stuff yourself on shish kebab, *kofta, ful,* and *taamiya* (skewered lamb, grilled spiced ground meat, savory beans, and bean fritters) for the price of a single bottle of beer at the Hilton.

In asking about food, approach someone this way: instead of "I'm thirsty, I need a cola," say, "I'm thirsty—what do local people drink?" You may end up with refreshing tea with mint, or fruit juice, or spring water.

Lunch Is Cheaper Than Dinner

Why is lunch cheaper than dinner, virtually everywhere in the world? It's simple: millions of people eat lunch away from home. Dinner is a discretionary meal: you can dine at home *or* in a restaurant. At lunchtime, however, most people are going about their day's work and would rather not traipse all the way home to eat. Local restaurants can depend on great volume, and can therefore offer more for less. The Business Lunch is now a world institution: a set-price, multicourse repast designed to attract officeworkers with good and plenteous food at moderate prices. If you only buy one meal a day, it probably should be lunch.

LOW-COST LUNCHES: Workers eat cheaply, and whether you're in Stockholm, London, Paris, or Rome, you'll find appetizing lunches at the least expensive prices at these insiders' restaurants. In England, of course, pubs traditionally offer simple, hearty fare. For French regional cooking at its finest, stop in at a *routier,* roughly comparable to the U.S. truck stop or roadside diner, distinguished by the traditional routier's white disk-like sign in front. In Rome, labor unions and branches of the military have centrally located restaurants, and Stockholm has its "bars," which are popular cafeteria-like establishments (there's one in the central city park).

Department stores provide a good source for inexpensive lunches or snacks. And at Paris's Samaritaine store, the view from the terrace café supplies a city backdrop that outdoes any of that city's four-star restaurants.

Do-It-Yourself Dining

Plan ahead to prepare at least half of your meals yourself. "Oh," a friend once said to me, "how sordid! There I was in my room, eating cheese, bread, sausage off a plastic bag!" It was his own fault if his impromptu meal was no gourmet's delight. The ingredients for an elegant picnic were probably just around the corner in the local market, but he didn't plan ahead or think creatively. He just bought a lump of some strange cheese, and an entire loaf of bread (of which he threw three-fourths away), and too much of a sausage he didn't really care for.

EVERYBODY DOES IT: At the very moment he was lamenting his plight, travelers all over the world were sitting down to picnics in their rooms. *Every* traveler eats in his room. *No one* likes eating in restaurants and snack shops all the time. The truth is that it's relaxing to be out of the struggle with waiters, strange dishes, worry about prices, mistakes on bills, concern over tipping, finding a good place. Your mistake is not that you're eating in your room; your mistake is that you didn't plan the meal properly.

A traveler is certainly limited when it comes to buying foodstuffs. Large items (whole melons, cuts of meat, pounds of pasta), items that must be prepared with utensils (ovens, colanders, frying pans, toasters, grinders), items that need constant refrigeration, or that can't take travel easily (fish, fresh eggs, many fruits and vegetables) are all out of the question for the traveler's picnic. But even a modest meal need not be boring if you prepare for it.

A DO-IT-YOURSELF PICNIC: Take a bag for shopping: set aside some time specifically for grocery shopping, just as you would before preparing a meal at home. Check through the markets, and shop as though you lived there: ask for a taste of the cheese or the olives, find out what's in the sausages, watch the locals buying bread. Does the bakery sell rolls? Does it sell half- and quarter-loaves? (In most countries with fresh-baked bread, bakeries sell a variety of sizes of loaves, or they will gladly sell you only a portion—they do it all the time.) Alternatives to bread include dry rusks (zwieback), plain crackers, unleavened bread.

Note: Besides purchasing your picnic fare at the markets you can often find delectable stand-up meals in or on the fringes of the market—spicy hot leberkase and all kinds of würst in Germany, hot tempting pizza in Italy, stir-fried vegetables and noodles from a cook-boat in Bangkok, or crisp fried pork cracklings with salsa verde at the massive market in Mexico City.

Back in your room, set up your meal just as you would at home. Have utensils (plastic ones from the plane will do; metal is nicer, but heavier), napkins, glasses (from the bathroom shelf), a bottle of wine, fresh wildflowers or a candle. Dining is a ceremony, and the best dinners are made not with just good cooking, but with pleasant ritual as well. You may then

---

Lunch is cheaper than dinner. . . . If you only buy one meal a day, it probably should be lunch.

---

feast on simple fare: good cheese, an interesting cold meat, pickled olives or vegetables, preserved seafood (sardines, pickled fish, canned oysters or octopus), nutritious raw vegetables and fruits, a glass or two of mineral water or the local table wine.

In places where good foodstuffs are abundant, you can truly feast. A Paris market yielded the following hotel room feast: *crudités* (raw vegetables with a dash of salt and vinegar), *terrine de lapin* (a delicious rabbit pâté), *pâté de faisan* (pheasant pâté), fresh camembert and *fromage de chèvre* (creamy, flavorful goat's milk cheese), *clemantine* (seedless tangerines), and *dattes de Tunisie farci* (dried Tunisian dates stuffed with walnuts). We accompanied our feast first with a cup of hot bouillon, then with an inexpensive local wine, and finished up with French coffee and cognac. How much would such a meal have cost in a Parisian restaurant? About $30 apiece. How much did we pay? About $8 each.

Think "picnic" when you're sightseeing too. Even in the heart of great cities there are parks, both large and "vest-pocket," where you can have a picnic lunch. Outside the cities, châteaux, castles, and other tourist attractions provide very pleasant picnic sites for their visitors. But even if there are no specific picnic areas on your route, you'll soon become adept at spotting likely picnic spots—along a grassy riverbank, at scenic mountain overlooks—even the ramparts of a medieval city can serve as your dining table.

BE PREPARED FOR YOUR PICNICS: You may want to build a small supply of kitchen tools, taking some from home and picking up others along the way. A multipurpose pocket knife with a corkscrew, such as a Swiss army knife, is good to have, plus a can opener; vegetable peeler, paper napkins, eating utensils, stores of a few spices and such condiments as salt, pepper, sugar, bouillon cubes, etc. A fine piece of screening or cloth, or an infusion ball ("tea egg") will allow you to make tea and coffee without leaves or grounds left in the cup. If you prefer instant, use that.

A tool I find indispensable is an immersion heater coil. Pick one up in a North American hardware or grocery store ($4 or $5) for 110 voltage and domestic trips. For the rest of the world, look for one abroad that operates on 220 volts, and keep it for later trips. I was appalled some years ago when I found a good sturdy 220-volt immersion heater in Greece—it cost an astounding $8! But since I bought it, that coil has heated water for about 1,000,000 cups of coffee, tea, bouillon, chicken noodle soup, hot toddies, sleeping potions (hot milk with honey), sore throat remedies (hot tea with lemon and honey), shaving when there's only a cold water tap, even mulled wine (red wine, orange slices, raisins, cinnamon stick).

SOME FINAL PICNIC TIPS: As you explore your travel destination, pick up bits of information that will help you to prepare your meals: detour into shops for ideas of what's available, ask locals to point out the nearest bakery, wine shop, grocery store, or market. Are there open-air markets? What are the market days? What local foods are good for a picnic? Is there a delicatessen, *charcuterie,* etc., in the neighborhood? Bring your supplies home inconspicuously so the hotel clerk doesn't raise a fuss. Clean up, and the clerk will never know.

Remember: many travelers are eating in their rooms; a good meal must be prepared, not thrown together; make it a ceremony, however informal; relax, and enjoy the luxury of dining with your shoes off, at your own pace, without having to flag down waiters or tot up restaurant bills—and at a fraction of the price.

THE PLEASURES OF A RESTAURANT

No one eats in restaurants all the time, but no one eats at home all the time either. For those occasions when you want to or must buy a meal, you should know that there are ways to get the maximum for your money.

Choosing a Restaurant

Finding the right restaurant is the most important step of all. Guidebooks, advertisements, a hotel concierge or clerk will all give you advice, but you won't know the restaurant is truly worthwhile until after you've eaten there. By then, it may be too late.

The greatest problem comes with standards. "Where's a good, cheap place to eat?" Well now, what does "good" mean to you? Definitions of good range from "I don't care so long as I don't gag and the portions are huge" to "The waiter must be all in black, of course, and the *quenelles* must come on a warm— but not hot—plate." Both definitions are valid. Just beware when you are using one and your advisor is using the other.

Of course your advisor is going to recommend a "good" restaurant. No one wants to rush off to a "bad" or "mediocre" restaurant, so avoid the word "good" completely when asking for a place to dine. Instead, be specific: how close is it, what does it serve, is there atmosphere, how much does an average meal cost? Have you eaten there, how long ago? Who eats there, tourists or locals? What are the other choices?

GET SEVERAL RECOMMENDATIONS: Get not one but several recommendations, and soon you will see a pattern emerge: no one has ever come away from the Grumbling Gravy dissatisfied; the Caviar-and-Cress is only for the expense-account crowd; the Fish Vat's food is not refined, but portions are big and prices are low. One meal in one restaurant is very scant evidence on which to base a universal judgment. By asking many people, you get the benefit of judgments by different judges who have dined there on different nights at varying times in the past.

Few countries look upon butter as a necessary table condiment. Having butter on the table morning, noon, and night would seem to them like our having a bowl of whipped cream always in sight. You can get butter anywhere. You will pay dearly for it.

Watch for self-interest: the desk clerk who gets a kickback, or who comes up with the same name for every guest; or the obliging soul who sends you where he thinks you want to go—to the place where all foreigners go (perhaps McDonald's or Kentucky Fried Chicken), rather than where he would go himself.

Checking It Out

Now that you've got some leads, go check the place out. Is there a menu posted outside the door? If not, no matter. Stroll in and ask to see one. Don't sit down, just stand out of the way and read it near the door. No one will mind. (I've had waiters at the Ritz bring a menu to the door so I could read it, which they did very graciously.)

Next: is it busy? Should it be? If it's empty in a busy downtown area at lunchtime, or in a resort on Saturday evening, those vacant places are shouting a warning at you. You can try it, but don't expect much.

Don't *ever* be afraid to get up and walk out if your sensors tell you that you're in for something that you won't enjoy. If you have ordered something, you should feel obligated to pay for it. But if you haven't ordered, you are free to leave, no matter how many glasses of water have been poured or napkins unfolded. Waiters are used to people leaving, especially in clip joints and bad places; even in good places it happens, as potential diners discover they "really wanted something fancier/cheaper, serving seafood/vegetarian food, with/without a liquor license."

Another assertion of your rights: Get a good table. Be understanding of the waiter's responsibilities, and don't monopolize a prime four-seat window table if you're alone; but also don't accept a table by the kitchen door or the silverware racks or the cash register, or in a draft, or right beside a loudspeaker, if there is an acceptable alternative. What you pay for your meal will be exactly the same whether you dine in the wind from the swinging door or at that cozy spot by the crackling fire. Get your money's worth.

Restaurant Rhythm

In much of the world, including North America, there is a specific weekly rhythm to restaurant life, dictated by the society's general lifestyle. Friday and Saturday are the busiest nights, Sunday afternoon is not bad. Monday is traditional closing day, though many restaurants will serve lunch for the business clientele. In fact, lunch Monday through Friday is fairly well attended; many places won't even serve lunch on Saturday or Sunday, only dinner.

What happens Tuesday and Wednesday evenings? Not much. Everybody in town is deep into the work week, and few people have the time or inclination for a big dinner with drinks and wine—they've got to get up early and be in top shape for a Wednesday- or Thursday-morning conference.

Tuesday and Wednesday evenings are thus the best time to look for bargain dinners. Astute restaurateurs will offer good if simple values on these evenings to attract more customers. Often the value will be an extra lavish set-price meal, or a normal meal at a discounted price.

You may even find a chance to "let them do you a favor"; as you stand at the door perusing the menu, a waiter (with time on his hands) may wander over and engage you in conversation, hoping to bring you in and seat you.

"Lots of good things on that menu," he says.

Sure, you say, "but prices are a little high for our budget; we'd have to forgo having wine with dinner."

"Hold on a minute," he says, and disappears. When

he emerges, it is to say "The chef will provide a carafe of house wine, on the house." Point of Mutual Advantage: The restaurant keeps its staff busy and *fills a table* (full tables lure other customers) in exchange for a few dollars' markup on the wine, while you get the meal you wanted, with free wine. All you did was make it easy for them to be generous. Everybody's happy.

EARLY-BIRD SPECIALS: In many tourist destinations, there is even an hourly rhythm to the restaurant day. A good number of people come for breakfast, the luncheon crowd comes between noon and 3 or 4 p.m., but then there's a lull until dinnertime. To keep their staff busy and the restaurant filled, some enterprising restaurateurs offer "Early Bird Specials" to patrons willing to dine between 5 and 7 p.m., before the big dinner rush begins. Usually the special is a good, set-price meal at a very good price. Look for this feature when you travel, and take advantage of it when you see it.

Menus, Delightful and Otherwise

Are all menus created equal? Of course not. What are the differences? How is a menu made?

A restaurateur wants a list of dishes that will both appeal to a large clientele and yield him a profit. The price charged for a particular dish may or may not reflect the cost of its preparation; it may or may not reflect the dish's quality and nutritional value.

Which offers the best value-for-money? A huge chef's salad for $10, or a plate of spaghetti for the same? Which costs more to make? On which is the profit the biggest?

Where is quality going to be the highest? In Texas cattle country, on steaks or seafood? The beef probably walked to the back door. The lobster was caught weeks ago in Maine, frozen like a rock, and brought by Boeing to the Texas restaurant's freezer.

THE BASIC STRATEGY: Here is my strategy for ordering from a menu, developed by long experience of restaurant-sampling. First, compare the menu with foods available in the region, giving preference to native ones. Try to remember which foods are in season, such as vegetables, fruits, game, shellfish, and fish. Ordering foods that are out of season means you will get lower quality, or higher prices, or both. If you've been following my advice and preparing some of your own meals, you know what's fresh in the markets.

Next, try to figure out which dishes are there to make a profit and which are there to make life interesting for the chef. Surf-and-turf, the popular small steak and lobster tail, is simple to prepare from frozen ingredients, and always carries a high price tag. Several other items at the top of the price range will be there for the same reason: not because they are particularly fine, but because they are exotic, or out of season, or chic, or because unselective diners are captive to them, as in "I want a big, juicy steak." Except in good steak houses, steak is usually on the menu to make a profit from people who will eat nothing but steak.

THE VERY BEST CHOICE IS . . .: The chef gets no creative thrill from preparing surf-and-turf or steak. He or she gets her kicks from delicate and interesting preparations, and from the items on the menu which change: the daily specials.

In the average, low- to middle-range restaurant, the menu might as well be carved in granite, except for the daily specials. The standard list of items is easy to store and prepare (freezer, microwave, etc.) and makes a good profit. The daily specials, or *prix fixe* meal, or *comida corrida,* or whatever it's called, is where the chef has fun and adds variety to her life. She buys less of the ingredients than she knows she can sell (tomorrow's special will be different—she wants today's to sell out and not take up storage room), so you're guaranteed freshness. She takes interest in its preparation. And she puts a price on the special that will guarantee not only a decent return, but also that it will sell out. By far, the daily special meal offers the best value-for-money. If you choose from the standard menu, you pay for the privilege whether the food is excellent or indifferent.

In a local Cairo restaurant you can stuff yourself on shish kebab, *kofta, ful,* and *taamiya* (skewered lamb, grilled spiced meat, savory beans, and bean fritters) for the price of a single bottle of beer at the Hilton.

Another selling point: daily specials are the dishes made from highly perishable ingredients such as fresh shrimp, or unusual ingredients, which come into the market that day but are gone the next.

If there are no daily specials, the chef is dead or is not a chef. Or locals never go to that restaurant. Locals demand variety.

Beware the six-page, handsomely printed, lavishly illustrated menu. If it offers an astounding array of dishes, it's likely that none of them will be fresh or tasty. In my experience the meals I've liked best were in restaurants where there were about six dinner-entree specials, with an even fewer number of appetizers and desserts. Each of the offerings was freshly prepared with loving attention, and was well worth its price. No restaurant can adequately handle many different kinds of dishes without suffering an accompanying loss of quality. In assessing a restaurant's menu, remember, less is more.

HOW MUCH WILL IT COST?

Want to estimate the total price of the meal before you sit down? Choose a main course you like, and double the price of it. If you want drinks before dinner or a bottle (not a carafe) of wine with your meal, add a bit more. Here's an illustration:

	cost
Soup or appetizer	$ 3
Main course: filet of sole	12
Cheese or dessert	3
Coffee	1
Large glass of wine	3
Meal tax	1
Tip	3

Notice that the tip is about 13%. To believe that 15% is required is silly. To give 20% is outrageous unless service has been spectacular. To give less than 10% borders on insult (which may be what you want to do). Average, as far as I'm concerned, is 11% to 13%, with 15% the reward for quite good service. In many foreign countries, percentages are much lower except in tourist joints.

One further point about tipping: always check on the menu before you order to see whether or not the service is included in the total price. That way you won't be embarrassed by having to ask the waiter after you've received the check or by having to ask to see the menu again.

Adding Up the Bill

Always do it. Banks take extreme care in adding up sums of money, and they still make mistakes. A busy restaurant waiter or cashier is even less dependable when it comes to figures. Beyond normal human fallibility, there is human cupidity, so your chances of encountering faulty addition, mistaken prices, unwarranted taxes, and mysterious extra charges on restaurant bills are actually quite enormous. If you are in doubt, have it explained. If you are still uncertain, appeal to the cashier, maître d', or manager. Are you pretty sure it's not an honest mistake, that you've been ripped off? Hang around and make a quiet fuss. If the rip-off is real, *they do not want you there*. They want to rip you off quietly and anonymously, and if you are not quiet and anonymous they will give in just to get rid of you. And you win.

One thing is certain: you can't travel inexpensively by allowing people to take your money for nothing.

11

Out on the Town

Nothing compares with the thrill that comes when you first enter Notre Dame, or approach the Taj Mahal, or hear the chimes of Big Ben. This is what travel is all about: fabulous sights, strange customs, new pleasures. These are the things which make any journey the trip of a lifetime.

Some travelers see more than others, dig deeper into the local culture, get to know the people better. Their experience is not a passive one, merely sitting on a tour bus as a lecturer speaks, but an active participation in the daily life of a different place. They really *get to know* a place, rather than just pass through it.

These are the people who, instinctively or by reading this book, follow the Four Laws in order to get the most out of their travels. These are the ones whose diaries, photographs, and tape recordings fascinate friends and family at home. Not only that, their wise use of travel resources, spending just the optimal amount, gets them exactly what they want, yet leaves them plenty of money for side trips and special adventures.

AN ACTION PLAN

Seeing sights consists of two things: getting there, and getting in. What one pays for each may range from $0 to infinity, which is surprising since sightseeing prices are mostly fixed like iron. How then, can one spend $0 to infinity?

To get from London to Blenheim Palace, Sir Winston Churchill's ancestral home, you can spend $0 by hitching a ride or a small amount by taking the bus. Or else you can let some sharp operator tell you that there is no bus to Blenheim, that the only way to get there is by chauffeur-driven Rolls-Royce, and that you will be a private guest of the duke and duchess and must pay accordingly. These examples sound absurd, especially in the context of orderly England, but they're not really. In Mexico City, tourists regularly let con men convince them that the only way to get to the Pyramids of Teotihuacán is by private taxi (not on the meter, either), and that they'll need a special guide—him—to fully appreciate the ruins.

In less well-traveled areas of the world, obviously sometimes you will require a guide. For instance, you'll need someone to help you negotiate the labyrinthine maze of streets in Benares or Fez, or to guide you up the paths of Mt. Kilimanjaro. In such situations, use common sense. Ask local English-speaking residents what the going rate for such services might be. In other words find out what local wages are and pay accordingly. Don't pay American salaries.

Your duty, then, is to pay no more than the sensible prices for seeing world-famous attractions. There are lots of ways you can pay a bit less too.

Getting There

The cheapest way to go is by public transportation. In some cities the public bus system provides special low-cost, far-ranging tourist jaunts (usually nonstop) that give you a useful orientation. For example, in Washington, D.C., tourmobiles run daily between the Mall and Arlington. For only a few dollars you can get on and off at any of 18 stops near the important museums and other major landmarks. Special buses run along Boston's Freedom Trail. Always use public transportation to visit individual sightseeing attractions; there is a bus or subway stop nearby, and with the help of a bus or subway map you'll find the nearest stop. A good guidebook should provide this kind of specific how-to-get-there information for the major sightseeing attractions.

Some Days Cost Less Than Others

Those who operate attractions have a problem. They want local people to enjoy and benefit from their attractions often, but they also want to get a fair return from visitors who come from out of town to visit only once. The most popular solution is discount days, when normal admission fees are reduced, or abolished altogether.

Saturday until noon, Wednesday after 5 p.m., all day Sunday—the discount period may be at any time. To benefit, you must know about several discount periods in advance, and then plan your sightseeing route so as to take advantage of as many as possible. Admission hours and fees change frequently and so guidebooks are loath to print them. But a good guide will give you help with discount periods. Failing that, look for local, current publications for data, or ask at tourist offices.

Ten for the Price of Two

Another popular discounting procedure is the all-inclusive pass or package, or "combination ticket."

American or Canadian national parks, Newport's grand mansions, England's National Trust properties—these and similar networks offer cut-rate passes that will save you a bundle if you visit more than just one or two.

Why do tourism officials dream up these discount schemes to tempt you into their lands? . . . They are giving something of value which costs them little: the museums must be kept up no matter how many people visit.

Some of these sightseeing discounts are available for just one travel season, others have been offered for several years. A long-standing offer from the Netherlands Tourist Office, for example, is the Holland Culture Card, available for $15 to North American residents only. The card permits free entry to over 250 Dutch art and historic museums and other important sites. Also, cardholders can buy reserved seats for concert, ballet, and opera performances up to 24 hours before curtain time. In nearby Belgium, there is a "Brussels Is Love" coupon booklet, with sightseeing discounts for those staying at participating hotels. Another good long-running offer is BritRail Travel's "Open to View" ($24 for adults, half-price for children 5 to 15) ticket. This one ticket entitles you to visit an impressive number of Great Britain's most exciting attractions—from the Tower of London to Edinburgh Castle—for a period of one month, starting from the date the ticket is first used.

Local tourism authorities are also zealous in putting together packages and combinations for a particular city or region. In New York City, for example, the Visitors' Bureau publishes a free directory of tour and hotel packages. Their "Ultimate Winter Vacation" package includes four nights' accommodation, theater tickets, bus or helicopter tour, two dinners, a visit to the Empire State Building, and free maps and other information.

Why do tourism officials dream up these discount schemes to tempt you into their lands? What's in it for them? Mutual advantage, for you will come if they put money in your pocket (which is what they're doing), and you will stay in their hotels and dine in their restaurants and perhaps buy their goods as souvenirs. They are giving you something of value which costs them little: the museums must be kept up no matter how many people visit, and the trains will run whether you are on board or not. Everybody wins.

Family Plans

Tourist authorities recognize that the burden of sightseeing costs is heaviest on families, as two adult and several children's tickets can add up to a hefty sum, particularly if the sight is a theme park (Disney World) or an elaborate "outdoor museum" such as Mystic Seaport or Old Sturbridge Village. Therefore you will usually find a "family" ticket or a "maximum fee" which will allow you in at a discount. If such a plan doesn't exist, make up your own and try it out on the ticket collector. What do you have to lose? Pay for parents and three kids, and let the other two sneak under the turnstile; or get all the children, even the teenagers, in for the under-10 rate.

Special Discounts

Senior citizens with proof-of-age identification and students with ISIC cards or other student ID can cut sightseeing fees by significant sums. See Chapter 14 for details on how to get these savings. Any traveler going abroad will do well to ask at tourist offices for what nonresident sightseeing discounts are currently available at their destination—in many cases these special discounts are sold only outside the offering country.

FREE ACTIVITIES

Unlike hotels and restaurants, most attractions are not set up to make a profit, and fees will be modest, to cover expenses. In addition, many sights are free. In London, for example, three of the most inspiring and awesome sights—the British Museum, a session of the House of Commons in the Palace of Westminster, and trials at the Old Bailey—are free.

Your duty, then, is to pay no more than the sensible prices for seeing world-famous attractions. There are lots of ways you can pay a bit less too.

Civic-minded groups sponsor walking tours, architectural tours, historical exhibitions. Municipal authorities will set up outdoor concerts and festivities. Check listings in local newspapers for specific details.

Industrial tours can be fun, interesting, even intoxicating (as in the case of the popular brewery tours).

These activities are slightly out of the ordinary, and thus the people you meet at them will be the more interesting and adventurous types. You will almost certainly get to meet local people as well, and you will truly participate in the daily life of the society—a thrilling experience.

Some of the most interesting—and memorable—free travel experiences take a bit of advance planning. Here's how some creative advance planning paid off for two far-sighted travelers. A professor of communications at a New York college wrote to the British Broadcasting Corporation before he went to London. When he was in England, he and his wife were given an insider's tour of the broadcast studios. Another creative traveler enjoyed an architectural tour of Seattle with a guide from the area's landmarks commission after she had written to express her interest in exchanging ideas about her favorite topic—historic preservation. Whatever your occupation, field of interest, or hobby, you can locate a counterpart in the place you're going to visit. A brief letter in advance of your trip can be the "open sesame" to the kind of experience no paid tour could possibly offer.

Servas

Servas is an organization that seeks to further international understanding. It sponsors a worldwide program of exchange visits for travelers in 90 countries including the U.S. Here's how it works: you apply and are interviewed; if accepted, you get a personal briefing, written instructions, a list of Servas contacts in the area you are going to visit, and an introductory letter. You arrange visits in advance with your host and are generally invited to stay one or two nights. For information, write to the U.S. Servas Committee, Inc., 11 John St., Room 406, New York, NY 10038 (tel. 212/267-0252). Servas asks for a donation of $45 for its services.

Make Up Your Own Free Adventures

If this paragraph results in your having just one fascinating and unforgettable experience, it will have accomplished its purpose: to get you to overcome language barriers, natural trepidation, and social conventions, and to go on an adventure.

Whatever your occupation, field of interest, or hobby, you can locate a counterpart in the place you're going to visit. A brief letter in advance can be the "open sesame" to the kind of experience no paid tour could possibly offer.

In the beautiful colonial Mexican city of San Luís Potosí, I once passed an ornate and elegant building on a side street. No sign, no clue to its use or purpose was evident. In fact, it was none of my business! But somehow I brought myself to try the door, which was open; somehow I got up the courage to tiptoe in. What I found was an elegant, opulent urban palace, perfectly preserved from a century ago. It was an exclusive men's club, I found out from a servant who approached me—to toss me out, I was sure. Instead of the bums' rush, I got a guided tour! My Spanish was not so good, but I came to understand which was the dining room and which the card room, what local luminaries had belonged here and which exciting events had been played out within the gilded walls. I will never forget it. A minor club in the eyes of the world, but a true Mexican adventure for me. I offered the servant a tip, which he strenuously refused (he had never given a tourist a tour before!)

Do not go where you are not wanted. Don't be impolite. But also don't anticipate hostility when there is none in sight. Oddly enough, it's true that "the best adventures in travel are free."

NIGHTTIME TREATS

Nighttime activities are among the most fertile areas for cutting costs. For one thing, clubs and shows are in the business to make big profits, and yet you can enjoy them for a lot less then you think.

There is hardly a major city in the world today where one cannot have a fascinating night on the town and spend next to nothing. No-cost or low-cost activities are all around you and, when you're in a strange place, they can provide almost as much novelty and excitement as the Folies Bergère.

Saving Money on Performance Tickets

Like so many other services today, the market for concert, theater, and show tickets is broken down into segments to yield the greatest return. The most expensive tickets are the ones for the best seats, sold well before the performance, at a ticket agency rather than at the box office. Conversely, the least expensive seats are the ones sold only minutes before the show, at the box office, for whatever seats are left.

Most theaters can predict how many people will just

show up on their doorsteps a half hour before the performance; also, they know how many seats have been sold in advance. To assure the least number of empty seats, they begin discounting a certain number of seats the day of the performance. Sometimes the discount sales begin in the morning, sometimes at noon, sometimes a few hours before curtain time. As an out-of-town visitor, these "rush" seats are perfect for you. More often than not, rush seats are sold in a special booth rather than at regular ticket agencies; or they may be sold only from the theater box office itself.

Ask around to find out where rush tickets are sold, and don't rest on the word of just one person. Not everyone knows about them, and many people have an interest in your buying a full-priced seat.

YOU'RE IN LUCK!: Another way to cut the cost of theater and concert tickets is to show up at the hall, circulate through the crowd, and find someone with tickets to sell. The vagaries of illness, broken dates, accidents, and so forth often yield rich rewards for the last-minute ticket buyer. Naturally, the unfortunate ticketholder who wants to recoup his costs will ask for the full price. For a crowded, popular show he might just get it, and so perhaps you'd better grab them. But for a normal performance, get to the hall 30 or 45 minutes before curtain time, identify the people with tickets to sell, and let them know you're in the market. Don't buy, but stand and wait instead. Are they selling their tickets? Time is on your side, and the price will drop constantly. Right before curtain time, if there are tickets left, you will get any price you mention. Still nothing satisfactory? Curtain time itself, and shortly thereafter, is when the most spirited bargaining takes place. A person running up to the door with unused and (for them) unusable tickets a few minutes after curtain time may even be satisfied with the good feeling of generosity, and give them to you for free.

Clubs and shows are in the business to make big profits, and yet you can enjoy them for a lot less than you think.

Don't forget the box office itself. Depending on policy (and the true policy may only come clear right at curtain time) you may be able to buy cut-price tickets at curtain time or just after. The ticket seller will probably wait until the crowd vacates the lobby. The theater doesn't want it generally known that it sells tickets for a third of the price, when all those other people have just paid full price! An important note: No matter how frantic the atmosphere, make sure the money is right. *Count your change carefully* (even slowly, if necessary); if you're doing all this in foreign currency, be all the more careful.

Saving Money at the Movies

Cinemas in many countries charge different prices for different times of the day or days of the week. Again, Tuesday and Wednesday are the slow nights. In countries with "early closing," the early closing day (usually Wednesday) features special cinema prices. Everyone gets off from work, and children get out of school, at noon or 1 p.m., and the cinemas would like to attract the business.

Another way to save money on cinema tickets is to look for "People's Day," a special time of the week when tickets sell at reduced prices just as they do at museums. And just like the museums, this cut-price period is often one in which the moviehouse would otherwise be very empty.

In countries with differing prices for the various sections of the theater—"orchestra," "parquet," "balcony," etc.—you needn't buy the most expensive seat for the best view of the screen. Many times the price is high for another reason. The balcony is a favorite spot for romantic encounters and explorations, and local adolescents will pay more for the privilege and privacy. They'll make their own entertainment. Who cares what's on the screen?

Saving Money at Nightclubs

This is tough, because clubs expect you to pay freely. Of course, you should sit or stand at the bar rather than at a table unless you plan to dine. At the World Trade Center in New York, this will save you a cover charge. Often there is no cover charge at the bar, or the charge is smaller, or the minimum is less. If you're single, this is where you'll meet new people in any case.

Clubs are usually quite responsive to supply and demand, eliminating the cover charge on slow nights, or sponsoring a two-drinks-for-the-price-of-one Happy Hour to lure customers. There are occasional opportunities for reductions, if you remember to ask. On busy nights, though, you may actually have trouble getting into a popular club. The bouncer at the door may demand a club membership card or ID. If you don't have one of these, a $5 or $10 bill will often do just as well.

12

Bring Home Something Memorable

Now for the good part! Shopping in mysterious markets, browsing in quaint old shops, trying on leather coats, suede vests, and natty suits, is a wonderful part of any adventure. Not only does travel bring you in contact with different things at lower prices, it adds special significance to everything you buy. Each purchase ends up being a treasured souvenir of your journey.

BARGAINING

The quaint custom of bargaining is usually associated with colorful peasants in outdoor markets, bearded patriarchs in Middle Eastern bazaars, or lively Oriental dealers in crowded stall-sized shops.

But bargaining is something we do frequently here at home. The difference is merely of size and frequency.

No one in his right mind would waltz into an automobile dealership near home and agree to pay the very first price put to him by the dealer. Likewise, no one purchasing a house or condominium wants to go through with the deal without at least trying to get a few thousand dollars knocked off the price, or some other concession. We haggle here at home, but only on the big items, which we buy only now and then.

Haggling is not just a quaint custom practiced by ignorant peasants who lack a pricing structure. It's a sophisticated mechanism for determining the current, up-to-the-minute price of something of value. We've seen in Chapter 7 how the value of a seat on an airplane dwindles to almost nothing as takeoff time approaches. Or how a hotel room that's empty at 11 p.m. is worth a lot less than a hotel room that's empty at 11 a.m. A Third World merchant will haggle with you over the price of a cheap trinket or bauble. Why? He paid very little for it: you want it and you're willing to pay according to your value structure. He has to find out how badly you want it, and what your value structure will allow you to pay before he decides what to charge. So he bargains.

Of course, haggling is much more than a pricing mechanism. Throughout the world, it is a social custom as well. A businessman taking clients out to lunch, or on a round of golf, is doing the same thing as a Turkish carpet merchant who invites you into his shop for tea or coffee. Just as no good businessperson here at home would think of discussing an important deal nonstop over a conference table, no self-respecting merchant in a Middle Eastern bazaar would think of waiting for more than 60 seconds to ask, "Coffee, tea or soda?" The difference is only one of scale.

A SHOPKEEPER'S PLEASURE

Half the fun of being a shopkeeper is dealing with people. The social dimension is almost as important as the price-setting one. Therefore you should train yourself to be patient, to enjoy chatting with shopkeepers, and to sharpen your bargaining skills. Time and patience are needed, but the payoff is an enjoyable experience, and a much lower price.

Although most of the bargaining you do will be abroad, you must keep your eyes open for opportunities when you travel at home. Just because you don't normally bargain over price for some items does not mean that the shopkeeper is unwilling to do so. For all you know, the person coming into the shop as you leave will use a few well-placed words and a keen assessment of the shopkeeper's situation to get a better price than you just paid.

Is Bargaining Appropriate?

The first thing to do is to determine if bargaining is appropriate. If the shop is very busy, it may not be good to bargain; perhaps you should return later, or pay the price asked. In some shops, usually the posh ones catering to the carriage trade, bargaining is simply not done. After all, people go to these places to

---

Bargaining is something we do frequently here at home. No one in his right mind would waltz into an automobile dealership and agree to pay the very first price put to him by a dealer.

---

spend large amounts in a genteel manner, so what's the point of bargaining?

It's simple to determine if bargaining is appropriate. Just begin: offer a decent price that's somewhat lower than the asked (or marked) price. If the shopkeeper won't bargain, he or she will tell you so right away: "I'm sorry, but the price is as marked." Whatever the reason for not bargaining—the price is already low, or it takes time, or it would "lower the tone" of the shop—your path is now clear. You buy, or you don't buy, at the price offered. No hard feelings.

Warming to the Task

On the other hand, if the shopkeeper budges, or even pauses for a moment, you'll know that his or her brain is whirring to digest the consequences of your offer. ("Can I sell it for that and still make a decent profit? How important is this sale to me? I've got to pay the rent tomorrow! Actually, I like this object and wouldn't mind having it hang around the shop for a few more weeks. . . .") That pause is your signal that bargaining is possible, and that in almost every case there will be accommodation, some searching for the Point of Mutual Advantage. You're in.

Determining Price

I was once visiting my sister in Morocco. I wanted some of the fine leather items being sold in Rabat's tidy bazaar. After wandering through its streets for a half hour, examining suitcases, handbags, and hassocks in various shops, asking prices, judging quality, I finally settled on the shop of an excitable but sympathetic old gent. He wore a formal outfit (tails) and a fez, spoke French as though he were firing a machine gun, and seemed only partly in possession of his wits. But he was indeed sympathetic, he stocked quality goods, and he seemed to have the lowest prices.

At the end of 45 minutes, we had finished numerous glasses of sweet mint tea, and had arrived at one final lump-sum price for what I wanted: a large suitcase, two handbags, two hassocks, various little purses and trinkets. He was happy. I was happy.

I proudly took my purchase back to my sister's house. When I told her what I had paid (that is, what a good deal I had gotten), she was ready to shove me into her car and go tearing right down to the bazaar. "That thief! That bandit!" she cried, "He's robbed you mercilessly! I won't let him get away with that!"

This is not what I wanted to hear. A man of the world, experienced haggler, who had once gotten the best of a master haggler in Istanbul's awesome Grand Bazaar—such talk from my sister was not good for my ego.

"Well, what would *you* have paid?" I asked her.

"Half of what you did, maybe a third," she replied in scorn.

"How was I to know?" I murmured weakly in self-defense.

How *does* one know what to pay? The best and surest way to know is to live there and to shop in the markets frequently. Then you know. But we don't live there, and we can't shop there frequently. The worry-free method is the one I use: tell yourself what an item is worth to you, and then stick to your price. Say to yourself, "A leather suitcase at home would cost $400; this one is not as high in quality, but it's 'rustic,' and I like it. I'd pay $140 for it at home; I'll pay $70 or $80 for it here." Do all this thinking *before* you have any idea what the shopkeeper wants.

Your price is $70 or $80. You ask the shopkeeper. He says, "For you, because you're from (blank), and because you're my special friend, and because it is such a beautiful day, and because my uncle's cousin's nephew's wife just had a baby, $100." Now your course of action is clear: bargain him down to $80 at least, $70 preferably, even lower if possible.

If he says, "For you, (etc.), $100," you counter with

Bargaining is not just a quaint custom practiced by ignorant peasants who lack a pricing structure. It's a sophisticated mechanism for determining the current, up-to-the-minute price of something of value.

"I will give you $70 for it and not a penny more, take it or leave it." Get out the money—in cash. If he hesitates, you're close, and if you can't get it for $75 you will get it for $80. If his eyes bulge, and his cheeks puff, and a boy runs to get him a glass of water, you know that your price was not reasonable to him. Too bad. It was a nice suitcase.

This method avoids the sort of disappointment I suffered in the bazaar in Rabat because you assume there is no fixed price; you learn some people may get lower prices, but you know what the item is worth to you, you know what you think is fair. You are satisfied because you are getting your money's worth.

The other method is to try and get the lowest price possible. This demands more skill, more patience, more time. The more time you can spend in shops, talking with shopkeepers, quizzing other tourists, examining goods, the better you will understand the market and its price structure.

The Really Good Prices

You're determined to get the best bargain you can. Good for you! Start by getting acquainted with the market as much as time will allow. Know the goods, their quality, now and then casually ask a price (but don't make a counter-offer, or you've begun bargaining).

Once you are acquainted with the market structure for the items you want to buy, choose the shop that appeals to you. Don't show too much enthusiasm for the items you want. In fact, *convince yourself* that you don't need them, that you could walk away empty-handed and completely happy. This is one of those biblical contradictions, similar to "The meek shall inherit the earth": the way to get it for the best price is not to want it at all.

After you've looked over the items in the shop and have chosen the ones you might buy, you're ready to begin talking prices in earnest. Ask the shopkeeper what he wants for all the items combined. Counter his offer with a price, which is very good for you, but which is not an insult. *Be ready to buy at that price*. It is very impolite to begin serious bargaining and not to buy if the dealer meets your price. He may jump at your offer, in which case it was probably too high. Too bad. By ancient custom and by modern law, you've come to an agreement and you've made a contract, and you must go through with it. Thus, make your counter-offer something you can live with.

The bargaining process after these opening bids have been stated is merely one of narrowing the gap. Reasons are given for each new bid: "If the leather were finer, I'd pay more, but as it is I'll go as far as $70." The shopkeeper replies, "But this leather is durable, it'll last a lifetime. I can't let it go for less than $100."

Next round: "How do I even know my friend will like it?"

"She probably will; this style is selling by the dozens these days."

"If she doesn't like it, it's useless to me. But I'll give you $75."

"If she doesn't like it, you can always give it as a gift. What about $85?"

Clinching the Deal

Now you must be patient and creative. Look for ingenious reasons, especially ones that allow both of you to save face.

"You know, my daughter would really like a bag like this, but I can't spend more than $75." By saying this, you're giving the shopkeeper the opportunity to be kindhearted to your daughter. He saves face, because he appears to be cutting the price out of generosity, not because the price was inflated in the first place.

"Okay, for your daughter then, $75. I hope she likes it."

Another tack is to let the shopkeeper do you a favor: "I have another candlestick just like this one, and the two would make a pair."

"Oh, well, then, you must have this one. I think I can give it to you for what you offered."

This gives the shopkeeper a chance to save face by being nice to you. But watch out! The price will be written in granite, or even raised, if you say something like "In my collection of 5,000 coins, this is the only one I don't have yet!" Your appeal should be one of sentiment, not of covetousness.

As in any dealing, the face-saving aspect can be as minor as a well-timed joke: you both chuckle and the deal is easily concluded. Or it can be an appeal to patriotism: "I wanted a nice souvenir of your beautiful city (or country)."

Don't belabor the point for only a few pennies. Price reductions decrease geometrically during haggling:

Tell yourself what an item is worth to you, and then stick to your price. . . . Get out the money—in cash. If he hesitates, you're close. . . . If his eyes bulge, and his cheeks puff, and a boy runs to get him a glass of water, you know that your price was not reasonable to him.

---

that is, you'll save tens or hundreds of dollars at the outset, but at the very end, just before the deal is concluded, you'll be bargaining over mere fractions.

If You Can't Agree

It may be that you just can't bring yourself to meet the shopkeeper's price, or vice-versa. All appeals to sentiment have been exhausted. However, there is one last tactic you can use: leave the shop. The shopkeeper must assume when you walk out that he will never see you again, that the deal is off. If he was truly undecided as to price, he may come running after you: "Okay, $75 it is." You have the advantage here, because if he fails to run after you, you will know that the last price was solid. If you want the item at that last price, you can always return (in an hour or a day) and buy the item at that price. You save face by saying, "I really can't afford this, but it is so beautiful," or "I won't buy that sweater I wanted; I'm putting the money toward this." The pressure is on the shop-keeper when you walk out, for you can always return, but the shopkeeper cannot always go out and find you.

Payment: The Secrets

Having agreed on a price, you must agree on a form of payment. This can be of real significance. Having made a deal and given you a good price on an item, a shopkeeper may not be willing to let you pay by credit card, because he must pay a percentage of the deal to the credit card company. He may demand cash in local currency, or in dollars. Surprisingly, personal checks are often readily accepted in foreign countries. The shopkeeper may require that you make it out to "Cash." In many areas of the world, your check will then pass between a hundred thumbs and forefingers, almost as though it were cash, before ending up in your check file at home.

Form of payment can be a bargaining point. Nothing speaks louder to a shopkeeper who has bills to pay than crisp banknotes crackling in your hand. Don't hand them over until the deal is clinched, though.

WHERE TO GET THE BEST PRICE

There is no real fixed price for any item in this world. A cigarette lighter which costs $10 in a discount store may cost $35 in a posh shop on New York's Fifth Avenue. When you're out shopping, at home or abroad, always keep in mind that location, style, clientele, overhead, supply, and many other factors that affect the store will affect the prices it charges.

Unfortunately, there are no easy, set rules to help you determine where to buy. It used to be that crafts sold in villages where they were made would be cheaper than crafts shipped to the city and sold right under the tourists' noses. But craft cooperatives, very popular in countries such as Mexico and Guatemala, may now set prices by sophisticated marketing theories. You may actually find the same crafts cheaper in big cities due to the volume of business there.

In general, fixed-location shops are most expensive. If they don't sell an item one day, the proprietor can switch off the lights, lock the doors, and go home. The item will be there tomorrow, and so will new customers.

Open markets are less expensive, particularly late in the day, because a merchant here must pack up his goods and carry them if he can't sell them. Have you ever bought fish from an open-air market late in the day? They almost give it away. It won't last, and the merchant doesn't want to bother storing it. It's yours for pennies, though it sold for $10 a pound a few hours before.

Street vendors offer excellent bargains if they are authentic. If Señor Gomez decides he could use some extra cash, and if he gathers some Guatemalan Momostenango blankets on consignment and takes the bus from Momostenango to Quezaltenango to hawk his beautiful blankets in the city park, you've got a dealer willing to give you a good price. But if Señor Gomez lives in Quezaltenango, leaves home each morning with an armload of blankets, and returns home with the unsold lot each evening, then he's actually a merchant without a shop. Coming in from the village, a vendor doesn't want to return with unsold goods. But living in the city, a vendor may not mind returning with unsold goods; he'll just head out again tomorrow. If Señor Gomez is always in evidence, speaks English, and is up-to-the-minute on exchange rates, you've got a businessman, not a vendor from the village. And this businessman has no shop to which you can return with defective goods, no address to which the Tourist Police can accompany you. He may offer you a good price nonetheless. Fine, take it. But *caveat emptor:* know your goods, and check his stock very carefully before you buy.

WATCH OUT AT DUTY-FREE SHOPS

Often you will hear the modern traveler's lament: "Duty-free goods used to be so cheap! Now those duty-free shops in airports are a rip-off." Is it true?

The question is, cheap for whom? You can get a good bottle of cognac in the United States for $20 or $25. In London you will pay $35 or $45 for the same bottle. Thus if the bottle costs $30 in a duty-free shop, it's cheap to a Londoner, but expensive to you.

Living in the midst of the world's largest market for consumer goods, Americans enjoy "volume discounts" on just about everything. On some "luxury" items such as liquor and tobacco, federal taxes haven't been raised significantly in 20 years, even though inflation has rendered the old tax rates ridiculously low. There is talk now of raising the taxes on luxury items, but until this is done, a "duty-free" purchase probably won't save you much over the normal U.S. price.

The whole rationale for duty-free shops has changed. They were first established to take advantage of "international waters." Ships that sailed out beyond territorial waters were subject to international maritime law, which imposed no luxury taxes nor forbade such things as gambling. Liners would stock luxury goods, make an agreement with national tax officials that the goods would not be opened or used within the national boundaries, and would be exempted from national taxes. It was a service to passengers on which the ships might make a modest profit, or at least cover expenses.

The airlines got into the act, though there was less rationale than with the ships. On a five-day crossing, one might conceivably use up goodly quantities of luxury goods; but how many cigarettes can you smoke, how much whiskey can you drink, how much perfume can you use on a six-hour flight? Still, it was a service to passengers, and an airline might lose passengers if it did not offer this service.

Now, with huge shopping centers in every airport, the duty-free shop has become not a place to save money, but a place to spend time between planes, or to buy last-minute gifts. You may save a few dollars by buying in a duty-free shop, but only if you know prices at home to compare. What did you last pay for that bottle of scotch, or perfume? What price will your local photo shop give you on a Nikon, or Canon, or Minolta? Duty-free shops are not places to do casual shopping. To get any good deal at all, you must be prepared, and careful.

Important Exceptions

Of course there are exceptions, places where duty-free goods are ridiculously cheap. Most of these places are islands (some Caribbean islands, the Canary Islands, etc.), and they use duty-free status to lure tourists. The Second Law operates here: they give up a little something in the way of taxes, but duty-free status helps convince tourists to spend the extra money for the longer flight, and to spend a few more days in local hotels, because tourists save significant sums on luxury items. Not bad.

Another exception is this. You like to have a drink before dinner, you've heard that your favorite drink is very expensive in Europe, and you'd like to have your own bottle. You didn't buy one at home (for $8), so you pick one up in the duty-free shop (for $10) because in Europe you've heard it costs $15.

Duty-free shops cater to one-way shoppers. No one goes to the airport, shops by comparing prices, and then returns home, ready to take advantage of a better price at a local shop. By definition, *you have to be going somewhere,* leaving the country, to use a duty-free shop. Comparison-shopping is difficult. They know this, so you must keep it in mind too. By the time you see their price, it's too late to go back into town and buy it for less.

Among the airports, Schipol in Amsterdam tends to be the least expensive, with many true bargains. London's Heathrow and Gatwick are about the most expensive. Why is this so? Well, the Dutch government wants people to use Schipol and to visit Holland, so they draw them with duty-free bargains. London, on the other hand, is the hub of the air-traffic world. The sheer mass of passengers filing through London's duty-free shops guarantees lots of business.

What about on airplanes? In general, prices are pretty good on planes flying international routes. Airlines are not in the liquor, cigarette, and perfume retailing business (as duty-free shops are), and they'd rather not trundle the stuff around if they can't sell it. So they charge decent prices and look upon the sales as a service to passengers.

HOW TO GET YOUR PURCHASES HOME

Nothing you've bought abroad does you much good if it never makes it out of Cairo, or Tel Aviv, or New Delhi. And all that wonderful bargaining you did will seem as nothing if U.S. Customs hits you with an enormous import fee. Believe it or not, big discounts are available through the bureaucratic machinery which oversees international movements of goods. You can save twice, because you will have to deal with two sets of Customs regulations, the first in the country you're leaving, and the second when you get home.

Getting yourself out of a country is usually no problem, but taking certain items out of a country can be difficult. Antiquities, works of art, precious items, which represent a significant transfer of wealth across borders—things like this, if discovered in your luggage, can cause problems. You may be delayed, or you may have to pay a fine, or the goods may be seized.

Big Foreign Tax Rebates

Most of us aren't bringing home Greek statues, or antique icons, or old carpets, or uncut diamonds. Rather, we will have bought tweeds in Britain, leather goods in Jerusalem, glassware in Venice, pottery in Mexico. Many countries in the world levy a Value Added Tax (VAT) on consumer purchases. The rationale is that any item goes through several stages in its progress from raw material to finished product, and that at every stage value is added to the item. The tax, then, is levied at every stage at which the "value" is added. So much for accountants' legerdemain. What the VAT amounts to is a super sales tax, often of 10%, 12%, or even 15% or 20%, levied on the final purchase price of most items (food, medicines, and some clothing are often excluded). To encourage foreigners to shop in their countries, many governments that levy a VAT also set up schemes whereby foreign visitors can claim reimbursement for VAT if they export the items they have purchased. Here's an example:

I go to Edinburgh, and I see a nice Harris tweed

jacket. I'd like to buy it, but it costs about 8% more in Edinburgh than it does at home in Boston, where I live. Well, the British government is willing to reimburse me for payment of VAT (15%) if I take the jacket out of the country and "consume" it elsewhere. (Obviously, if they simply knocked off the VAT at the time of sale, I'd buy the jacket and then sell it to Jack McCoy, my Scottish friend, tax free. The government would be cheated out of the tax.) First, I must make sure the store participates in the VAT reimbursement plan, and I then tell the shopkeeper I'm going to take the jacket out of the country, and that I'd like forms to fill out for VAT reimbursement. I pay full price for the jacket, including VAT, to the shopkeeper. At the airport I show the forms and the jacket to the Customs officer before I board my plane. I give the forms to the Customs officer who signs (testifying that the jacket has indeed been exported) and mails them first to the Customs office and then to the shopkeeper who sold me the jacket. The shopkeeper is exempted from paying VAT on my purchase; instead, he mails me a check for the amount of the VAT: 15% of the price I paid.

With such a scheme, the jacket, which would have cost 8% more than at home, ends up costing 7% less.

Complicated? Well, it was thought up by a government bureaucracy. Slow? Yes. But it does work, and it does provide you with substantial discounts. Who offers it? Not all countries, and not all shops. And the shops that participate do not always announce the fact in foot-high letters in their front windows. Most of them would rather not put up with all the paperwork, though they will do it if they think it will get them a sale.

Therefore, if you are in a country that levies a VAT, and that has VAT rebate plans, *you must ask* in a shop (preferably before you buy) if they can get you the

VAT rebate. When you've done all that's required for your rebate, don't hold your breath waiting for the check. It may take months. But it will come.

One reader of this book wrote and offered a special answer to a thorny problem. She was obviously following the First and Third Laws:

"Everything I have read about VAT rebates assumes that the traveler will be leaving the country by plane. But when crossing a border by train or bus, sometimes a Customs officer comes aboard, sometimes not. The forms showing you exported the goods have to be stamped by a Customs officer. After having gone through all the trouble of arranging for the forms to be filled out, I hated to lose the discount. So I decided that proof of entry into the United States would be just as good as proof of export from France. On two separate occasions the American Customs officer said it wasn't usual procedure, but he stamped my forms anyway. I mailed them to Paris myself, and got my refund both times."

Must I Pay a Lot in Customs Duty?

The second Customs hurdle comes when you return home. The U.S. Customs officer at the airport or border crossing is empowered to enforce a complicated body of regulations imposing duties (taxes) on various goods brought into the country. These taxes are aimed at the wholesale, commercial importer, and are meant to be an important source of revenue for the federal government. (Customs duties are among the most ancient forms of taxation.)

You may not be a commercial dealer, but the goods you bring in may have to be taxed as though you are. The government does grant exemptions from the Customs duties, so let's look at those.

First and most familiar is the "personal exemption,"

which allows U.S. residents to bring in up to $400 worth of goods bought abroad without paying any Customs duties whatsoever. Then there are the special exemptions on luxury items: one liter of liquor, tobacco products (one carton of cigarettes), perfume, jewelry. Here, you can bring in certain small quantities without paying duty.

Customs regulations are extremely complex, and unless you are a specialist you will simply depend on the Customs officer to determine the amount of duty you owe. For instance, he will discover from his computer screen that cigarette tobacco is taxed at a low rate, but cigarettes themselves are taxed quite high; normal table wines are taxed at one rate, fortified wines such as sherry and port are taxed at another, sparkling wines at yet another. There is little for you to do at this point but wait, then pay.

What's the GSP?

You can save money if you plan your souvenir purchasing ahead, however. Customs, in its wisdom, has established what's known as the GSP (Generalized System of Preferences), special regulations which exclude certain goods from certain countries from being subject to duties. The GSP is actually a bit of foreign aid to various developing countries. Industries in these countries, which do not compete directly or seriously with our own, are encouraged by granting their products duty-free status. Thus most ceramicware you buy in Mexico—even if you buy $1,000 worth—will come into the U.S. free of Customs duties. Baskets from Guatemala will likewise be duty free, as will guitars. Duty-free items change from country to country, and you will have to ask Customs (or a U.S. consulate abroad) if a certain item from a certain country is free from duties.

What this all means is that you may be able to buy $500, $600, or even $1,000 worth of goods abroad, and bring them all into the country duty free. If you have $500 of GSP items, and $500 of dutiable items, you will end up paying duty on only $100 worth of goods (remember, you get $400 worth of goods in free under your personal exemption). The remaining $100 will be taxed at 10%. This flat rate (10%) applies for the first $1,000 of taxable goods. Applying a flat rate like this saves time and expense for both you and Customs. As you can see, you may well return home with $2,000 worth of goods, and end up paying only $110 in duty.

Note that special, higher duty-free limits apply if you are returning to the U.S. from a U.S. possession such as the U.S. Virgin Islands, Guam, or American Samoa. That makes shopping in these places an even greater bargain.

By the way, you can now pay any Customs duties by charging them to your VISA or MasterCard credit card.

Mailing Gifts Home

If you mail a gift from a foreign country to the U.S., it will not be subject to duty if its value is $50 or under. Mark the gift package "Gift—under $50" if that's what it is.

Horrible Foreign Bugs!

Be very careful about bringing agricultural and animal products into the country. The government wants to prevent certain bugs, plant and animal diseases, etc., from attacking our crops and flocks. It used to be that if you had some prohibited item, it would merely be seized, or you would be fined up to the value of the item. But now you may have to pay a $25 or $50 fine right to the officer who discovers the prohibited goods;

or up to $1,000 if you go before a hearing panel. Play it safe.

Free Information

A way to have all of your Customs questions answered is to order "Know Before You Go" from U.S. Customs. This is a brochure describing every aspect of U.S. Customs which is of interest to travelers. It includes liquor import restrictions of each state (it may make a big difference if you travel from Mexico into Texas, rather than into California, for instance) and rules governing duty on gifts. Write or call the Department of Treasury, U.S. Customs Service, Room 6306, 1301 Constitution Ave. NW, Washington, DC 20229 (tel. 202/566-8195).

Can You "Fool" the Customs Officer?

One last note on Customs. Imagine that you are a Customs officer at a U.S. port of entry. Every day you deal with hundreds of people returning from abroad; every day you inspect suitcases being brought in from the Middle East, Africa, South America, Europe, the Orient. After a while, you know all the stories, all the pained expressions, all the nervous laughs, all the tricks. You can predict in two seconds what a person may have in that suitcase. Now, as a returning tourist, is this the sort of person you want to try and fool?

But . . . How Do I Get It Home?

Getting your goods home can be expensive and troublesome, but only if you're not careful. Friends of mine recently traveled to India. They bought a rug, and wisely made arrangements to have it shipped C.O.D. Obviously, they weren't about to pay a substantial sum to a man in India, then fly home and wait for the rug to arrive. It might never do so. So the dealer proposed an ingenious solution. "I will ship it in care of your bank," he said, "with instructions that it be released only after the bank has received your authorization to transfer payment to me." Wonderful, fine, let's do it.

The problem was this: the Indian dealer did not know that in the U.S. there are different types of banks (merchant, commercial, savings, savings and loan, etc.) and that a savings bank—such as my friends patronized—could not by law perform commercial-bank transactions, like dealing with international rug payments. So the rug sat in Customs while everyone spent lots of time working out a solution.

This is not the first time that international shipment of goods has caused expensive and time-consuming problems. In fact, international shipment very often seems to cause problems. You can avoid them, though.

Take things with you. If you simply can't (as with the rug), try your best to have them shipped with you on the *same plane*. If this is impossible arrange to have them shipped so as to arrive at the U.S. point of entry *when you do;* or to have them arrive a day or two earlier. By following these suggestions, you can limit the number of people and procedures and locations involved in a shipment, and thus hold down the possibilities of complicated screw-ups. Air freight may cost more than sea freight for very heavy or large items; but sea freight charges are usually subject to a minimum size or weight, so that shipping 50 pounds of goods by sea costs about the same as shipping 500 pounds (that is, you must pay a minimum charge, 500 pounds minimum). Thus air freight may not cost any more than the slower sea freight for 50 or 100 pounds, and you can arrange to pick up your item and guide it through Customs at the airport when you reenter the country. And by dealing with your items yourself, you avoid the costs of a Customs broker.

WHERE TO BUY WHAT

Local goods are cheapest. But of course, that's obvious. Or is it?

You are in Florence, and you've just seen Michelangelo's magnificent *David*. You'd like a copy of it, however primitive, for a friend at home. Right outside, a street vendor has dozens of small copies. Every single one has been made in Taiwan.

It is not at all easy these days to determine which goods are local and which are transported or imported. But ever since I learned that the Stetson hat company was founded in Pennsylvania, and that hula skirts were exported from Britain, I've wondered about "local goods." What about the time I tried to buy V.S.O.P. cognac in a small town in France? "Where do you think you are," sniffed the woman behind the counter, "London, or New York? You may find it in Paris, but it will be expensive. Wait until you get home—it's cheaper!" French tax laws, and export pressures, do indeed make cognac cheaper to buy in New York than in Paris!

It's fun to shop in the local equivalent of a variety store or a department store—you'll get more insights into a nation's lifestyle than you'd find in an armload of sociology textbooks, plus substantial savings on the kind of merchandise sold only in overpriced specialty shops back home.

What you should do is follow the Third Law and "Look Beyond the Obvious." For instance, I got a nice, useful, inexpensive souvenir of Cairo by seeking out the shops where local people shopped. Instead of looking at jewelry in Khan Khalili (which is what most visitors do), I went around the corner to a local caftan shop. A lady was bargaining vigorously with the store-keeper and, having learned the numbers from one to ten in Arabic, I could understand enough to know roughly what she was paying for it. I tried one on (good as a nightshirt), and when the shopkeeper tried to charge me four times as much, I indicated that I had overheard what the local lady paid. I got my price.

13

What to Do If Anything Goes Wrong

The joy and excitement of traveling in strange places can turn to misery when problems arise. Where do you find a doctor? What do you do if your wallet is lost or stolen? How do you react when a foreign official demands that you pay a bribe? Besides misery, you can be in for a good deal of expense. Accidents and mishaps cannot be avoided. But some problems can be anticipated, and you can prepare yourself to deal with them quickly and inexpensively. Get into training to deal with crises by reading over the following pages, which examine the most common travel problems and ways to make them go away.

SOLVING MONEY PROBLEMS

Money matters take up more of your time while traveling than they do at home. Also, you've got your money-handling problems worked out at home: the supermarket will take your personal check, the gas station will take your credit card, the bank will provide you with cash at any time of the day or night from its computerized teller machine.

Handling money abroad can be very expensive, which is why money matters are an appropriate subject for this book. For instance, in some countries—including several in Europe—banks may charge you 3% or even 5% to change your money. That means you give the foreign exchange teller in the bank $100 in U.S. dollars, and you get back only $95 to $97 in local currency!

The same thing happens when you change local currency back into dollars as you leave the country. Thus on at least part of your money you've paid the bank 6% to 10%!

Exchange Rates Revealed

The exchange rates quoted in the daily newspapers may not be the ones applied to tourist transactions. The *New York Times,* for example, lists the rates applicable for exchanges between commercial banks for amounts of $100,000 or more. Naturally, the bank will not give you such a preferential rate if you are only changing $100. But the commercial rate is still a good approximation of the rate you'll get.

In some countries, rates vary considerably from bank to bank and from bank to hotel or travel agency or money-changer. Look at it this way: you are selling a commodity (the dollars or other currency you hold) and you want to get the best price for it. If one bank offers you 6 French francs for it, and another bank offers you 6.2 francs, you sell to the latter and get more francs for your dollar.

I wish it were always as simple as going from bank to bank looking for the best rate. But it's not. Many banks give a better rate for traveler's checks than for cash. Most charge a fee for the transaction, and the fee may differ from one bank to the next. The black market may offer much better rates of exchange, and may be perfectly safe—or perilously unsafe.

The fastest international transfers are made by telegraph or telex. . . . The slowest way to get money is to wait for a personal check to clear through international banking channels. You must have lots of time for this—six weeks or more—and hitches and problems can develop.

What I can say here is that you must shop around, and you must always be aware of the *actual amount of cash which ends up in your hand*. In Jerusalem, you can exchange dollars for Israeli shekels at banks (both Palestinian and Israeli) or at money-changers. The money-changers, a colorful medieval holdout, are grouped around Damascus Gate. Transactions are very simple: no forms to fill out, no route through several tellers and cashiers to follow. The man or woman behind the counter pulls open a drawer and pays out cash for the money you've put down. The rate of exchange is not as good as at the bank. *But there is no fee*. If you are changing $1,000, you may do better at a bank, for the fee is a small set amount, which may equal only 1/10th or 1/20th percent of $1,000. But for amounts around $100, you do better at the money-changers, for the fee at the bank may be 1%

or 2% of $100. Thus at a money-changer you walk away with more cash in your hand. In Jerusalem this is all perfectly legal.

Can I Play the Black Market?

In many countries, black market currency transactions are punishable by long sentences in jail and large fines; in some countries these punishments are even meted out. But in others the black market is accepted as a fact of life, and participants are rarely prosecuted.

It's a tempting prospect, but look at it this way. It's true that if there is black market activity, then black marketing can be done and people do it daily without getting caught. But they're familiar with the local scene, and you're not. Just because you are approached on the street by someone who whispers "Change money?" in passing doesn't mean that's the way it's done. Could you tell a plainclothes police officer from the dealer? Do you know whether exchange transactions can be safely carried out in public places in broad daylight? In the final analysis, don't do it—change your money at a bank or money-changer where you'll still get a good rate—and safe exchange.

What to Do When You Run Out of Money

If you run out of money you pay a hefty price. You will have to spend vacation time standing in lines at banks and telegraph offices. You will probably have to stay in one place longer than you desired. You will have to pay for telegrams, telephone calls, bank fees, etc. You may have to change hotel and transportation reservations.

TURN PLASTIC INTO CASH: If you have a major credit card, and if you are careful always to have some credit available on it, there's no reason you should want for money either at home or abroad.

Details on how to best use the services of your credit card are given in Chapter 5 under "What You Didn't Know About Credit Cards."

For American citizens abroad, there is a quick way to handle financial emergencies with the help of the nearest American embassy or consulate. Call your family (or friends) back home and ask them to draft a Western Union money order payable to the Department of State, and a telegram with your full name, the exact district of the overseas consular office, and the sender's full name and address. This should be sent to the Department of State, Citizens Emergency Center, Room 4811, 2201 C St. NW, Washington, DC 20520 (tel. 202/647-5225, weekdays 8:15 a.m. to 10 p.m.; for after-hours emergencies, 202/634-3600). The Department of State must receive payment before you can receive any money at the consular office; payment is made in local currency. The transaction takes about 24 hours once the money order has been received in Washington.

TURN A WIRE INTO CASH: The fastest international transfers are made by telegraph. Sometimes the telegraph office acts as a transfer bank (this is true in countries where the post office, telephones, and telegraph are operated by the government; the post office is usually a savings bank as well). You go to the telegraph office with your passport (for identification), ask them to wire your bank with an order to pay you a certain amount, and then wait for it all to come true. It may take hours, it may take weeks. Several days is the usual time. The telegraph office may have to work through several banks. For instance, if your account is in a savings bank, that bank will have to apply to a commercial or merchant bank for help since savings banks don't normally engage in such transactions. All this takes time, and each bank—as well as the telegraph office—will charge you for its time.

In my experience, the cheapest way to transfer funds is by a commercial bank transfer wire, that is, a telex message sent from one bank to another. For instance, I once had to transfer $1,500 to a foreign country. I explored various methods. A telegraph-company transfer (see below) would have been very fast, but would have cost upwards of $100 (the actual fee was a *percentage* of the funds being transferred). An international money order, bought from a savings bank or savings-and-loan association, would have taken at least a week, and would have cost $35 for the money order, and $7 or $8 for registered international airmail postage, or a total of $42 or so. But a local commercial bank would transfer the funds by international telex in a matter of hours for $17. In the United States, a telex transfer from one bank to another normally costs about $10.

There is another important way you can transfer emergency funds, however. Using the Western Union International Funds Transfer Service, you can have someone call a toll-free number, give them their VISA or MasterCard number, and have them send up to $1,000 anywhere in the world. You (the recipient) can normally pick up the funds at a foreign bank or post office, in local currency, one or two business days after the call is made. The amount transferred, and the Western Union charges, will appear on the monthly credit card statement. To send an International Money Order by Western Union, call toll free 800/325-6000; in Missouri, 800/342-6700; in Alaska, Hawaii, Puerto

Rico, and the U.S. Virgin Islands, 800/648-4590. The person who calls must give full details of where the money is to be sent: city, bank and *branch* (address). If for some reason it seems best to do it through the U.S. consulate on the spot, you can do it that way (see the boxed copy). For more information, contact Western Union at 1 Lake St., Upper Saddle River, NJ 07458 (tel. 201/825-5569).

By the way, Western Union will transfer funds from one point in the U.S. to another, as well.

ANY BANK IS "YOUR" BANK: Plan ahead, and you can save lots of time and money. Just write a letter to your bank asking them to transfer a certain amount to a certain bank (and branch) abroad. If you don't know a bank, just walk into one and ask if they will be able to accept the transaction. But what if you're in Budapest and you want the money delivered in Stockholm? Then tell your bank this, and give them an address in Stockholm (Poste Restante will do) where they can reach you. When you get to Stockholm, go to the Poste Restante and pick up the bank's reply, which will contain the name of the bank to which the transfer has been sent. Go to the bank with your passport and the bank's letter, and pick up your money.

THE SLOWEST WAY: The slowest way to get money is to wait for a personal check to clear through international banking channels. You must have lots of time for this—six weeks or more—and hitches or problems can easily develop.

OFFICIAL HELP: "Well, I can always cash a personal check at the U.S. consulate." Wrong. The embassy or consulate will not accept your check—personal or traveler's—and will not lend you money (but they *will* pass on money sent by someone else—see the boxed copy). People in dire circumstances have been helped by their fellow citizens in diplomatic service, but this is a private effort. Diplomatic personnel will sometimes chip in to a charity fund to be used for the relief of Americans who run into problems abroad. This is definitely charity, though.

What about those stories of people who ran out of money and were flown home at government expense? This does happen. Here's how: you apply for repatriation at a consulate, and if you are accepted, you turn in your passport and agree to *pay back the loan* (with interest), which the government will make to you in the form of a commercial airline ticket. When you pay back the loan, you get your passport back—not before. Other security may be demanded as well. It's no fun.

What to Do about Losses and Thefts

The chilling moment comes when your purse or wallet is not where it should be. You've forgotten it somewhere, or it's been stolen. In either case, you have a chance to get it back.

Retrace your steps. Ask as many people as possible. Mention where you're staying, so they can notify you if it turns up. If you think it's been stolen, check in wastebaskets, bushes, gutters—a thief doesn't want the evidence of the crime on his person, and after extracting your cash and traveler's checks he may dump the item quickly. Notify the public officials nearby of the loss: subway or bus people (they always have a special lost-and-found office), policemen on the beat (if they still exist), even street sweepers if you see them. Tell them your name and where you're staying, always. About half the time, something comes back to you—the empty wallet, or wallet and personal items, or maybe even credit cards. About 10% of the time you get your money back too!

GET MONEY BY REPORTING THE LOSS: You will probably suffer some permanent loss, monetary or personal, if your wallet or purse disappears. Report it to the police, get a copy of the report (or at least a summary or note), and make a claim against your traveler's or homeowner's insurance when you return home. Yes! Homeowner's insurance will cover many such losses.

For lost traveler's checks, you apply to the issuing bank or its representative. You will need your passport, and perhaps the police report of the loss.

SOLUTIONS TO MEDICAL PROBLEMS

Nothing is quite as scary as getting sick when you're far from home. Besides the uncertainty of "What's wrong with me?" there is the problem of whom to consult. Where is the doctor? When can I get an appointment? Will there be a language problem? How much will all this cost? See Chapter 5 under "What Happens If I Get Sick?" for some tips on reference books to consult before you leave. But if you're suddenly taken ill:

Finding an English-Speaking Doctor

If you haven't obtained a list already (see Chapter 5), contact your embassy or consulate for the name of a recommended local physician who speaks English. The consulate won't guarantee good service; but any doctor, hospital, or clinic that occasions complaints is removed from the list. A diplomatic duty officer is on call even when the consulate or embassy is closed. The number may be in the telephone book; in some cases, it's posted on the door of the consulate building, and you may have to send someone to go look for it.

Your hotel may also be able to provide the names of doctors and clinics with which you can deal in English, and which have proved satisfactory.

In an emergency, remember: most hotels have doctors on call; that taxis are a cheaper, and many times faster means of reaching a hospital than ambulances; that as a general rule, public hospitals abroad have 24-hour service, a larger range of facilities, and better-trained staffs than do private ones.

Be warned that payment for medical treatment abroad must nearly always be made by you directly to the doctor or hospital. Make sure that you obtain itemized statements for your insurance company.

Toothache!

The same rules apply for finding a dentist: check with the local consulate. Dental practices vary somewhat from country to country, but you needn't fear that you'll have to settle for the sidewalk dentist in the bazaar of Fez who sits you on a stool, takes an ordinary pair of pliers, and extracts the tooth with a violent jerk. On a plastic sheet set out in front of him are the dental relics of all his former patients. Some of these unfortunate souls may still be alive!

"Well, I can always cash a personal check at the U.S. consulate." Wrong. The embassy or consulate will not accept your check—personal or traveler's—and will not lend you money.

Rather, you are more likely to run into a dentist trained in the United States or Europe. In Istanbul, I had dental work done by a man who attended the same American college I did. We spent half the time chatting about professors, football seasons, and the rowing team.

Eyeglasses and Contacts

If you've brought your prescription with you, it should be fairly simple to get replacement glasses. Any major city will have a well-equipped and modern optometrist's shop. It may be expensive.

Contact lenses may not be so easy to find, however. You may have to arrange for them to be sent from home.

AIR TRAVEL SOLUTIONS

Lost Airline Tickets

What if you lose the return portion of a round-trip airline ticket? A simple matter to replace it by checking with the airline computer? *Not* if you don't have the number of the original ticket! Most likely, you'll be required to purchase another return ticket, sometimes at prices higher than the initial cost. A simple precautionary measure is to record the number of your round-trip ticket right along with your passport number and traveler's checks information and tuck it away in a safe place. With the ticket number, the computer goes into action, and your ticket can be reissued in little or no time. No expensive repurchase or layover days waiting for records to be checked.

Some airlines follow this procedure: they will ask you to buy a new ticket for your return. After a certain time, if your old ticket has not been used by anyone, the airline will refund to you the amount of the unused portion.

What about Baggage?

Just when we thought we had baggage allowances down pat, some of the airlines are looking at the whole question of checked and carry-on bags and tightening or changing existing regulations. Most major lines still adhere to the dimensions rule—free checking of two

---

Do complaints help? Yes. An unqualified yes. They always help.

---

pieces of 62 and 55 inches (the sum of the length, width, and height of each case) and one carry-on of 45 inches, that will fit under the seat. Excess baggage charges vary widely from line to line. *Always* check with your reservation agent for current allowances. There may have been a change since your last flight!

What happens if your luggage is lost? Well, first of all, let's talk about some things you can do to prevent that kind of disaster. There is, of course, the obligatory identification tag which all airlines require on each piece of luggage, whether checked or carry-on. Tags are available at no charge at all airport check-in desks. Before affixing a new tag, *be sure to remove all old destination labels*—otherwise, some harried baggage handler may send your suitcases back to where you've already been instead of where you're headed. It's a good idea, too, to supplement the outside tags with some form of identification—a business card or label with your name and home address and telephone number—taped firmly to the inside of your bags. It will speed up their return enormously in case the outer tags are missing when your bags go astray.

There are a few simple precautions you can take at the check-in desk. First of all, ask the agent the code letters for your destination, then check to see if your bags have been marked correctly for destination and flight number. *Always* compare the stubs you're given to those on your bags to be sure they correspond. And above all, don't pack valuables or irreplaceable papers or medicines in luggage you plan to check—those should travel with you in carry-on bags.

Now, if in spite of everything, you wind up one place while your luggage takes off for parts unknown, proceed immediately to the airline desk to fill out the required claim form. Do this *before you leave the airport*. Give the most accurate description you can of each bag and its contents and insist on a copy of the form for your own records. The airlines have a pretty good record of tracing and returning lost baggage and have recently installed sophisticated computer systems to increase the speed with which you and your luggage will be reunited. Still, there are those cases when bags simply disappear. If that happens to you, you may be in for a six-week to three-month wait for compensation (carriers are under no time limit to settle a claim), and if you feel the reimbursement falls short of actual value, your only recourse is to sue in a small claims court.

For detailed information on how to deal with lost—or damaged—luggage, as well as a number of other airline emergencies, write for the U.S. Department of Transportation's helpful booklet called "Fly-Rights," which by rights should be part of your carry-on luggage on every flight. It's available for $1 from the Consumer Information Center, Pueblo, CO 81009.

HOW TO PAY (AND *NOT* PAY) A BRIBE

The scene was Mexico's mountainous jungle state of Chiapas, on a sweltering hot summer day. I was approaching the Guatemalan border, my head filled with horror tales about the rapacity of Central American border officials. But I was prepared: my car was an immense Ford LTD station wagon, a used car to me but to Central Americans a sign of unequalled wealth and power. Dressed in a suit and tie, I donned a pair of intense black sunglasses. A scowl curled my lip. I was ready.

Everyone was respectful, deferential, polite, but still official. I paid the official $1 fee for insecticide spraying of my car, and the official $1 fee for my Tourist Card. And that was all.

Several years later the scene was quite different. I approached the selfsame border station in a red VW minibus, dressed in a sport shirt and blue jeans, a smile brightening my countenance. The border officials took their time, scowled at me. I paid dearly for my pleasant attitude and informal appearance.

The point is this: not everyone pays bribes, and not everyone pays in the same amount or with the same frequency. What you want to do is to become part of the crowd that doesn't pay. Though Central American border officials do indeed have a well-earned reputation for rapacity, you can frequently get by them if you're prepared. Officials in other developing countries have similar mind-sets, and you can deal with them in the same manner.

First, look important, respectable, serious, and wealthy. I was able to wear a suit on that first venture into Guatemalan officialdom because the Ford had an arctic air conditioner. The VW did not, hence the necessity for less formal dress. In many situations it's impossible to dress formally, but at least one can look austere or sinister, perhaps by wearing lightweight black clothing. Sunglasses are a great help. Always

---

Not everyone pays bribes, and not everyone pays in the same amount or with the same frequency. What you want to do is to become part of the crowd that doesn't pay.

---

scowl, say little, and affect an air of mild annoyance and impatience.

Be careful, though! Maintain an attitude of correctness and civility, and never raise your voice, get angry, or insult an official! Not only does this blow your cool, it threatens his dignity, which, for most Third World officials, is worth more than the paltry official salary. If his dignity is threatened, he will be forced to take steps to protect it, such as not letting you enter the country (minimum) to tossing you in the slammer (maximum, to start).

A border official (Customs officer, immigration officer, border patrol officer) will put the touch on you if you look pliable, gullible, friendly, or frightened. If, on the other hand, you stand your ground and allow him his dignity, he will usually let you through without paying. He doesn't want trouble, he wants easy money. If you look important—perhaps as though you have important friends in the capital city—he'll want to stay out of your way. Often the officials at airports will not hit you for bribes, as people who fly are assumed to be rich and important. And airports are places that specialize in speed, efficiency, the modern outlook. But at a highway or railroad border crossing or international wharf, thousands of simple local people will be crossing with you. Each of them will be made to pay a pittance. After so many pittances, you will look like King (or Queen) Croesus to an underpaid border official.

A textbook, real-life example of how to beat the high cost of bribery: the Mexican government maintains a commercial frontier between the Yucatán peninsula and the rest of Mexico. Commercial vehicles must stop here to have their cargoes and papers inspected. Tourists are also flagged down by the sole officer, and are asked to show their papers. One used to need two official papers to drive through Mexico: a Tourist Card and a Temporary Vehicle Import Permit. Later, these were merged into a single document, and there was some confusion for people used to having two papers. The Yucatán frontier officer devised an ingenious scheme by which to earn extra cash. He exploited the confusion.

Like everyone else, at first I had assumed I lost one of my papers, or an official had neglected to return one to me. But I discovered in Mexico City that the single document I possessed was dual-purpose. So when I encountered the mercenary Yucatán frontier official, I felt sure of my ground.

"You must have two permits, Señor." he said.

"One, Señor," I answered. "It used to be two, but now it is one."

"I have always seen two; where is your other one?"

"I have no other one because it is no longer issued. If you read the one I have, you will see that it is sufficient." I was firm, but very polite.

"Well, how can I be sure. . . .?" He saw his bribe slipping away.

"I am certain, Señor. Thank you very much. Please excuse me. Goodbye."

I bowed politely and left. Later that day the official claimed $5 from a friend who drove through and who did not stand his ground.

Please, please make the distinction between official fees and bribes. An official fee or tax, no matter how silly, stupid, unfair, or rapacious, *must* be collected by an officer. Arguing with him over such a fee is useless. He'll tell you, in so many words, "go tell Congress." But if it is truly an official fee, you have a right to receive a receipt, and you should ask for one if it is not provided automatically. A bribe, on the other hand, is something he can collect or not collect as he likes.

HOW TO FIGHT BACK

It would be wonderful if I could tell you that by following the advice of this book, you would avoid all disappointing situations. Alas, the world is too complicated a place to avoid all bad times. But it is certainly true that keen-eyed and clear-thinking travelers avoid many unpleasant situations encountered by their less aware fellow travelers.

It is not unusual for an emergency call from a hotel in a foreign city to the U.S. to cost upward of $100. Obviously, this is outrageous.

Each year I receive hundreds of letters from readers of my guidebooks detailing their travel experiences both in the United States and Canada, and abroad. Corresponding with readers is one of the most pleasurable and satisfying parts of my work, and also one of the most informative. About 85% of the letters describe enormously satisfying and rewarding trips, with perhaps one or two hitches along the way. Perhaps one will say, "The Hotel Palace was fine, but the Restaurant Delicatesse must have a new chef—all the food tasted as though it had been boiled for hours." Another 10% of the letters is devoted to one particular travel experience that was upsetting: "The bus from the capital to the ruins is woefully inadequate for the crowds; the driver always overcharges; and it's always several hours late—please warn your readers!" The last 5% are the unfortunate people who have had a bad trip, and who tend to blame all those connected with it—airlines, hotels, restaurants, travel agents, and guidebook writers—for the disaster.

Do complaints help? Yes. An unqualified yes. They always help. They may not get you your money back, and indeed you might not even be able to see direct results from your complaint, but a complaint always registers. Eventually, action is taken.

If I get a complaint about any establishment mentioned in one of my books, I check it out extra carefully on my next inspection trip. I ask around and find out from others if there have been more complaints. If I receive two or three complaints, the establishment had better have some very redeeming features, or a change of heart, if it is to be included in the next edition of the book. More than three complaints, and I'm pretty sure the place is a loss, though I feel that out of fairness it must be reinspected with an impartial eye.

This is the concrete effect your complaint has on the opinion, and product, of a guidebook writer. Similar effects register with travel agents, local tourist boards or chambers of commerce, or governmental tourist authorities. Think of it this way: a complaint is a vote. One vote alone means little, but the effect of many votes can be overwhelming.

Why don't writers, managers, and officials pay even more attention to complaints? Why not just close a place down, or exclude it from publication, or black-ball it, on the basis of a well-voiced complaint? If it could happen to one person, it could happen to a million. The reasons are that all complaints are not equal, and that conditions change frequently.

When a chef falls ill or goes on vacation; when a hotel changes manager or hires new staff; when equipment breaks down unexpectedly; when there are too many visitors for facilities to handle—this is often the time when things go wrong. Such situations are understandable and sometimes excusable. But there are two sides to every story and also to every complaint. The hotel manager may say, "I'm terribly sorry the water's off, but there's nothing we can do about it—the city main burst." Still, it is disappointing to be cheated out of a shower after a long day of sightseeing. Or to dream of a romantic dinner, and find you're next to a huge table of birthday-party revellers.

Your bad experience can depend partly on your frame of mind. If you've saved and saved for years so you can fly off to Paris, stay at the Crillon, and dine at Maxim's, everything had better be perfect, completely perfect. When you have a wonderful memory of a city, or a restaurant, you want to return and have it be exactly the same. And if your standards of cleanliness and service are high, you may find it hard to understand that the best place in town is a dump. One week, I received two letters from readers describing their experiences at exactly the same hotel. "The place was so beautiful, the food was so interesting and delicious; the owner and his wife showed us everything in their own car!" The other letter said, "The room was dusty, there was grit in the halls, the dinky light bulbs left everything in perpetual near-darkness, and the owner could have cared less—he was never around!" Both of these descriptions are probably accurate.

This is not to suggest that you should not register your complaint. You should, you must. But if you think that your complaint is meeting with indifference, it may just be that the person to whom you complained is waiting for more evidence.

It matters greatly *where* you lodge your complaint. A reader once blamed me because her room did not have a view of the sea, and I had described the hotel as having "windows looking either onto the bay or the inn's lush grounds." Her request for a room with a sea view should of course have been lodged with the hotel reservation clerk. Or, upon arrival, she could have asked for such a room when she registered.

It also matters greatly *how* you lodge your complaint. A polite but firm request should be met with satisfaction or a reasonable excuse, and you have every right to expect such. But the person to whom you complain has every right to expect that you will be reasonable and polite. If you aren't, they will feel as though they have a right to ignore you. Besides, there are always those times when they are right and you are wrong. If you've lodged your complaint politely, you have nothing to regret.

Successful Complaints

Successful complaints come about through a process of escalation.

Complain at once. Get satisfaction as soon as you notice something is wrong. Any time that passes works to the advantage of the other side: "The customer put up with it this long, it must not be important." When the waiter puts that unordered tray of delicacies on your table, or that expensive bottle of mineral water, speak up: "Excuse me, we didn't order this. Is it on the house? How much does it cost? Would you take it back, please?" Or when you notice your room is noisy, or the lock doesn't work, or there is no light bulb, bring these things to the attention of the front desk at once. Give them a chance to save face and make it right by fixing things or by giving you another room.

Be polite and civil, but firm and persistent. Do not shout or use threats. Rather than saying "I'll report you to the manager!" if the waiter or desk clerk ignores your request, do just that—report him to the manager. Do it without the clerk's knowing, so he won't get to the manager first with excuses.

Be reasonable. Determine if the other side has a legitimate case. Service was slow at the restaurant, and you almost missed the first act at the opera? For the romantic couple lingering over each course in that dusky corner, service was probably too fast. Perhaps you should have mentioned to the waiter that you had to make an 8 o'clock curtain, and asked for his suggestion on how you might order. Or if that hotel in the jungle is too expensive for what it is, consider what it must be like to run a hotel in the jungle. The people who work at the hotel probably view it as the height of luxury. Perhaps they think it's silly to pay $50 (a fortune!) for a concrete-block room when one can sleep under a tree for nothing. That's when you must decide if it's worth it to pay $50 so you don't have to sleep under a tree.

If you've truly been cheated, join battle to win. Now you're sure it's not just a mistake, or an accident, or your bad mood, or some other person's bad mood. These people are out to get you, and that overcharge is premeditated and deliberate, or they have no intention of providing what they promised. Proceed quietly and deliberately. Set aside time to do it. Keep appealing to higher authority as necessary, from the waiter to the maître d' or hostess, from them to the manager or

---

> The inflexible law of tipping is this: the person who importunes you the most will need the tip least. . . . Never allow yourself to be shamed into tipping or into tipping big.

---

chef, from them to the tourism bureau or chamber of commerce, from them to the national authorities; to guidebooks, travel agents, newspapers. Let word get around. Persist.

Remember, complaints *always* help. I'd estimate that in 60% of the cases you'll get full and immediate satisfaction if you lodge your complaint according to these rules. The rest of the time you'll attain satisfaction eventually, or you'll influence someone who will see to it that the wrong is made right.

Finally, don't rule out the use of humor to get what you want. A well-placed joke can defuse an antagonistic situation, melt a heart of stone, or make everyone see the lighter side of life. Make someone laugh, and they've got to like you. And if they like you, they'll do anything for you.

Getting Satisfaction from an Airline

What do people complain about most to the airlines? At the top of the list are gripes about flight cancellations and delays, lost or damaged baggage, and red-tape problems in getting refunds. How many people complain? The Department of Transportation receives anywhere from 20,000 to 40,000 official complaints a year. Airlines that are the worst offenders receive about two or three complaints for every 10,000 passengers carried; the best airlines receive one complaint for every 1,000,000 passengers carried. But only about 1/2 of 1% of the public "officially" responds to bad treatment. This may mean that for every 10,000 people carried by an airline with poor service, 400 to 600 walk away might unhappy.

Here's the procedure for complaints against airlines. First, complain to the airline itself. About 90% of the time, the airline's consumer relations representative will help you to resolve the complaint. If you get no satisfaction, report your complaint to the U.S. Department of Transportation's Office of Intergovernmental and Consumer Affairs, 400 Seventh St. SW, Washington, DC 20590 (tel. 202/366-2220). Though this office does not act as a mediator and will not actually go to bat for you in your complaint, it does something to urge the airline toward satisfying you: the office records your complaint in its official Travel Consumer Complaint Report, and an official notifies the airline that your complaint has officially been lodged against them. The official will also help you to get a response from the airline. If the airline has violated consumer protection laws, as in cases dealing with false or misleading advertising, overbooking, or smoking complaints, your complaint could lead the Department of Transportation to begin an investigation and possibly to sue the airline for civil penalties. Even if this doesn't happen, your complaint becomes a "vote" against the airline, and the tally of all such votes is published in various travel media. Sooner or later, it becomes apparent that certain airlines are mistreating their passengers. Make your complaint as soon as possible, and then be patient. The Office of Intergovernmental and Consumer Affairs sometimes receives as many as 300 complaints a day, and it may take some time for them to get to your request.

Embassies and Consulates— What They Can Do

An embassy is the diplomatic representative of one government to another government. A consulate is charged with the welfare of its nations' citizens and business interests in a foreign city.

Embassies deal with governments; consulates deal with people and firms. Consular officers will do their best to see that you receive equitable treatment under the laws of the foreign country in which you find yourself. They can recommend lawyers, visit you in prison, petition the foreign authorities. But they cannot guarantee your safety, cannot get you out of jail or out of the country, make travel arrangements, forward your mail, or act as a bank.

A consular officer will gladly renew your passport, advise you of Customs regulations in the U.S., warn you of dangers in the country, or provide business materials dealing with the foreign country. You can register at a consulate abroad, and if there is trouble they will attempt to contact you and let you know what to do.

TURNING MOUNTAINS INTO MOLEHILLS

Everything that's so cheap and easy at home seems to turn into a chore when you're on the road. Famous Nobel laureates and people who rule vast commercial empires can turn to imbeciles when faced with a foreign pay telephone: How do you get the cursed thing to work? Where can I get my laundry done? What do you mean, it will take five days? Travel tips to cover these sorts of daily concerns may not solve all your problems. But the selected hints mentioned below will certainly save you money.

Easy Laundry

I always have supplies to do my own, just in case. Elaborate supplies can include a bottle of concentrated liquid detergent, a small string for a clothesline, aluminum or inflatable hangers for drip-dry shirts, a drain stopper for those budget hotel rooms that always seem to lack them, a small brush for getting out spots and stains. Simple supplies are just the bath soap found in the room, hangers from the closet, and a rolled-up sock to plug the drain.

In some cities, all this is unnecessary. Pull into any big shopping center and there will be a coin laundry complete with washers, dryers, and vending machines selling everything from detergent powders to fabric softeners to laundry bags. In foreign countries, coin laundries (laundromats, washeterias, whatever your favorite term) may be scarce, but good old hand laundries may be common. You may get a jolly *señora,* or a dignified Chinese man, or a bevy of dark maidens to do your laundry for a very reasonable sum, and perhaps even deliver the freshly ironed garments to your hotel. Conversely, there are many countries in which the laundry bill is higher than the value of the clothes. In Switzerland one can pay $30 to have two shirts and some underwear cleaned; in Israel, I paid $15 to have a $20 pair of blue jeans washed and ironed.

Your hotel will always be able to arrange for laundry and dry cleaning, and will almost always take a cut of the action. In most cases it's better to make your own arrangements. Ask a café or query a taxi driver, and find the location of a nearby laundry. Even if you don't speak the language, even if the sign is in Arabic or Swahili, laundries are pretty much the same the world over. What changes is price and time. The clerk can write the price for you, and you can count out the day when it will be ready in sign language, or point to a calendar. Same goes for dry cleaning. But ask the price before you commit yourself.

You *Can* Get Mail!

Mail presents a dual problem: receiving letters and sending letters.

To receive mail, the most dependable way is probably through a branch of American Express. You must be a customer of that company (that is, you must hold their credit card, or use their traveler's checks, or sign up for one of their tours), and there must be an Amex office in town.

Also dependable is Poste Restante (General Delivery). You will need your passport to collect your mail, and you may have to pay a small fee for each letter. In cities with more than one post office, your Poste Restante will be sent to the main or central post office unless addressed otherwise. You may have to apply for your mail at certain hours—don't assume you can pick it up anytime the post office is open.

In other countries Poste Restante is not as dependable as having your letter sent to a hotel. In Egypt, for instance, this is the case.

To send mail in foreign countries, do it in post offices. Hotel clerks may or may not know the proper postage for foreign letters. If they don't, it's not their letter that comes back, postage due—it's yours. Besides, hotels usually charge extra for their stamps, not to mention for their postcards. Often you'll find hordes of inexpensive postcard sellers around the post office.

Remember that foreign post offices provide all the usual services: registered letters, special delivery (express), general delivery (poste restante), and money orders. These services may or may not apply to letters leaving the country; that is, if you pay for express service from Brazil to the U.S., the U.S. Postal Service will probably honor the special delivery provision. But a special delivery letter sent from the U.S. to Brazil may not be delivered extra quickly at that end.

A Fortune for a Phone Call!

The major problem with telephones abroad is the cost of using them. In many countries, simple local calls are amazingly cheap—the equivalent of 5¢ or 8¢—but long-distance and international calls are fantastically expensive, costing several dollars per minute. In addition, most hotels add a surcharge if you call from your room or from a booth utilizing the hotel switchboard or operator. It's not unusual for a call from a hotel in a foreign city (even in Mexico) to the U.S. to cost upward of $100. Obviously, this is outrageous. But how can you avoid it?

WAYS TO PROTECT YOURSELF: A long-distance call from a Paris phone booth to your stateside home might cost $3 per minute. But from your Paris hotel room, it might cost $10 a minute. The difference is the hotel's surcharge, a rapacious fee it collects just because it provides you with the occasional use of a telephone line. How can you protect yourself from such robbery?

Before you call long distance from a foreign hotel, ask to see if it is a member of AT&T's Teleplan. If it is, the hotel will add only a small flat-fee surcharge of $1 or so to your call, and may not add any surcharge at all. Furthermore, the hotel may offer its guests a direct connection to an AT&T operator in the United States.

There may even be a separate phone with a direct line to AT&T's circuits right in the hotel lobby. Teleplan hotels are found in Cyprus, England, Germany, Ireland, Portugal, Panama, Israel (all hotels), and several countries of the Pacific region and the Far East. In addition, all Hilton International Hotels and Marriott Hotels are members of Teleplan.

Another way to avoid the surcharge is to use AT&T's service called USADIRECT. What you do is call a local number in the city where you're staying, punch in an access code, and you're immediately connected to AT&T in the United States. You can use your AT&T credit card to make calls through this line, or you can call collect. You'll be billed on your AT&T credit card account at the operator-assisted international calling rate. The only charge you pay the hotel is for the local call.

The USADIRECT access code can be used from most telephones in certain foreign countries (Australia, Belgium, the British Virgin Islands, Denmark, France, West Germany, Great Britain, Holland, Japan, and Sweden), not just from hotel phones. In other countries (23 of them), you must use the special AT&T telephones. For information on international calling in general and USADIRECT in particular, including a list of access numbers, call AT&T toll free at 800/874-4000.

If for some reason you cannot use either of the plans above, try placing the call through the regular channels and charging it to your AT&T credit card. Many countries will accept this form of payment if your card has an "international billing number" on it, and you will be billed at a station-to-station rate. To get an international billing number, call your telephone company. The number will be issued to you for free.

If the local operator won't let you use your card, try calling collect. This is more expensive than a credit card call, as you will be billed at the person-to-person rate. But that rate may still be lower than the foreign-billed rate. When your party answers at home, give them your number and location (including hotel room number) and ask them to call you back. This results in most of your conversation being billed at the lowest possible rate, the one used when someone in the United States dials a foreign number directly.

Also, keep in mind that foreign telephone companies have special rates for special calling times, just as we do. Calls may be cheaper at night and on weekends. Check a local telephone directory, or ask for help at your hotel, to determine the cheapest calling times, which may be quite different from what you're used to at home.

Another thing to know is that AT&T is not the only American telephone company providing international long distance service. The rival companies such as MCI and US Sprint may provide similar services at very competitive rates. Contact those companies for details.

A final word: after almost two decades of writing guidebooks to Mexico (including *Mexico on $20 a Day*), I must warn you that Mexico's long distance and international telephone rates are perhaps the highest in the entire world. It is quite possible that a 20- or 30-minute call home will cost you $100 or more. Be very careful when calling internationally from Mexico; try to avoid such calls if possible.

If you can't call from your hotel, where *can* you call from? In many foreign countries, the post office operates the telephone service. Many post offices have special long-distance telephone stations or booths. It may seem like a bother to find one, but remember—those hotel surcharges and taxes can be truly breathtaking.

MYSTERIOUS FOREIGN PHONES REVEALED: First, a note about "taxiphones": in many countries you will find ingenious pay telephones called "taxiphones." The odd name comes from the phone's "meter," which automatically calculates time and distance for the call and charges you accordingly. The usual procedure is to approach one of these telephones (in a café, terminal, or hotel) with a pocketful of the sort of coins or tokens which the phone will accept. You load a quantity of coins into the phone, and they appear in a little glass chute. As you speak, the coins slowly drop, gone forever. When the chute is empty, the call is disconnected, so you must keep replenishing the supply of coins in the chute as you talk. Often there will be several chutes for the several sizes of coins.

Though taxiphones in some countries accept only small-denomination coins good for local calls (making it difficult to call long distance—how would you like to load 300 tiny 5¢ coins?), many in Europe accept high-value coins. In France, for instance, you can walk up to a phone booth on a Paris streetcorner, load in some coins worth several dollars apiece, and dial a friend in the United States.

As for other types of pay phones, the rule is: don't insert your money until you're sure the phone won't work without it, as some phones are designed without coin-return provisions. If you get a dial tone, then dial. If it rings, let it ring. When the person answers, the phone may go dead, or you may hear blips—*that is the time* to insert the coin, or push the plunger, or whatever it seems required to do, and not before. If you push in a coin before that point, it may be gone for good and you may get nothing in exchange.

Note that in some countries you pay for every second the receiver is off the hook—whether you get a busy signal, or an incomplete call, or an unknown number from the operator.

DEBIT CARD PHONES: In some foreign countries, notably in France, the telephone company has installed telephones which accept debit cards to pay for calls. A debit card looks like a credit card: it's a little rectangle of plastic. But there's a difference. A debit card actually has a tiny computer memory and battery in it. This memory is "filled" by the telephone company with credits for phone calls, and the card is sold to a telephone user at a price equal to the amount of the credits.

For instance, you can buy a card in Paris good for FFr50 or FFr100 worth of telephone calls. You pay the telephone company FFr50 or FFr100, take your card, and go to a phone booth. Slip the card into the telephone slot and dial away, to another street, another city, another country, or another continent. The telephone will automatically subtract credits from the card's memory as you talk. When you finish your call and remove your debit card from the telephone, the total cost of the call has been debited from the card. Your FFr50 card may now be worth only FFr43. It's an excellent system, and it saves you the trouble of having the right coins, and loading them into the telephone, and being cut off when you run out of the right coins.

Here's a bonus. An American friend of mine who lives in Paris says that French telephone users often forget their debit cards, and just walk away from the phone booth. He says that he never buys cards. He just glances in every phone booth he passes, and collects enough cards with enough credits to make all the calls he wants!

Telegram or Telex?

The alternative to the telephone is the telegraph or Telex. What's the difference? Well, a telegram can be sent to anyone, anywhere; but a Telex can be sent only to someone with a Telex machine (teleprinter or computer with a Telex hookup). Telex machines are widely used in offices and hotels. In effect they provide "written telephone service." One dials a number just like the phone, and when the other party answers, one types the desired message on the keyboard.

Telexes have a distinct advantage over the telegraph in terms of cost, though. With a Telex, the operator can encode your message on tape beforehand, and when the call goes through to its recipient, the tape can be played at high speed, thus saving time on the line. Therefore if you can send a Telex, always do so in preference to a telegram. Don't know the Telex number? Most Telex offices have libraries of directories listing Telex numbers for the entire world.

As for telegraph service, you can save money by requesting that your message be sent as a "Night Letter." This service is available in many countries. Your message is delayed only until the slack period for telegraph traffic arrives (sometime late at night). There is a maximum delay time, and if your message is still waiting to be sent at that time, it is sent whether traffic has abated or not. Night Letters give you more words for your money, and have a higher minimum word limit. This means that they are particularly good for longer messages. Your message may be only one line, in which case you might as well send it by normal service. When asking for Night Letter service, just write "NL" for the clerk if you can't speak his language—that seems to be the universally accepted abbreviation.

Secrets of Tipping

This is always a problem in a strange society. Most of us feel that we should observe the customs of the country. We don't want to disappoint anyone, or insult them. At the same time, it's our hard-earned money that we're handing out, and we'd like very much to avoid giving more than is generous or necessary.

The inflexible law of tipping is this: the person who importunes you the most will need the tip least. The taxi driver who berates you for stinginess, the bellhop who scoffs at your proffered coin, the street beggar who asks for some larger coin, or two or three—they're on the take, and they're taking from you. They've seen that putting a tourist to shame can produce big money fast, and they're hooked on this source of income. Compare them to the quiet country man who is a guard at some remote archeological site. Not often seeing tourists, he feels delighted and honored when you visit. He would not think of besmirching his hospitality by begging, unless he is in real need. And even if he truly needs some money, *you* may have to beg *him* to take it. In some cases, a small gift of something "foreign" (an American ballpoint pen or keychain, for instance), or a photograph or a postcard sent after you return home, will mean more to your newfound acquaintance than cash.

In any case, never allow yourself to be shamed into tipping, or into tipping big.

WHO GETS THE TIP?: If you leave a tip on your dinnertable, or pay it into the hand of one of several helpers, who gets it? That's hard to say. The best policy is to pay each person directly if you truly want to express your gratitude. A restaurant in Istanbul used to employ the following rapacious tactic: a service charge was added to the bill, and you were expected to leave a tip on top of that. But this tip went only to the maître d' while the poor waiter got nothing. The tip was very important to the waiter as he was the lowest-paid member of the staff, and he would work hard to get it. How did he get his just returns? He stood by the door as you left, wishing you a good evening and hoping you'd figure out the unjust tipping system in time to give him a little something.

This system was close to robbery, but when one understood it, one knew to leave very little on the table, and a much larger amount in the hand of the waiter himself.

HOW MUCH?: How much does one tip? This is the most difficult question of all. Many people think 15% is the minimum, and 20% the norm, especially when the pressures of operating in a foreign society produce fear and guilt. This fear and guilt may be costly, because local custom may dictate a tip of 3%.

I tend to think of 10% as the norm, 12% as good, 15% as tops. I think 20% is outrageous, and is in effect begging for love. In places where there is a service charge, no tip may be necessary; on the other hand, the service charge may go to the owner alone, and the staff may be expecting tips. Give something extra in this case, but not 10% or 15% extra.

What if you notice local people leaving only a few small coins on the table? Well, it may be that a small amount is sufficient—in Egypt, the equivalent of 65¢ will buy a workingman a bounteous repast of *fuul, taamia,* pickled vegetables, tomato salad, fresh bread, hummus, and spring water—all he can eat. Or it might be that tipping is not an important matter, or is almost frowned upon, as in Switzerland and Israel.

Wherever you go, you will encounter people who will want bigger and bigger tips. You will find them even in countries where tipping is not important. Why? Because previous travelers have tipped out of fear and guilt, and have corrupted the outlook of these service people. From wanting nothing, or very little, the waiters and cab drivers and guides want all they can get, and would gladly accept a tip of 100%. Why not? Tourists are giving money away, why not take it?

Oh, God . . . JAIL!

The thought of ending up in a foreign jail is the farthest thing from our minds. And, in fact, it rarely happens by mistake. If you don't buy, carry, or use drugs, trade on the black market, insult a foreign official or his country, or otherwise engage in illegal activities, why should you end up in jail?

If it happens to someone you know and love, don't panic. Foreign jails are not often the horror holes portrayed in movies. These horror tales make thrilling cinema, but they are hardly accurate. While foreign jails may be less comfortable than hometown jails, more basic and simpler, foreigners are usually treated *better* than local people, though *all* inmates will be treated as though they are suspected (or have been convicted) of criminal behavior. Don't get into a panic just because it's a foreign jail. Have you ever seen a jail at home? It's not much better, if at all.

There are things you can do to help.

The person on the spot, in jail, will understand best of all what happened and why. The only thing to do is to remain calm, and request permission to contact the nearest U.S. consular officer. The consular officer can make sure that you receive proper and equal treatment, can help to arrange for a lawyer, and can advise you on the best way to defend your case.

The person at home can get more information on what happens by ordering a 16-page booklet called "The Hassle of Your Life: A Handbook for Families of Americans Jailed Abroad," from Contact, Inc., P.O. Box 81826, Lincoln, NB 68501. The booklet was prepared by the International Legal Defense Counsel of Philadelphia, and costs $2.

14

Special Travelers

For many people, travel presents special problems and opportunities. What about women traveling alone? What about families traveling with children? Or the handicapped? What about single travelers, in a world set up to handle couples? These and other special situations can be turned to your advantage. Special strategies apply for saving money if you're not precisely the middle-class, middle-aged couple that the travel industry so often expects and equips itself to serve.

In this chapter you'll find information and suggestions for dealing with these special situations in a cost-effective way: first, youth and student travel, and educational travel, then senior citizen's travel, then families traveling with children. After dealing with family travel problems, we'll look at ways to overcome the solo traveler's problems before taking a look at special-interest vacations, from archeological digs to working on a kibbutz, which leads naturally to the ultimate value of all—working abroad.

YOUTH AND STUDENT TRAVEL

When it comes to cost-effective travel, young people rule the road. Willing to take chances, to do without frills and comforts, and to forget considerations of rank and status, students can and do travel the farthest on the least. One reason for this is the vast network of youth hostels, student hotels and flights, discounts on ships and buses, inexpensive university cafeterias, even student travel bureaus.

A young person's passport into the worldwide network of student travel organizations is the International Student Identity Card, described in detail in Chapter 5. Once you're plugged into the network, you can get hold of the CIEE's *Student Work-Study-Travel Catalog,* and also the *Update* to the catalog, which is mailed out later in the year when travel prices have solidified.

> A young person's passport into the worldwide network of student travel organizations and discounts is the International Student Identity Card.

The catalog is free. It contains a complete list of International Student Travel Conference (ISTC) offices abroad, information on books and guidebooks, an application form for the International Student Identity Card, and full information on student travel opportunities. An added feature of the catalog is a large section on "Work Abroad" in countries throughout the world. The CIEE has negotiated agreements with many countries, which make it possible for students to work in foreign countries for limited periods without hassling over normal work permits (sometimes impossible for foreigners to obtain). Finally, the catalog deals in detail with opportunities for study abroad. Note that CIEE activities are of interest to high school as well as college students.

If you want even more information than the 64-page catalog provides, go to any bookstore and pick up the CIEE's *Work, Study, Travel Abroad: The Whole World Handbook*. The price is less than $10, and for that you get over 400 pages of tips, addresses, directions, and opportunities. Note that the *Handbook* is no replacement for the aforementioned catalog and update, because it does not carry the same current information as do the smaller publications. The *Update,* for instance, is almost all totally full of charts of airfares for student flights. If you're traveling in the United States, get hold of a copy of CIEE's *Where to Stay USA,* available in bookstores. Make sure you contact the **Council on International Educational Exchange** at 205 East 42 St., New York, NY 10017 (tel. 212/661-1414).

EDUCATIONAL JOURNEYS

Many organizations known for sponsoring student travel abroad are actually not limited to a student clientele. In many cases, anyone with an interest in education or a vacation as a "learning experience" can sign up to go. Get hold of a copy of *Learning Vacations*, published by Peterson's Guides, P.O. Box 2123, Princeton, NJ 08543 (tel. 609/924-5338). A copy costs $10.95, and is available in libraries, bookstores, or from the publisher. It lists and describes lots of educational trips directly supported, organized, or sponsored by universities, museums, and similar cultural institutions. On these excellent educational trips, you usually spend part of the day in the classroom and the rest of the day exploring directly and first-hand the subjects you've just learned about. Tours are often cheaper than normal because they are organized by non-profit institutions.

There are many other organizations dedicated to providing travelers of all ages with memorable, educational, fulfilling vacations abroad. Here are some of them:

American Field Service, International/Intercultural Programs, 13 E. 43rd St., New York, NY 10017 (tel. 212/949-4242); AFS has numerous programs in almost 70 countries, where students stay with local families.

American Institute for Foreign Study, 102 Greenwich Ave., Greenwich, CT 06830 (tel. 203/869-9090); they sponsor foreign student travel programs, with stays in foreign homes and campuses.

American Intercultural Student Exchange, 7728 Lookout Drive, La Jolla, CA 92037 (tel. 619/459-9761); they'll set you up with a family in Latin America, Europe, and the Asian/Pacific region.

Amigos de las Americas, 5618 Star Lane, Houston, TX 77057 (tel. toll free 800/231-7796); they organize volunteer work situations, with stays in local homes in Latin America.

Children's International Summer Villages, Inc., 206 N. Main St., Casstown, OH 45312 (tel. 513/335-4640); they arrange for youth aged 11 to 18 to stay and work in many foreign countries.

Experiment in International Living, Brattleboro, VT 05301 (tel. toll free 800/451-4465); "the

Experiment" is among the best-known organizations, arranging stays in foreign homes in 23 countries.

Future Farmers of America, P.O. Box 15160, Alexandria, VA 22309 (tel. 703/360-3600); they'll set you up with work on a farm in any of 25 foreign countries.

National 4-H Council, 7100 Connecticut Ave., Chevy Chase, MD 20815 (tel. 301/656-9000); homestays with emphasis on farming, in 17 foreign countries.

Open Door Student Exchange, 124 E. Merrick Rd., Valley Stream, NY 11582 (tel. 516/825-8485); they'll arrange a foreign home for you in Europe, the Middle East, or Latin America.

Operation Crossroads Africa, 150 Fifth Ave., Room 310, New York, NY 10011 (tel. 212/242-8550); their specialty is volunteer work programs in Africa and the Caribbean.

People to People International, 2420 Pershing Rd., Suite 300, Kansas City, MO 64108 (tel. 816/421-6343); they do stays in local homes and tour itineraries in Europe and East Asia.

Youth for Understanding, 3501 Newark St., NW, Washington, DC 20016 (tel. toll free 800/833-6243); the emphasis here is on sports clubs and athletic training activities.

SENIOR CITIZEN SAVINGS

The rationale for giving discounts to older people runs like this: "Here we have this large group of citizens who have come to enjoy the finer things in life, but who now are living on limited retirement incomes. They have the time and the inclination to travel, but perhaps not as much money as they'd like. Seniors represent a vast pool of customers for airlines, trains, buses, hotels, and restaurants. They're good customers too: no vandalism, robberies, or bad times with seniors, by and large. The way to attract this large clientele is by offering discounts."

Well, that's the rationale. And it works, though senior discounts are sometimes small and sometimes cancelled when trade is brisk—the bright side is that you don't have to work hard to get them.

Senior Citizens' Organizations

First thing to do is to join a recognized senior citizens' organization. The dues are a small amount, and the benefits are substantial. Best-recognized is the **American Association of Retired Persons** (AARP), affiliated with the **National Retired Teachers Association,** 1909 K St. NW, Washington, DC 20049 (tel. 202/872-4700); another big one is the **National Council of Senior Citizens** (NCSC), 925 15th St. NW, Washington, DC 20005 (tel. 202/347-8800).

For senior citizens, the first thing to do is join a recognized senior citizens' organization. The dues are a small amount, and the benefits are substantial.

Why does it help to be a member? Because firms are much more likely to give discounts to members of a group that number in the tens of thousands, hoping to attract more and more members to their services. And seniors' organizations can negotiate with firms on that basis as well. Also, you can often slip in under the wire on discounts that are given out to "retired persons" (i.e., over 65) because you can join the AARP at age 55 and reap the benefits.

Senior Discounts

If you've followed the advice of this book and have sent away for the directories of the budget motel chains, you already have a head start on senior discounts. Many hotel, restaurant, and transportation firms require that you hold their own identification card or join their own seniors' club in order to get discounts, and the directories tell you how to get them. Often this costs nothing (or just a dollar or two). The entire procedure seems designed to get your loyalty, thinking that you won't bother to send away for the other chains' cards, and will only use theirs.

Be careful, and calculate exactly what you'll be getting with your senior discount, whether the deal is for a motel room, airfare, or train ticket. Stipulations will be made, such as that you must reserve one of the nicer (and pricier) rooms in order to get the 10% discount, or that you must fly on a certain flight, or pay in advance. All this may be fine, but you also may be able to do better by ignoring the senior discount and looking for normal cost-cutting deals as described in this book. For instance, if a hotel is offering a special weekend rate, that rate will usually be much better than the normal "rack rates" minus 10%. The same goes for transportation: if you must pay full fare to get the 10%, you may do better by signing up for an excursion or promotional fare.

Another stipulation often made is that one must arrange in advance to get the discount. You can't just pull off the highway at a chain motel (in some cases) and sign up for a room at a 10% discount. They want you to help them plan their workload by reserving in advance. In theory, that's the way it works. In practice, they won't turn you—or your request for the discount—down if they have the space and it looks as though it'll go unused.

> Be careful and calculate exactly what you'll be getting with your senior discount. . . . You may do better by ignoring the senior discount and looking for normal cost-cutting deals as described in this book.

THE UNITED STATES GOLDEN AGE PASSPORT: The United States government issues a Golden Age Passport to those 62 and over that entitles holders to enter all National Monuments and National Parks for free. Proof of age is required. For general information call 202/343-4747. State and city governments also offer a variety of discounts. Find out about them by checking with the local Office for the Aging or look up the number of the Senior Hot Line—most major cities have one.

THE EUROPEAN INTER-RAIL SENIOR PASS: All kinds of senior citizen discounts on transportation are available. In Europe one of the best, but *for European residents only,* is the Inter-Rail Senior Pass, which may be purchased in 17 countries for first- or second-class travel. It is valid for one month, and allows you to pay 50% of regular fare in the country of purchase, then ride free in all others. Obviously, it's best to buy it in a small country like Luxembourg. These passes can be purchased at any railroad ticket office (you'll need proof of at least six months' residency in a European country) in the participating countries: Austria, Switzerland, France, Germany, Luxembourg, Belgium, the Netherlands, Greece, Portugal, Denmark, Sweden, Norway, Finland, Hungary, Yugoslavia, Rumania, and Spain.

ELDERHOSTEL: One exciting program offered to the over-60s is the remarkable Elderhostel program, which enables seniors to study at various colleges and universities throughout the U.S., Canada, Britain, and Scandinavia. Courses range from dance, literature, and art to astronomy, finance, ecology, and sociology. Although the courses are given year round, during the summer months more programs are offered and the costs may be a little lower because dorm accommodations are available. Prices from $225 a week cover room, board, tuition, and some extracurricular activities. To find out more about Elderhostel, contact the state and provincial offices nearest you (check your phone book, or information in the nearest large city), or write to Elderhostel, Suite 400, 80 Boylston St., Boston, MA 02116 (tel. 617/426-7788).

PLEASANT FAMILY TRAVEL

When I was in junior high school, my parents debated taking a vacation to Montréal and Québec City. This was a great adventure for us, because as children we had always gone on vacation to the same lovely state park in Pennsylvania. My father charged me with gathering information for the trip, and started me off by pointing out the coupons attached to travel advertisements in magazines and newspapers. In no time I had a bulging file of maps, color brochures, French phrase books, historical walking tours, and technical explanations of the wondrous St. Lawrence Seaway. I loved it.

My father hated to be bothered with making travel plans. When he traveled, his corporation made all the plans and reservations. By "unloading" the vacation planning task on me, he made the vacation a child's adventure dream come true. What a stroke of luck that he hated planning! I can imagine how boring it would be for a child to be loaded into the car with no more idea about the destination than the strange word "Québec." Endless miles of driving, hotels popping up from nowhere, unfamiliar food, other children who didn't speak my language. It could have been a disaster. Instead, it was a dream-come-true. As soon as I got home, I used my new-found capabilities as a travel planner to chart make-believe trips throughout the world, using those marvelous coupons that said "Send for a free color brochure." Years later, I actually took many of the trips.

Actively involving the rest of your family in travel planning is absolutely necessary for a good trip.

Even adults can suffer from a powerful sense of being lost, in limbo, when they have had no active part in travel planning. If you're the one who has everything all mapped out, you may find it difficult to comprehend the problem. Showing others an itinerary may not be enough. They've got to be involved in the trip; it must mean something to them. There must be a mental panorama: tomorrow and the next day we'll be in Montréal, a city I know from travel folders and historical booklets; after that to Québec City, which looks medieval and has quaint, winding streets and horse-drawn carriages. Not only must your family be able to picture the destinations, they must have a sense of where they will be, when. No one likes living in ignorance of where he will be in approximately a week's time.

Actively involving the rest of your family in travel planning is absolutely necessary for a good trip. Be especially careful to do this if you are the take-command type. Delegate responsibilities, and then accept the results gracefully. It is not the actual trip that is important here, but each family member's mental picture of it. One cannot enjoy even the best vacation trip when forced to live in an eternal present jammed up against an inscrutable future.

THE PRICELESS GRIPE-AND-GRUMP NOTEBOOK: Children often find long trips boring and unsettling, and the irritation of boredom and unfamiliarity may sometimes come out in complaints, battles with siblings, and general moaning and groaning.

To save yourself having to listen to every gripe and grump, prepare beforehand by providing each child with a little pocket notebook and a pencil. Have the children label their notebooks "Gripes and Grumps," and make a rule that each child must write down complaints rather than voicing them during the trip. Tell the children, "We'll read and listen to all the complaints at the end of the trip, and then we'll decide who's right and who's wrong."

Each time during the trip that a child becomes grumpy, everyone in the family can say, "Put it in your notebook!" Writing the complaint down will, in most cases, dissolve the grump entirely after only a few minutes. And at the end of the trip, when the

children are back among their friends in familiar surroundings, the gripe-and-grump notebooks will probably be forgotten altogether.

Reducing Family Expenses

Traveling with children can be dauntingly expensive. All those restaurant meals—whether fully eaten
or not—must be paid for, and if you want privacy at
the end of the day, you'll need two hotel rooms, one
for you and one for the children. The advantage you
have as a family is bargaining power: the hotel, restaurant, or attraction you patronize is getting twice as
much business, so they should be willing to give a
discount.

TRANSPORTATION: Airlines have strict rules about
who must pay, and how much, when it comes to
children. There are family discounts, but they are not
too exciting (except for the occasional super promotions—spouse goes free, children pay half fare, etc.).
Airlines would just as soon try to attract singles or
couples for those empty seats.

Trains are better, and family plans help here. Children tend to enjoy trains more than airplanes as there
is more room to get up and stroll around, meet new
people, and play with other children.

But a family's best bargain is a car. It costs little
more to transport five or six than it does one. Whether
it's your family car or a rental car, a private auto is the
cost-effective way to go. It allows you to stop when
you want (or must), and to camp if you like. An even
better choice would be a mobile camper (your own or a
rental).

SAVING ON ACCOMMODATIONS: Every hotel and
motel that features two double beds in a room should

allow your children (teenage or younger) to stay for free. (Many extend the privilege to under-18s). At most, they should charge only $10 or $20 extra. If they charge more, they have a reason for discouraging children as guests: perhaps the resort rate structure dictates that each bed must yield maximum income.

Most of the large hotel and motel organizations feature family plans that allow kids to stay in their parents' room for free. If your chosen hotel has no such policy, work one out with the clerk or manager. Unless the place is full, they will be willing to haggle. Often the best arrangement is to take a suite or junior suite at normal price (which is less than two normal double rooms) and have it set up to sleep all of you. Another arrangement is to get two double rooms for the price of two singles—you save a little money, and you get a lot more luxury. Remember: what you are trying to do is utilize hotel space that would otherwise go empty, because that's how you'll get a good price. What the hotel clerk is trying to do is get your business without giving up other business. He is used to making special arrangements for families (though you may not be used to it), and the suite-for-price-of-a-room or two-doubles-at-singles-price arrangements are just face-saving devices. In fact, he's simply dropping the price for you. If the hotel is not full, he'll be willing to do so. Remember that.

Families sometimes end up staying in the more luxurious hotels and motels for good reasons. They need extra convenience and the larger hotels tend to have better family services: babysitters, bassinets and cribs, bottles and diapers.

OVERCOMING THE SOLO TRAVELER'S PROBLEMS

During the research for my guidebook on Turkey, I came across an old Victorian-era hotel in Istanbul. Prices were low, but so they should have been as the rooms were well worn and somewhat drab. Still, I gave the aged Hotel Bristol great play in my guide. Why? Because the Bristol, built to house British commercial travelers, had dozens of single rooms.

Except for YMCAs and those odd Japanese "capsule hotels," no lodgings being built are designed to accommodate the single traveler. When it comes to air, rail, or bus tickets, entry to a museum or cinema, the single traveler does as well as anyone else. But in lodgings and to a lesser extent in restaurants, the single traveler is at a distinct disadvantage.

There are two ways of looking at the lodging problem, as there are two ways of viewing a half-full glass of water. Just as the glass can be seen as either half full or half empty, a hotel room in a modern lodging establishment can be seen as underutilized if occupied by one, or super-efficiently utilized if occupied by two. Those faded single rooms at Istanbul's Hotel Bristol had *bathrooms* the size of today's standard-size hotel bedroom, so actual floor space has little to do with it. Rather, it is the hotel management's attitude that matters.

We've already studied some of these attitudes. One of them is "It costs us little more in the way of sheets, towels, water, and electricity to lodge two people instead of one, so the double price should be only a bit higher than the single price." Another is "We could lodge two people where that one person is staying, so the one person will have to pay almost as much as two—no sense losing that profit just because we agree to put up a single traveler."

Alas, all too often it is the second attitude that prevails, and as a single traveler you can expect to meet with it. You enter the lobby, approach the desk, ask if there are any rooms, and the clerk answers your question with another question: "For one or two persons?" As there are hardly any one-person rooms in existence, the question really is an answer: "For two persons I have rooms; for one person, maybe not."

In a situation where rooms are in short supply, your battle is all uphill. Forget about getting discounts. The clerk hesitates even to give you a room, let alone a discount. Your attitude at this point should be the first of the two mentioned above, namely that the single-room price is very adequate compensation for the use of the room; the two-person price is gravy, and the hotel shouldn't demand it.

> If they won't rent you a room at the single rate, try something like "Then, I'm afraid I'll have to go elsewhere," and start walking away.

If they won't rent you a room at the single rate, try saying something like "Then, I'm afraid I'll have to go elsewhere," and start walking away. More often than not this will produce a quick reaction and a room for you at a fair price.

If the hotel is not busy, a single traveler has as much chance of getting a discount as a couple. Indeed, the whole idea of "commercial rates" was to give a break to the frequent, single business traveler. Some of the big hotel and motel chains have direct arrangements with big commercial firms regarding discounts: the firm's travel department books all company travelers into the chain's facilities at special rates. But most hotels and motels will take a chance that you're a commercial traveler (why else would you be traveling alone?) and that you'll come back again. So look like you're there on business, and then ask for a commercial discount. They'll ask what company you work for. They'll also probably ask for an ID. Your company identification card or a business card of some kind should do the trick.

An informal survey of hotel chains turned up this information: rates are usually set not by the chain, but by each individual hotel manager, based on the competition at the time. You might want to review Chapter 9 on this point—there is much you can do to get the rate down.

Avoiding the Single Supplement

Although it seems very unfair to penalize the single traveler, it is done, and only by taking action yourself can you hope to avoid paying a single supplement on such items as package tours. When booking a tour, if you're willing to share with another single, always ask the tour operator (or have your travel agent ask the tour operator) to match you up with another solo traveler. Also, know that there are organizations founded specifically to help the single traveler. For example, Frommer Books operates a Travel Club that publishes a quarterly newspaper containing several columns for readers—including a share-a-trip column used by travelers seeking companions to share expenses. There are many other organizations that will perform similar services for a small fee. Cruises and tours strictly for people traveling alone (no couples or families accepted) are run by Singleworld, 444 Madison Ave., New York, NY 10022 (tel. 212/758-2433 or toll free 800/223-6490). Singles may choose private accommodations or can share rooms if they wish.

On cruises, there is much you can do. For instance, Cunard Line has established a plan whereby single travelers can apply for single-occupancy standby. Thirty days or less before departure, if places are available, a single pays only the normal rate (no single supplement) for a whole cabin.

Another Cunard plan will match you up with another traveler. If you do this, there's no need to wait on standby.

The Cunard Line has also set aside 100 single cabins on the *QE2*, in an attempt to please single passengers.

Even though other lines may not offer these plans formally, you may propose such arrangements. In many cases, cruise lines will be happy to cooperate.

Another service for joining up would-be travelmates is Travel Share International, P.O. Box 30365, Santa Barbara, CA 93130 (tel. 805/682-9955). Founded by Adele Rosen, Travel Share is a membership club. You pay an annual fee of $99, or a lifetime fee of $299, send in a photo, a short biography, and your goals in travel, and you receive a directory (published every two months) entitled *Key to Adventure* filled with the photos, first names, biographies, and travel goals of all the other members. After you've chosen a likely traveling companion from the directory, Travel Share sends you a complete profile, and you then contact the prospective partner on your own. Travel Share does not guarantee suitability or compatibility, but their approach gives you a good head start toward finding someone who shares your interests and tastes. Art lovers, adventure buffs, fishing enthusiasts, sports lovers, gourmands can all look for simpatico friends to share the trip—and banish the dreaded "single supplement." The main concern here is companionship, not romance, though the latter does break out from time to time.

Enjoying a Table for One

In my guidebook research, I often must dine in restaurants alone. It's not nearly as much fun as dining with another, and it demands special precautions. I have a pleasant, somewhat gullible look about me, I never confess that I'm inspecting the restaurant for a guidebook, and so I frequently am asked to sit next to the kitchen doors, or the silverware racks, or the drafty doorway, or the cash register. Consequently, I am now a master at the steely look and the tense but even tone of voice that communicates to the hostess or maître d' that such a table is unacceptable. Unspoken, but looming large behind that statement, is the question "Do you want my business, or not?" If so, then I had better get a more acceptable table.

The table by the kitchen door, or street door, or silverware clatter, is for customers who arrive later, when the restaurant has filled and when no alternative is available. They can then choose, on the basis of what's available, whether they wish to dine there or not. They can always wait for a better table to be vacated. This whole business has absolutely nothing to do with single or double.

It is proper and polite to accept a small table, well positioned, if you're dining alone. And if the little table is not horribly placed, why not? Asking for the very best table in the house, and asking for a decent table, are two completely different things. But if the management has lacked foresight and placed all the little tables in bad places, why should you be asked to give up your dining pleasure? They won't charge you any less because you're at a bad table. If things get tense, and they won't give you a decent table because it's larger, tell them you would be glad to have them seat someone else there as well. They then have no excuse for not giving in. Besides, this way you might meet someone interesting, which brings us to one of the great advantages of traveling alone.

Single Travel Is More Adventurous

Traveling in twos is more comfortable, but single travel is more adventurous. Traveling by yourself, you will definitely miss having someone along when that exquisite scene comes into view, or the theater performance is superb, or the cuisine is fantastic. You will also feel very alone when you miss the train, or sprain an ankle, or walk back to your hotel at 1 a.m., or can't speak the local language. That's the way it is. But you must dismiss the idea that single travel is any less rewarding than traveling with others. It's not. Besides, there are things you can do when you're lonely.

The first is to write. Take time and set down your experiences, or pour out your heart, if that's what's needed, into a diary or into a letter to someone you love. The act of writing is cathartic, and more than that, it is a very real way of enjoying that communication you lack. Although there is a time lag, you are in fact sharing that beautiful view or that frustration over the language with someone you love. And it is much better to write than to telephone, because a phone call catches a person unaware and unready. They may be busy with something else, and it will certainly take them some minutes (at what seems like $1,000,000 each) to come around and figure out who it is that's calling, and from where, and why. Phone calls have their place, of course. They are certainly a quick way of reassuring yourself that your world still exists, and that there are indeed familiar places and faces back home, not just this strange, unintelligible, and horribly *indifferent* foreign world.

If it's any comfort, couples traveling together also feel homesick and lonely for familiar sights and friends. It's just a bit more poignant when you're alone.

But being alone has its compensations. The possibilities for new acquaintances, experiences, and adventures are virtually unlimited for the single traveler. Even the most outgoing couples tend to insulate themselves against the world outside—that's where the comfort of traveling together comes from. And if you insulate yourself, you automatically limit the scope of your experiences.

Other ways to fend off loneliness are to spend part of your time making careful documentation of your trip. Draw up plans for a show of your photographs, or design (on paper) a recording you'd like to edit from live sound taping you've done. As you see the sights and explore new experiences, you will have a context and a purpose. Your show or recording can give people back home a comprehensive and balanced view of your travels. To make sure it does, you've got to go out of your way to get those extra photos that will fill gaps in the story. With an active purpose such as this, you forget at once the docile and disheartening role of passive sightseer. This is for real. You don't have to be going to some romantic spot or wild jet-set haven. Virtually anyplace in the world can be of interest to someone who hasn't been there, as each place has its own particular character, things to see and do, culinary quirks, and states of mind.

Singleness Loves Company

The oldest answer to singleness is also the simplest: other singles. You must make yourself realize that there are many others in precisely your situation at this very moment, thinking your thoughts and feeling what you feel. And in this well-traveled world, there are probably several such people very close by. All you need to do is find them. Cafés, restaurants, pubs, promenades, lookouts, beaches—these are places people go to see and be seen. If you can just get up the courage to break the ice, you'll be able to dispel the sense of loneliness at once. How to do it? The direct approach is usually best. When you notice someone who is probably your type, go right up and ask the time, or if they know a good restaurant nearby, or a good hotel, or what there is that's interesting to do. If it's obvious to the other person that you're only after conversation, the approach automatically becomes a compliment ("You look interesting—I'd like to find out more about you"). Don't be discouraged when you find that the person is waiting for someone else, or that she needs to be alone, or that he doesn't speak your language. That's going to happen. Remember: you're looking for one of the numerous people who need just what you do—warmth and human conversation. When you meet them, you'll know it right away. They'll respond just the way you would if someone approached you. The eager response says it all.

The Single Woman

Yes, it is more difficult for a woman traveling alone. (And I suppose it's no compensation to know that a man traveling alone will have more problems too. Traveling in a couple is safer for *both* parties!) But it's done all the time with minimal risk, and you can do it too.

Many women have written to me regarding their experiences in Mediterranean countries, certainly among the world's most bothersome for single women. From most of these travelers the message was the same: common sense and awareness will suffice; paranoia is unnecessary. Unpleasant situations will appear. Most will contain no real danger. But all will affront your self-respect and independence as a capable, liberated woman. There may be little you can do about it, and the sense of annoyance and frustration may be very great.

The frustration may be greater because you don't have enough acquaintance with the local culture to interpret the signs and signals present in such a situation. What about the taxi driver who tells you to sit up front with him so you can see the view? Is he truly being nice? Will you miss something pretty? Or is it an improper suggestion? Do Mediterranean women get pinched and followed all the time like this? If not, how do they get rid of it?

The only way to find out is to learn more about the culture. This may not bring satisfaction in the form which you would prefer. You might find out that local custom demands a single woman should never go to the beach alone. Rather, she should go with other women friends, or with relatives, or in a mixed group. "But there's all that gorgeous beach out there, and I just want to be alone on it!" you say. That may simply be impossible. To the locals, it may appear as odd as someone undressing on a Fifth Avenue bus in summer. That too would be natural and seemingly rational—on a sweltering day—but it's just not done, and that's that. To a nudist from Polynesia, such a benighted attitude toward comfortable Fifth Avenue bus travel might be completely incomprehensible, but the Polynesian would have to conform to local custom in any case.

With time, many such problems can be solved in accordance with local custom. You will find others with whom to share the beach, or will attach yourself—for cultural purposes—to an existing beach group. You will learn such things as train-compartment etiquette, whereby an older couple may "adopt" a single woman for the duration of the trip, looking after her honor and dignity, and assuring her respectability. Their icy stares and even, well-chosen words

---

If you're going to be spending thousands of dollars on a once-in-a-lifetime trip, make sure that you'll be getting what *you* want. Compare itineraries. . . . Then look at the other items. . . . Ask questions.

---

will drive off any interlopers with questionable intentions—they're doing for you what they expect your parents would do for their daughter in your country.

Perhaps the fastest way to learn the customs of a country is to appeal to an older woman who lives there. Even if she doesn't speak your language, you can get your message across. The situations are universal and age-old, quickly comprehensible, and almost as quickly disposed of by someone familiar with them.

TRAVEL INFORMATION ESPECIALLY FOR WOMEN: As I write this, plans are being finalized for publication of *Woman Traveler*, a national full-color magazine addressing the pleasures and problems of being a woman on the road. Publisher Jeanine Moss founded a women's travel newsletter entitled *Connections* in 1983, and the idea for *Woman Traveler* grew out of the success of that effort. Subscription rates and information will be available by the time you read this. Write to *Woman Traveler*, P.O. Box 6117, New York, NY 10150 (tel. 212/832-2052).

Unmarried Couples

In this modern world, there is little obstacle presented to traveling couples who are not married. No matter what the reason for your traveling together, most hotels will accept you without question. In foreign hotels, where you may have to present your passports to register, simply present both passports at the desk. In these days of liberal associations, and women who retain their maiden/professional name even in marriage, having two different names checking in raises no problem. You would not normally be expected to have two separate rooms.

The exceptions might be in particularly religious or conservative areas or hotels, or in a few bed-and-breakfast inns where the proprietors are particularly worried about propriety. But these are few and far between.

SPECIAL-INTEREST TRAVEL

What about something offbeat for your next trip? These days it's possible to sign up for a ten-day birdwatching trip to Iceland, a trek by dogsled across Greenland, a bicycle tour of the People's Republic of China, or a Land Rover expedition in Yemen. Shoot the rapids on the Euphrates in eastern Turkey, dive to inspect coral off the coast of Sinai, or hike through ancient kingdoms in the Himalayas. The world is open to you for exploration more than you may have realized!

Some of the fields of adventure for which there are

organized tours are these: adventure cruises, archeological digs, astronomy and eclipse-chasing, balloon-
ing, beer-lover tours, cycling, dog sledding in Alaska,
fishing, golf, hang gliding, health, horseback riding,
kayaking, mountain climbing, music and bands, natural history, nature excursions, parachuting, rail adventures and steam trains, safaris, sailing, scuba diving,
skiing, trekking, white water rafting, and yacht chartering. Ask your travel agent about these tours, or look
for them in the books described a bit farther along in
this section.

Many of these special expeditions are expensive,
however. Small groups, specially organized and accompanied by an experienced group leader, flying to
infrequently visited places, are going to pay more than
mass travelers on heavily traveled routes to mass-
production resorts. You must select your adventure
trip carefully, and perhaps ask for references from
satisfied customers—if you're about to put out $1,000
or $2,000 for a few weeks' travel, you have a right to
get opinions.

Consider any adventure destination and you'll find
several companies offering almost identical itineraries
at very similar prices. For example, there are half a
dozen or so companies operating safaris to East Africa. Don't just compare the overall price. If you're
going to be spending thousands of dollars on a once-in-
a-lifetime trip, make sure that you will be getting what
you want. Compare itineraries. One may visit several
game parks; another may visit only one or two game
parks and spend more time in Nairobi, let's say. Select
the itinerary for you. Then look at the other items. Are
all meals included in the price? Is transportation included both from the United States and within Africa?
If you have any questions or doubts in your mind,
query the company (it's always wise to get the facts in
writing, by the way).

For the skiing enthusiast the best values are available to members of ski clubs. For information on clubs in the eastern United States, write to the **U.S. Ski Association,** P.O. Box 727, Brattleboro, VT 05301; for other regions, the **U.S. Ski Association Sports Division,** P.O. Box 100, Park City, UT 84060.

Another wonderful way to really get to know the country you're visiting and save money over a regular vacation is to study there. Many, many summer programs are offered the world over. For a comprehensive guide, send $19.95 for a copy of *Vacation Study Abroad* to the Communications Division, Institute of International Education, 809 United Nations Plaza, New York, NY 10017 (tel. 212/984-5412). It contains programs for all ages. If you do study abroad, the college or institution will often be willing to find you lodgings with a family for a very low price. This is one way to really capture the flavor and life of the people.

Believe it or not, many companies, universities, societies, and nonprofit organizations sponsor varied programs of special-interest travel. You can help save endangered wildlife, take part in an expedition to record data on an eclipse, witness new volcanic activity—almost anything imaginable. Most of these organizations work through travel agents, so ask your agent about trips by Sobek, University of California at Berkeley ("Berkeley Expeditions"), Earthwatch, Mountain Travel, etc.

The Adventure Book, published by Sobek's International Explorer's Society (P.O. Box 1089, Angels Camp, CA 95222), is a beautiful introduction to the world of adventure and special-interest travel. Another guide, designed more for travel agents, is the *Specialty Travel Index,* published by Specialty Travel Index, 305 San Anselmo Ave., Suite 217, San Anselmo, CA 94960 (tel. 415/459-4900). It's mailed to travel agents, for free, twice a year. Individuals may order it for $5 per year. Finally, *Archaeology* magazine has a directory of 75 active archeological sites, all over the world. For a copy of the directory, write to *Archaeology*, 53 Park Pl., New York, NY 10001.

Another book filled with adventure possibilities is *Adventure Travel Abroad*, published by Adventure Guides, Inc., 36 East 57th St., New York, NY 10022 (tel. 212/355-6334), for $14. The book is over 200 pages long, listing more than 350 adventure trips, from jeep expeditions through those by elephant, camel, luxury barge, or mule caravan.

THE ULTIMATE TRAVEL VALUE: WORKING ABROAD

Early in his eventful life, Ernest Hemingway recognized that you never really know a place until you've earned your living there. Even staying a month in some city or country will tell you less than if you must get along on your own wages for a week.

Working while you travel is the most cost-effective travel of all. Stories abound of intrepid types who set out with $100 in their pockets and return two years later with $800, having traveled to the tip of South America, or across Asia, or 10,000 miles in North America. To do this, one needs a high tolerance for uncertainty and inconvenience, plus a lot of time. If your time is limited, you've got to plan well in advance.

The big hurdle to employment abroad is the work permit. As unemployment is a worldwide problem, no country wants foreigners to come in and take jobs from its own people. Usually you need exceptional qualifications—some skill that cannot be found in the native job market—to procure a work permit legally.

However, there are ways that you can work abroad, particularly if you just want to work a short time (several weeks or months). You can often get a job by talking to the boss, arranging for payment in cash, and setting up an excuse for why you're there. Scandinavian women easily get seasonal jobs as hostesses in Mediterranean resort bars and lounges; college-educated North Americans, Britons, and Australians can often support themselves by giving English lessons in non-English-speaking countries (talk to executives at banks and trading companies—they're the best prospects). Small-scale, short-term employment can be and is carried out this way.

There are lots of other possibilities, though. You can work for a voluntary service organization (they sometimes help pay expenses), or participate in an internship program, or work at an archeological dig, or lead a group of young people, or participate in the life of a kibbutz.

To work on a kibbutz, contact the Kibbutz Aliya Desk, Jewish Agency, 27 West 20th St., 9th Floor, New York, NY 10011 (tel. 212/255-1338).

The best source of information is the *Whole World Handbook,* put together by the Council on International Education Exchange and sold in the travel sections of bookstores (under $10).

If you're a student you can take advantage of the special arrangements made by the Council on International Educational Exchange for students to work abroad during vacations.

DISABLED GLOBE-TROTTERS

Much has been done to open the world to the handicapped. There are now numerous guidebooks on the market describing the ease or difficulty of access, the special facilities available, and the steps necessary in vacation travel for those who are blind, hearing-impaired, in wheelchairs, or have suffered from stroke or another debilitating illness. Some guides deal with the subject of handicapped travel in general, and others give lots of detailed information on specific destinations. Check at your local library and bookstore. If you don't find what you need, look in *Books in Print* at the library or bookstore under the "Travel" and "Handicapped" headings.

There are also special tours for disabled globe-trotters operated by several travel companies, including these:

Evergreen Travel Service, 19505 44th Ave. W., Lynnewood, WA 98036 (tel. 206/776-1184).

Flying Wheels Travel, 143 West Bridge, P.O. Box 382, Owatonna, MN 55060 (tel. toll free 800/533-0363).

Whole Person Tours, Bayonne, NJ (tel. 201/858-3400).

APPENDIX

Travel Resources

The Four Laws are fully sufficient to get you what you want in the way of travel information. But in gratitude for your interest and patronage, I've included here several comprehensive lists of information sources. Using these lists will speed you on your way to more rewarding, less expensive travel. If you find a new item which should be included in any of these lists, please write to me, personally, and bring it to my attention. My address is at the end of Chapter 2.

1. Tourist Offices of Foreign Countries
2. State Tourism Departments and City Convention and Visitors Bureaus
3. Travel Bookstores and Outfitters
4. Car Rental Companies

APPENDIX 1:
TOURIST OFFICES OF FOREIGN COUNTRIES

Remember that many countries maintain information offices in numerous cities, so you might want to check your local telephone directory for a nearby office if you live in a major urban area such as Chicago, Los Angeles, Miami, New York, or Toronto. Another tip is to contact the major airline which flies to your destination; in some instances, the national airline acts as a country's tourism office as well. In any case, you can always get what you want from the addresses below.

North America

BERMUDA: Bermuda Department of Tourism, 310 Madison Ave., New York, NY 10017 (tel. 212/818-9800).

CANADA: Tourism Canada, 1251 Avenue of the Americas, 16th Floor, New York, NY 10020 (tel. 212/757-4917).

MEXICO: Mexican National Tourist Council, 405 Park Ave., Suite 1002, New York, NY 10022 (tel. 212/755-7261).

Caribbean and West Indies

CARIBBEAN: Caribbean Tourism Association, 20 East 46th St., New York, NY 10164 (tel. 212/682-0435). Here's a list of the association's member countries; an asterisk (*) indicates that the country also has its own tourism information office, listed below: Anguilla, Aruba*, Barbados*, Belize, Bonaire*, Cayman Islands*, Curaçao*, Dominica, Dominican Republic*,

French West Indies* (Guadeloupe, Martinique, St. Barts, St. Martin), Haiti*, Jamaica*, Montserrat, Panama*, Puerto Rico*, St. Kitts/Nevis*, St. Lucia*, St. Vincent and the Grenadines*, Surinam, Turks and Caicos Islands*, U.S. Virgin Islands*, Venezuela*.

ANTIGUA: Antigua Department of Tourism, 610 Fifth Avenue, Suite 311, New York, NY 10020 (tel. 212/541-4117).

ARUBA: Aruba Tourism Authority, 1270 Avenue of the Americas, Suite 2212, New York, NY 10020 (tel. 212/246-3030 or toll free 800/862-7822).

BAHAMA ISLANDS: Bahamas Tourist Office, 150 East 52nd St., 28th Floor, New York, NY 10022 (tel. 212/758-2777).

BARBADOS: Barbados Board of Tourism, 800 Second Ave., New York, NY 10017 (tel. 212/986-6516).

BONAIRE: Bonaire Tourist Information Office, 275 Seventh Ave., 19th Floor, New York, NY 10001 (tel. 212/242-0000).

BRITISH VIRGIN ISLANDS: British Virgin Islands Tourist Board, 370 Lexington Ave., New York, NY 10017 (tel. 212/696-0400 or toll free 800/835-8530).

CAYMAN ISLANDS: Cayman Islands Department of Tourism, 420 Lexington Avenue, Suite 2312, New York, NY 10170 (tel. 212/682-5582); also offices in Atlanta, Chicago, Dallas, Houston, Los Angeles, Miami, Seattle, and Toronto.

CURAÇAO: Curaçao Tourist Board, 400 Madison Ave., Suite 311, New York, NY 10017 (tel. 212/751-8266).

DOMINICAN REPUBLIC: Dominican Tourist Information Center, 485 Madison Avenue, New York, NY 10022 (tel. 212/826-0750).

FRENCH WEST INDIES: French West Indies Tourist Board, 628 Fifth Avenue, New York, NY 10020 (tel. 212/757-1125). Members: Guadeloupe, Martinique, St. Barts, St. Martin.

GRENADA: Grenada Tourist Board, 141 East 44th St., New York, NY 10017 (tel. 212/687-9554).

HAITI: Haiti National Office of Tourism, 1270 Avenue of the Americas, New York, NY 10020 (tel. 212/757-3517).

JAMAICA: Jamaica Tourist Board, 866 Second Avenue, New York, NY 10017 (tel. 212/688-7650 or toll free 800/223-5225).

PUERTO RICO: Puerto Rico Tourism Company, 1290 Avenue of the Americas, Suite 2230, New York, NY 10104 (tel. 212/541-6630).

ST. LUCIA: St. Lucia Tourist Board, Suite 315, 41 East 42nd St., New York, NY 10017 (tel. 212/867-2950).

ST. MAARTEN / SABA / ST. EUSTATIUS: St. Maarten / Saba / St. Eustatius Information Office, 275 Seventh Ave., 19th Floor, New York, NY 10001 (tel. 212/989-0000).

TRINIDAD AND TOBAGO: Trinidad & Tobago Tourist Board, 400 Madison Ave., Suite 310, New York, NY 10017 (tel. 212/838-7750).

TURKS AND CAICOS ISLANDS: Turks and Caicos Tourist Board, Box 592617, Miami, FL 33159 (tel. 305/577-0133 or toll free 800/411-4419).

U.S. VIRGIN ISLANDS: U.S. Virgin Islands Division of Tourism, 1270 Avenue of the Americas, New York, NY 10020 (tel. 212/582-4520).

Central and South America

ARGENTINA: Embassy of the Argentina, 1600 New Hampshire Ave. NW, Washington, DC 20009 (tel. 202/939-6400).

BOLIVIA: Embassy of Bolivia, 3014 Massachusetts Ave. NW, Washington, DC 20008 (tel. 202/483-4410).

BRAZIL: Brazilian Tourism Office, 2 West 45th St., Room 1409, New York, NY 10036 (tel. 212/840-3320).

CHILE: Embassy of Chile, 1732 Massachusetts Ave. NW, Washington, DC 20036 (tel. 202/785-1746).

COLOMBIA: Colombian Government Tourism Office, 140 East 57th St., New York, NY 10022 (tel. 212/688-0151).

COSTA RICA: Costa Rican National Tourist Board, 200 S.E. 1st Street, Suite 402, Miami, FL 33131 (tel. 305/358-2150 or toll free 800/327-7033); or 3540 Wilshire Blvd., Suite 802, Los Angeles, CA 90010 (tel. 213/382-8080 or toll free 800/762-5909).

ECUADOR: Ecuatoriana Airlines, 1290 Avenue of the Americas, New York, NY 10104 (tel. 212/399-1180).

EL SALVADOR: Embassy of El Salvador, 2308 California Ave. NW, Washington, DC 20008 (tel. 202/265-3480).

GUATEMALA: Embassy of Guatemala, 2220 "R" Street, NW, Washington, DC 20008 (tel. 202/745-4952).

HONDURAS: Embassy of Honduras, 4301 Connecticut Ave. NW, Suite 100, Washington, DC 20008 (tel. 202/966-7700).

NICARAGUA: Embassy of Nicaragua, 1627 New Hampshire Ave. NW, Washington, DC 20009 (tel. 202/332-1643).

PANAMA: Panama Government Tourist Bureau, 630 Fifth Avenue, Suite 1414, New York, NY 10111 (tel. 212/869-2530).

PARAGUAY: Embassy of Paraguay, 2400 Massachusetts Ave. NW, Washington, DC 20008 (tel. 202/483-6960).

PERU: FOPTUR, Peru Tourist Office, 50 Biscayne Blvd., Suite 123, Miami, FL 33132 (tel. 305/374-0023).

URUGUAY: Embassy of Uruguay, 1918 "F" St. NW, Washington, DC 20006 (tel. 202/331-1313).

VENEZUELA: Contact any office of VIASA, Venezuela's national airline.

Europe

AUSTRIA: Austrian National Tourist Office, 500 Fifth Ave., New York, NY 10110 (tel. 212/944-6880).

BELGIUM: Belgian Tourist Office, 745 Fifth Ave., New York, NY 10151 (tel. 212/758-8130).

BULGARIA: Bulgarian Tourist Office, c/o Balkan Holidays USA Ltd., 161 East 86th St., New York, NY 10028 (tel. 212/722-1110).

CYPRUS: Cyprus Tourism Organization, 13 East 40th St., New York, NY 10016 (tel. 212/213-9100).

CZECHOSLOVAKIA: Czechoslovakia Travel Bureau, 10 East 40th St., 19th Floor, New York, NY 10016 (tel. 212/689-9720).

DENMARK: Danish Tourist Board, 655 Third Ave., New York, NY 10017 (tel. 212/949-2333).

FINLAND: Finnish Tourist Board, 655 Third Ave., New York, NY 10017 (tel. 212/949-2333).

FRANCE: French Government Tourist Office, 610 Fifth Ave., New York, NY 10020 (tel. 212/757-1125).

GERMANY, DEMOCRATIC REPUBLIC (EAST): German Democratic Republic Travel Bureau, Postfach 77, 1026 Berlin, East Germany.

GERMANY, FEDERAL REPUBLIC OF (WEST): German National Tourist Office, 747 Third Ave., New York, NY 10017 (tel. 212/308-3300).

GREAT BRITAIN: (See "United Kingdom," below.)

GREECE: Greek National Tourist Organization, 645 Fifth Ave., New York, NY 10022 (tel. 212/421-5777; in Chicago, tel. 312/782-1084; in Los Angeles, tel. 213/626-6696).

HOLLAND: (See "Netherlands," below.)

HUNGARY: IBUSZ Hungarian Travel Bureau, 630 Fifth Ave., Suite 520, New York, NY 10111 (tel. 212/582-7412; or Tourinform, V. Petofi Sandor u. 17–19, Budapest, Hungary).

ICELAND: Iceland Tourist Board, 655 Third Ave., 18th Floor, New York, NY 10017 (tel. 212/949-2333).

IRELAND (EIRE): Irish Tourist Board, 757 Third Ave., New York, NY 10017 (tel. 212/418-0800, or toll free 800/223-6470).

ITALY: Italian Government Travel Office, 630 Fifth Ave., New York, NY 10111 (tel. 212/245-4822).

LUXEMBOURG: Luxembourg National Tourist Office, 801 Second Ave., New York, NY 10017 (tel. 212/370-9850).

MALTA: Consulate of Malta, 249 East 35th St., New York, NY 10016 (tel. 212/725-2345).

MONACO: Monaco Government Tourist & Convention Bureau, 845 Third Ave., New York, NY 10022 (tel. 212/759-5227).

NETHERLANDS: Netherlands Board of Tourism, 355 Lexington Ave., New York, NY 10017 (tel. 212/370-7360).

NORWAY: Norwegian Tourist Board, 655 Third Ave., New York, NY 10017 (tel. 212/949-2333).

POLAND: ORBIS Polish Travel Bureau, Inc., 500 Fifth Ave., New York, NY 10110 (tel. 212/391-0844); or 333 N. Michigan Ave., Chicago, IL 60601 (tel. 312/236-9013).

PORTUGAL: Portuguese National Tourist Office, 548 Fifth Ave., New York, NY 10036 (tel. 212/354-4403).

ROMANIA: Rumanian National Tourist Office, 573 Third Ave., New York, NY 10016 (tel. 212/697-6971).

SPAIN: National Tourist Office of Spain, 665 Fifth Ave., New York, NY 10022 (tel. 212/759-8822); also offices in Beverly Hills, Chicago, Houston, and St. Augustine.

SWEDEN: Swedish Tourist Board, 655 Third Ave., New York, NY 10017 (tel. 212/949-2333).

SWITZERLAND: Swiss National Tourist Office, 608 Fifth Ave., New York, NY 10020 (tel. 212/757-5944).

TURKEY: Turkish Culture & Tourism Office, 821 United Nations Plaza, New York, NY 10017 (tel. 212/687-2194); or Turkish Information Center, 2010 Massachusetts Ave. NW, Washington, DC 20036 (tel. 202/833-8411).

UNITED KINGDOM: British Tourist Authority, 40 West 57th St., New York, NY 10019 (tel. 212/581-4700).

U.S.S.R.: Intourist (USSR), 630 Fifth Ave., Suite 868, New York, NY 10111 (tel. 212/757-3884).

YUGOSLAVIA: Yugoslav National Tourist Office, 630 Fifth Ave., New York, NY 10111 (tel. 212/757-2801).

Middle East and North Africa

EGYPT: Egyptian Tourist Authority, 630 Fifth Ave., New York, NY 10111 (tel. 212/246-6960; in San Francisco, tel. 415/781-7676).

ISRAEL: Israel Government Tourist Office, 350 Fifth Ave., New York, NY 10118 (tel. 212/560-0650).

JORDAN: Jordan Information Bureau, 2319 Wyoming Ave. NW, Washington, DC 20008 (tel. 202/265-1606).

MOROCCO: Moroccan National Tourist Office, 20 East 46th St., New York, NY 10017 (tel. 212/557-2520).

TUNISIA: Tunisian Information Office, 2408 Massachusetts Ave. NW, Washington, DC 20008 (tel. 202/234-6650).

TURKEY: (See under "Europe," above.)

Africa South of the Sahara

KENYA: Kenya Tourist Office, 424 Madison Ave., New York, NY 10017 (tel. 212/486-1300).

SOUTH AFRICA: South African Tourism Board, 747 Third Ave., New York, NY 10017 (tel. 212/838-8841 or toll free 800/822-5368).

TANZANIA: Embassy of Tanzania, 2139 "R" St. NW, Washington, DC 20008 (tel. 202/939-6125).

ZIMBABWE: Zimbabwe Tourist Office, 1270 Avenue of the Americas, Suite 1905, New York, NY 10020 (tel. 212/307-6565 or toll free 800/621-2381).

Asia and Oceania

AUSTRALIA: Australian Tourist Commission, 2121 Avenue of the Stars, Suite 1200, Los Angeles, CA 90067 (tel. 213/552-1988; in New York City, tel. 212/687-6300; in Toronto, tel. 416/487-2126).

BHUTAN: Bhutan Travel Service, 120 East 56th St., New York, NY 10022 (tel. 212/838-6382).

BRUNEI DARUSSALAM: Embassy of Brunei Darussalam, 2600 Virginia Ave., NW, Suite 300, Washington, DC 20037 (tel. 202/342-0159).

BURMA: Embassy of Burma, 2300 S St., NW, Washington, DC 20008 (tel. 202/332-9044).

CHINA, PEOPLE'S REPUBLIC: 60 E. 42nd St., Suite 465, New York, NY 10165 (tel. 212/867-0271).

COOK ISLANDS: Cook Islands Tourist Authority, P.O. Box 3647, Auckland, New Zealand; P.O. Box R177, Sydney, NSW 2000, Australia.

FIJI: Fiji Visitors Bureau, 6151 W. Century Blvd., Suite 524, Los Angeles, CA 90045 (tel. 213/417-2234 or toll free in CA 800/338-5686; in US 800/621-9604; in CN 800/647-7700).

HONG KONG: Hong Kong Tourist Association, 548 Fifth Ave., New York, NY 10036-5092 (tel. 212/869-5008); 421 Powell St., Suite 200, San Francisco, CA 94102-1568 (tel. 415/781-4582); 333 North Michigan Ave., Suite 2323, Chicago, IL 60601-3966 (tel. 312/782-3872).

INDIA: India Tourist Office, 30 Rockefeller Plaza, Suite 15, New York, NY 10112 (tel. 212/586-4901; in Chicago, tel. 312/236-6899; in Los Angeles, tel. 213/380-8855; in Toronto, tel. 416/962-3787).

INDONESIA: Indonesia Tourist Promotion Office,

3457 Wilshire Blvd., Los Angeles, CA 90010 (tel. 213/387-2078).

JAPAN: Japan National Tourist Organization, 630 Fifth Ave., Suite 2101, New York, NY 10111 (tel. 212/757-5640; in Chicago, tel. 312/332-3975; in Dallas, tel. 214/741-4931; in Los Angeles, tel. 213/623-1952; in San Francisco, tel. 415/989-7140; in Toronto, tel. 416/366-7140).

KIRIBATI: Government of the Republic of Kiribati, Ministry of Natural Resources Development, Box 261, Bairiki, Tarawa.

KOREA: Korea National Tourism Corp., 460 Park Ave., Suite 400, New York, NY 10022 (tel. 212/688-7543; in Los Angeles, tel. 213/623-1226; in Chicago, tel. 312/346-6660).

MACAU: Macau Tourist Information Bureau, 608 Fifth Ave., Suite 301, New York, NY 10020 (tel. 212/581-7465; in Honolulu, tel. 808/536-0719; in Los Angeles, tel. 213/851-3402 or toll free in CA 800/331-7150; in Toronto, tel. 416/593-1811).

MALAYSIA: Malaysian Tourist Information Center, 818 West Seventh St., Los Angeles, CA 90017 (tel. 213/689-9702).

MALDIVES REPUBLIC: Maldive Permanent Mission to the United Nations, 820 Second Ave., Suite 800C, New York, NY 10017 (tel. 212/599-6195).

MARSHALL ISLANDS REPUBLIC: Marshall Islands Government Washington Office, 1901 Pennsylvania Ave., NW, Suite 1004, Washington, DC 20006 (tel. 202/223-4952).

NEPAL: Embassy of Nepal, 2131 Leroy Place, NW, Washington, DC 20008 (tel. 202/667-4550); Nepal Consulate-General, 820 Second Ave., Suite 1200, New York, NY 10017 (tel. 212/370-4188); Nepal Consulate-General, 310 Dupont St., Toronto, ON M5R 1V9 (tel. 416/968-7252).

NEW ZEALAND: New Zealand Tourist & Publicity

Office, 630 Fifth Ave., Suite 530, New York, NY 10111 (tel. 212/698-4680; in Los Angeles, tel. 213/477-8241; in San Francisco, tel. 415/788-7404; in Vancouver, tel. 604/684-2117).

NORTHERN MARIANA ISLANDS COMMONWEALTH: Office of the Washington Representative, Commonwealth of the Northern Mariana Islands, 2121 "R" St., NW, Washington, DC 20008 (tel. 202/673-5869).

PAKISTAN: Contact Pakistan International Airlines offices in New York, Washington, Chicago, Houston, San Francisco, or Toronto; or the Pakistan Tourism Development Corp., House No 2, St. 61, F-7/4, Islamabad, Pakistan.

PALAU REPUBLIC Palau Liaison Office, 1441 Kapiolani Blvd., Suite 1120, Honolulu, HI 96814 (tel. 808/941-0988); or Palau Liaison Office, Hall of the States, 444 N. Capitol St., Suite 308, Washington, DC 20001 (tel. 202/624-7793).

PAPUA NEW GUINEA: Air Niugini, 5000 Birch St., Suite 3000 West Tower, Newport Beach, CA 92660 (tel. 714/752-5440).

PHILIPPINES: Philippine Ministry of Tourism, 1617 Massachusetts Ave., NW, Suite 304, Washington, DC 20036 (tel. 202/842-1664); or 556 Fifth Ave., New York, NY 10036 (tel. 212/575-7915; in Chicago, tel. 312/782-1707; in Los Angeles, tel. 213/487-4525; in San Francisco, tel. 415/956-4060; in Toronto, tel. 416/922-8880).

SINGAPORE: Singapore Tourist Promotion Board, 342 Madison Ave., New York, NY 10173 (tel. 212/687-0385); or 8484 Wilshire Blvd., Beverly Hills, CA 90211 (tel. 213/852-1901).

SOLOMON ISLANDS: Solomon Islands Mission to the United Nations, 820 Second Ave., New York, NY 10017 (tel. 212/599-6193).

SRI LANKA: Ceylon (Sri Lanka) Tourist Board, 2148

Wyoming Ave., NW, Washington, DC 20008 (tel. 202/483-4025).

TAHITI: Tahiti Tourist Promotion Board, 12233 W. Olympic Blvd., Suite 110, Los Angeles, CA 90064 (tel. 213/207-1919).

TAIWAN: Taiwan Visitors' Association, 1 World Trade Center, Suite 8855, New York, NY 10048 (tel. 212/466-0691 or 466-0692; in San Francisco, tel. 415/989-8677; in Chicago, tel. 312/346-1037).

THAILAND: Tourism Authority of Thailand, 5 World Trade Center, Suite 2449, New York, NY 10048 (tel. 212/432-0433); in Los Angeles, tel. 213/382-2353.

TONGA: Tonga Visitors Bureau, Box 37, Nuka'alofa, Tonga.

VANUATU: Director of Tourism, Republic of Vanuatu, Port Vila, Vanuatu.

APPENDIX 2:
STATE TOURISM DEPARTMENTS AND CITY CONVENTION AND VISITORS BUREAUS

The following is a selected list of state, territorial, and city tourism offices. Where a toll-free 800 number is available, it is given. However, the numbers are subject to change.

For a free directory of more than 250 convention and visitors bureaus in the U.S. and abroad that are members of the International Association of Convention and Visitor Bureaus, contact the association at P.O. Box 758, Champaign, IL 61820 (tel. 217/359-8881).

ALABAMA: Alabama Tourism and Travel Bureau, 532 So. Perry Street, Montgomery, AL 36104 (tel. 205/261-4169, or toll free 800/252-2262).

ALASKA: Alaska Division of Tourism, P.O. Box E, Juneau, AK 99811 (tel. 907/465-2010).

ALBERTA: Travel Alberta, 10025 Jasper Ave., 15th Floor, Edmonton, AB T5J 3Z3 (tel. toll free 800/661-8888).

AMERICAN SAMOA: American Samoa Office of Tourism, P.O. Box 1147, Pago Pago, American Samoa 96799

ARIZONA: Arizona Office of Tourism, 1480 E. Bethany Home Rd., Phoenix, AZ 85014 (tel. 602/255-3618 or toll free 800/528-8460).

Phoenix: Phoenix & Valley of the Sun Convention and Visitor's Bureau, 505 North 2nd St., Suite 300, Phoenix, AZ 85004 (tel. 602/254-6500).

Tucson: Tucson Visitor's Bureau, 450 West Paseo

Redondo, Suite 110, Tucson, AZ 85702 (tel. 602/792-1212).

ARKANSAS: Arkansas Dept. of Parks and Tourism, One Capitol Mall, Dept. 7970, Little Rock, AR 72201 (tel. 501/371-7777).

Hot Springs: Hot Springs Advertising & Promo. Commission, Convention and Visitors Bureau P.O. Box K, Hot Springs, AR 71902 (tel. 501/321-2277 or toll free 800/543-BATH).

BRITISH COLUMBIA: Tourism British Columbia, 802–865 Hornby St., Vancouver, BC V6Z 2G3 (tel. 604/660-2300).

CALIFORNIA: California Office of Tourism, 1121 "L" Street, Suite 103, Sacramento, CA 95814 (tel. toll free 800/862-2543).

San Francisco: San Francisco Convention and Visitor's Bureau, P.O. Box 6977, San Francisco, CA 94101 (1390 Market Street, Suite 260, San Francisco, CA 94102) (tel. 415/391-2000).

COLORADO: Colorado Tourism Board, 1625 Broadway, Suite 1700, Denver, CO 80202 (tel. 303/866-2205 or toll free 800/433-2656).

CONNECTICUT: Connecticut Travel Office, 210 Washington St. Hartford, CT 06106 (tel. 203/566-3385 or toll free 800/243-1685).

DELAWARE: Delaware Tourism Office, 99 Kings Hwy., P.O. Box 1401, Dover, DE 19903 (tel. 302/736-4254 or toll free 800/441-8846; in DE 800/282-8667).

DISTRICT OF COLUMBIA: Washington DC Convention & Visitors Association, Suite 250, 1575 Eye Street, NW, Washington, DC 20005 (tel. 202/789-7000 or toll free 800/422-8644).

FLORIDA: Florida Division of Tourism, 107 W. Gaines St., Suite 410-D, Tallahassee, FL 32301 (tel. 904/487-1462).

Miami: Greater Miami Convention and Visitors Bureau, 4770 Biscayne Blvd., Miami, FL 33137 (tel. 305/573-4300).

GEORGIA: Georgia Tourist Division, 230 Peachtree St., Suite 605, Atlanta, GA 30301 (tel. 404/656-3590).

GUAM: Guam Visitors Bureau, Box 3520, Agana, GU 96910; or Office of Congressman Ben Blaz, 1130 Longworth House Office Bldg., Washington, DC 20515 (tel. 202/225-1188).

HAWAII: Hawaii Visitors Bureau, 2270 Kalakaua Avenue, Suite 801, Honolulu, HI 96815 (tel. 808/923-1811).

IDAHO: Division of Tourism & Travel Development, State House Mall, Boise, ID 83720 (tel. 208/334-2470).

ILLINOIS: Office of Tourism, 620 East Adams, Springfield, IL 62701 (tel. 217/782-7139).

Chicago: Chicago Tourism Council, 806 N. Michigan Ave., Chicago, IL 60611 (tel. 312/280-5740).

INDIANA: Indiana Department of Commerce, Tourism Development Division, One N. Capitol Ave., Suite 700, Indianapolis, IN 46204-2288 (tel. 317/232-8860).

IOWA: Iowa Department of Economic Development, Tourism and Film Office, 200 E. Grand Ave., Des Moines, IA 50309 (tel. 515/281-3100 or 281-3679).

KANSAS: Kansas Division of Travel and Tourist Development, 400 W. Eighth St., Fifth Floor, Topeka, KS 66603 (tel. 913/296-2009).

KENTUCKY: Kentucky Department of Travel Development, Capital Plaza Tower, Frankfort, KY 40601 (tel. 502/564-4930 or toll free 800/225-8747).

LOUISIANA: Louisiana Tourist Development Commission, Box 94291, Baton Rouge, LA 70804 (tel. 504/925-3860).

New Orleans: Greater New Orleans Tourist & Convention Commission, 1520 Sugar Bowl Drive, New Orleans, LA 70112 (tel. 504/566-5011).

MAINE: Maine Publicity Bureau, Box 2300, 97 Winthrop St., Hallowell, ME 04347 (tel. 207/289-2423).

MANITOBA: Travel Manitoba, 7-155 Carlton St., Winnipeg, MB R3C 3H8 (tel. 204/945-4096).

MARYLAND: Maryland Office of Tourist Development, 45 Calvert St., Annapolis, MD 21401 (tel. 301/269-3517).

MASSACHUSETTS: Division of Tourism, 100 Cambridge Street, 13th Floor, Boston, MA 02202 (tel. 617/727-3201 or toll free 800/942-6277).

Boston: Greater Boston Convention & Visitors Bureau, Prudential Plaza, Box 490, Boston, MA 02199 (tel. 617/356-4100 or toll free 800/858-0200).

MICHIGAN: Michigan Travel Bureau, Department of Commerce, Box 30226, Lansing, MI 48909 (tel. 517/373-1195 or 800/543-2937).

MINNESOTA: Minnesota Office of Tourism, 375 Jackson Street, 250 Skyway Level, St. Paul, MN 55101 (tel. 612/296-5029 or 800/328-1461).

MISSISSIPPI: Department of Tourism & Development, Box 849, Jackson, MS 39205 (tel. 601/354-3414 or toll free 800/647-2290).

MISSOURI: Missouri Division of Tourism, Truman Office Bldg., P.O. Box 1055, Jefferson City, MO 65102 (tel. 314/751-4133).

MONTANA: Montana Travel Promotion, Department of Commerce, 1424 Ninth Ave., Helena, MT 59620 (tel. 406/449-2654 or toll free 800/548-3390).

NEBRASKA: Nebraska Travel & Tourism, P.O. Box 94666, Lincoln, NB 68509 (tel. 402/471-3796 or toll free 800/228-4307).

NEVADA: Nevada Commission on Tourism, Capitol Complex, 1100 E. William Street, Suite 106, Carson City, NV 89710 (tel. 702/885-4322 or toll free 800/237-0774).

Las Vegas: Las Vegas Convention and Visitors Authority, 3150 Paradise Rd., Las Vegas, NV 89123 (tel. 702/733-2323).

NEWFOUNDLAND: Newfoundland and Labrador Department of Development and Tourism, P.O. Box 2016, St. John's, NF A1C 5R8 (tel. toll free 800/563-6353).

NEW BRUNSWICK: New Brunswick Department of Tourism, Recreation and Heritage, P.O. Box 12345, Fredericton, NB E3B 5C3 (tel. toll free 800/561-0123).

NEW HAMPSHIRE: New Hampshire Office of Vacation Travel, 105 Loudon Rd., P.O. Box 856, Concord, NH 03301 (tel. 603/271-2343).

NEW JERSEY: Division of Travel and Tourism, CN 826, Trenton, NJ 08625 (tel. 609/292-2470).

Atlantic City: Greater Atlantic City Chamber of Commerce, 1301 Atlantic Ave., 2nd Fl., Atlantic City, NJ 08401 (tel. 609/345-2251).

NEW MEXICO: Economic Development & Tourism Dept., 1100 St. Francis Dr., Joseph Montoya Bldg., Santa Fe, NM 87503 (tel. 505/827-0291 or toll free 800/545-2040).

NEW YORK: Division of Tourism, New York State, 1 Commerce Plaza, Albany, NY 12245 (tel. 518/474-4116 or toll free 800/342-3810).

New York City: New York Convention & Visitors Bureau, 2 Columbus Circle, New York, NY 10019 (tel. 212/397-8200).

NORTHWEST TERRITORY: Travel Arctic, P.O. Box 1320, Yellowknife, NT X1A 2L9 (tel. 403/873-7200).

NORTH CAROLINA: Travel & Tourism Division, Department of Commerce, 430 N. Salisbury St., Raleigh, NC 27611 (tel. 800/847-4862).

NORTH DAKOTA: North Dakota Tourism Promotion, Library Memorial Bldg., 600 East Blvd., Bismarck, ND 58505 (tel. 701/224-2525 or toll free 800/437-2077).

NOVA SCOTIA: Nova Scotia Tourism Department, 136 Commercial St., Portland, ME 04101 (tel. toll free 800/

341-6096); or P.O. Box 456, Halifax, NS B3J 2R5 (tel. 902/424-5000).

OHIO: Ohio Office of Travel and Tourism, P.O. Box 1001, Columbus, OH 43216-1001 (tel. 614/466-8444 or toll free 800/282-5393).

OKLAHOMA: Tourism Promotion Division, 505 Will Rogers Bldg., Oklahoma City, OK 73105 (tel. 405/521-2464).

ONTARIO: Ontario Travel, Eaton Centre, 220 Yonge St., Toronto, ON M5B 2H1 (tel. toll free 800/268-3735).

Toronto: Metro Toronto Convention and Visitors Association, Eaton Centre, 220 Yonge St., Suite 110 (P.O. Box 510), Toronto, ON M5B 2H1 (tel. 416/979-3133).

OREGON: Oregon Tourism Division, 595 Cottage St., NE, Salem, OR 97310 (tel. 503/378-6309 or, toll free 800/547-7842; in OR 800/233-3306).

PENNSYLVANIA: Bureau of Travel Development, 416 Forum Bldg., Harrisburg, PA 17120 (tel. 717/787-5453 or toll free 800/847-4872).

Philadelphia: Convention & Visitors Bureau, 1515 Market Street, Suite 2020, Philadelphia, PA 19102 (tel. 215/636-1666).

PRINCE EDWARD ISLAND: Prince Edward Island Tourism, 105 Rochford St., Charlottetown, PE C1A 3T6 (tel. 902/892-7411).

PUERTO RICO: Puerto Rico Tourism Development Co., P.O. Box 3072, Old San Juan Station, San Juan, PR 00913 (tel. 809/721-2400).

QUÉBEC: Tourisme Québec, 770 Sherbrooke St. W., 14th Floor, Montréal, QC H3A 1G1 (tel. 514/873-2308).

RHODE ISLAND: Rhode Island Tourism Division, 7 Jackson Walkway, Providence, RI 02903 (tel. 401/277-2601).

SASKATCHEWAN: Tourism Saskatchewan, 2103 Eleventh Ave., Regina, SK S4P 3V6 (tel. 306/667-7191).

SOUTH CAROLINA: South Carolina Department of Parks, Recreation and Tourism, 1205 Pendleton St., Suite 106, Columbia, SC 29201 (tel. 803/734-0122).

SOUTH DAKOTA: South Dakota Dept. of Tourism, Capitol Lake Plaza, Pierre, SD 57501 (tel. 605/773-3301 or toll free 800/843-1930).

TENNESSEE: Tennessee Tourist Development, P.O. Box 23170, Nashville, TN 37202 (tel. 615/741-2158).

TEXAS: Travel & Information Division, State Dept. of Highways, 11th & Brazos Sts., Austin, TX 78701 (tel. 512/475-7123).

UTAH: Utah Travel Council, Council Hall, Capitol Hill, Salt Lake City, UT 84114 (tel. 801/533-5681).

VERMONT: Vermont Travel Division, 134 State St., Montpelier, VT 05602 (tel. 802/828-3236).

VIRGIN ISLANDS: Division of Tourism, P.O. Box 6400, St. Thomas, VI 00801 (tel. 809/774-8784).

VIRGINIA: Virginia Division of Tourism, 202 North 9th St., Richmond, VA 23219 (tel. 804/786-4484).

WASHINGTON: Washington State Tourism, 101 General Administration Bldg., Olympia, WA 98504 (tel. 206/753-5600 or 800/541-9274; in WA 800/562-4570).

Washington, DC: (See "District of Columbia," above.)

WEST VIRGINIA: West Virginia Department of Commerce, Division of Tourism, Bldg. 6, Capitol Complex, Charleston, WV 25305 (tel. 304/348-2286 or 800/225-5982).

WISCONSIN: Division of Tourism Development, P.O. Box 7606, Madison, WI 53707 (tel. 608/266-2161).

WYOMING: Wyoming Travel Commission, I-25 at College Dr., Cheyenne, WY 82002-0660 (tel. 307/777-7777 or toll free 800/225-5996).

YUKON: Tourism Yukon, P.O. Box 2703, Whitehorse, YK Y1A 2C6 (tel. 403/667-5340).

APPENDIX 3:
TRAVEL BOOKSTORES
AND OUTFITTERS

These are the places that stock more than the standard selection of travel guides. They know more about travel, and travel guides, and maps, and travel equipment, than normal stores. They should be your first stop when you set out shopping to prepare for a trip. Most will happily answer your questions and fill your orders by mail or telephone as well as in person, making them nationwide resources, really. If you know of a travel bookstore or travel outfitter that is not included below, write and tell me so that I can include it in the list in future editions of this book.

Nationwide Suppliers

AYH Travel Store, American Youth Hostels, P.O. Box 37613, Washington, DC 20013-7613 (tel. 202/783-6161). This is not really a store, but a service to provide hostellers (of any age) with important materials such as the *International Youth Hostel Handbook,* the *American Youth Hostels Handbook*, sheet sleeping sacks to be used in hostels, and membership in the American Youth Hostel organization.

Banana Republic, P.O. Box 7737, San Francisco, CA 94120 (tel. toll free 800/772-9977). The famous travel and safari clothing and gear outfitter, with numerous stores in major cities across the country, also has many stores with special travel book departments. Look for the book sections in the stores in Phoenix, Ariz.; San Francisco, Beverly Hills, and Santa Barbara, Calif.; Boulder, Colo; Farmington, Conn.;

Georgetown in Washington, D.C.; Boca Raton, Fla.; Atlanta, Ga.; Schaumburg, Ill.; Annapolis, Md.; Boston, Mass.; Grosse Pointe, Mich.; Minneapolis, Minn.; St. Louis, Mo.; East Princeton, N.J.; two in New York City, N.Y.; Ardmore and Philadelphia, Pa.; Austin and Houston, Tex.; Seattle, Wash.; and Milwaukee, Wis. By the time you read this, there will probably be travel book sections in the stores in these cities: Winter Park, Fla.; Chicago, Ill.; Ann Arbor, Mich.; Kansas City, Mo.; Riverside, N.J.; Santa Fe, N.M.; Manhasset, L.I., N.Y.; Burlington, Vt.; and Salt Lake City, Utah. You can also order books from their Travel Bookstore Catalogue. For information, call the toll-free number given above.

Dial-A-Book, 512 S. Baldwin Ave., Marion, IN 46953 (tel. 317/662-0403 or toll free 800/448-2665). Owners Anne and Phil Haisley are experienced travelers and owners of the retail bookstore named Redbeard's Books (tel. 317/662-0403). When you "Dial-A-Book," they'll ask you to describe your travel plans; then they'll prepare an appropriate list of pertinent guides, histories, novels, etc. to get you going.

Eagle Creek Travel Gear, 143 S. Cedros (P.O. Box 744), Solana Beach, CA 92705 (tel. 619/755-9399 or toll free 800/874-9925). Eagle Creek specializes in guidebooks, packs, security accessories, clothing, and sleep gear for young and adventurous travelers. They have a second retail store at 7560 Eads Ave., La Jolla, CA 92037.

Forsyth Travel Library, 9154 West 57th St. (P.O. Box 2975), Shawnee Mission, KS 66201 (tel. 913/384-0496 or toll free 800/367-7984, that's 800/FORSYTH). Forsyth carries all sorts of guides, maps, and travel materials—far more than are listed in their free catalogues. So ask them. In addition, they can issue EurailPasses, or rail passes for individual countries (Austria, Finland, France, Germany, Great Britain, Italy, Switzerland); they can even arrange special reduced tickets for museums, castles and mansions in England, and unlimited-mileage passes on the London Transport system.

Arizona

Places & People, 2623 N. Campbell Ave., Tucson, AZ 85719 (tel. 602/577-9620). Besides travel books and maps, and foreign magazines, they have travel accessories, and a good collection of interesting crafts from many foreign countries.

Wide World of Maps, 2626 W. Indian School Rd., Phoenix, AZ 85017 (tel. 602/279-2323); also 1526 N. Scottsdale Rd., Tempe, AZ 85281 (tel. 602/949-1012); and 1440 S. Country Club Dr., Mesa, AZ 85202 (tel. 602/844-1134). They have travel books, maps, and globes; their collection of maps covering Arizona and the Southwest is particularly strong.

California

Book Passage, 57 Post St., San Francisco, CA 94104 (tel. 415/982-7866 or toll free 800/321-9875). Elaine Petrocelli, owner of Book Passage, will send you a free catalogue, and, if you mention your itinerary, will prepare a list of suggested books for you, including travel guides and background reading.

Easy Going, Shattuck Commons, 1400 Shattuck Ave., Berkeley, CA 94709 (tel. 415/843-3533). Easy Going carries travel guides and travel accessories and clothing.

European Book Company, 925 Larkin St., San Francisco, CA 94109 (tel. 415/474-0626). This is basically a foreign language book company, with books written in French, German, and Spanish, and also magazines and newspapers from Europe in those languages. The periodicals are very recent, with some newspapers arriving the day after publication. They also have lots of teach-yourself language aids and some travel books (on the second floor).

Geographia Map & Travel Book Store, 4000 Riverside Dr., Burbank, CA 91505 (tel. 818/848-1414). Right near the famous film studios you'll find this store's good selection of travel guides for all the world, including local California sights and destinations, plus language books and tapes, lots of picture books, world atlases and road atlases to various countries, lots of maps (including California topographics, city maps, and National Park maps), and travel accessories, lightweight luggage, and some travel videos.

Gourmet Guides, 1767 Stockton St., San Francisco, CA 94133 (tel. 415/391-5903). Besides travel guides, maps, and the Thomas Cook railway timetables, they have lots and lots of cookbooks and restaurant and food guides.

John Cole's Book Shop, 780 Prospect St., La Jolla, CA 92037 (tel. 619/454-4766). John Cole's is a general bookstore with an especially large travel book section, including guides, picture books, histories, and other travel-related titles.

Le Travel Store, 295 Horton Plaza, San Diego, CA 92101 (tel. 619/544-0005). Owners Bill and Joan Keller run a store geared to the independent international traveler, and their lines of books cover a lot of offbeat destinations as well as the familiar routes. Foul weather gear, travel accessories, day packs and luggage are specialties, and they carry only very functional items, no fluff or shoddy. Write for their catalogue.

Map Center, 2440 Bancroft Way, Berkeley, CA 94704 (tel. 415/841-6277). Lots of guides, especially for the outdoors, plus maps, including topographic maps of California.

Map Centre, 2611 University Ave., San Diego, CA 92104 (tel. 619/291-3830). Besides lots of maps (including nautical charts), the Map Centre has a good selection of Michelin guides and other travel guides.

Pacific Travellers Supply, 529 State St., Santa Barbara, CA 93101 (tel. 805/963-4438). The name says it all: they cover all the bases with travel guides and maps, travel packs, luggage, and accessories.

Phileas Fogg's Books and Maps for the Traveler, 87 Stanford Shopping Center, Palo Alto, CA 94303 (tel. 415/327-1754 or toll free 800/533-3644; in CA, 800/233-3644). Phileas Fogg, as all good travelers know, is the peripatetic hero of Jules Verne's *Around the World in Eighty Days*. The store bearing his name carries over 7,000 guidebooks and maps to all areas of the world. It also publishes area-specific catalogues to the world's various regions, listing all of the store's many titles. Catalogues cost $1 apiece, or $5 for the full set of 10 catalogues.

Plan-It Travel Store, 777 S. Main St., Orange, CA 92668 (tel. 714/973-8979). Plan-It (get the pun?) has a complete selection of travel guides for the entire world, plus maps from both domestic and foreign publishers, and a complete line of travel accessories, including everything from electrical adaptors to toothpaste.

Quo Vadis, 427 Grand Ave., Carlsbad, CA 92008 (tel. 619/434-4301). Come here for travel books and maps, luggage, backpacks, and accessories.

Rand McNally Map Store, 595 Market St., San Francisco, CA 94105 (tel. 415/777-3131). They have travel books and maps, plus a few accessories.

Sierra Club, San Francisco Bay Chapter, 6014 College Ave., Oakland, CA 94618 (tel. 415/658-7470). The club's San Francisco Bay chapter operates a bookstore with many books and maps for travel in North America and abroad. The emphasis, of course, is on outdoor activities; they have a fine selection of foreign birding guides, for example.

Thoms Bros. Maps and Books, 603 W. Seventh St., Los Angeles, CA 90017 (tel. 213/627-4018), and also 550 Jackson St., San Francisco, CA 94133 (tel. 415/981-7520). The Thomas Bros. stores carry an excellent selection of travel guides, maps for both business planning and travel, globes, language tapes, and some travel accessories.

Travel Market, 130 Pacific Avenue Mall, San Francisco, CA 94111 (tel. 415/421-4080). Travel gear and accessories.

Travel Store, 56-1/2 N. Santa Cruz Ave., Los Gatos, CA 95030 (tel. 408/354-9909). Travel books and accessories.

Travel Suppliers, 727 N. Placentia Ave., Fullerton, CA 92631 (tel. 714/528-2502). They'll supply you with travel guides (2,400 titles), language books and tapes, maps (several thousand titles), and travel accessories.

Word Journeys, Lomas Santa Fe Plaza, 971-C Lomas Santa Fe Drive, Solana Beach, CA 92075 (tel. 619/481-4158). Here at Tony and Susan Childs' store you'll find a fine selection of travelogues and guides, both up-to-date and historical, plus language aids, international cookbooks, adventure travel books, and fiction set in foreign lands.

Colorado

Tattered Cover Book Store, 2955 E. First Ave., Denver, CO 80206 (tel. 303/322-7727 or toll free 800/833-9327; in CO 800/821-2896). This is a large and very active general bookstore with a particularly strong travel collection of 6,500 titles, plus 3,000 maps.

Connecticut

Traveler's Checklist, Cornwall Bridge Road, Sharon, CT 06069 (tel. 203/364-0144). Send for a catalogue of their travel accessories.

District of Columbia

Lloyd Books Ltd., 3145 Dumbarton St. NW, Washington, DC 20007 (tel. 202/333-8989). Lloyd has a full selection of up-to-date travel guides, and also sells antique and rare travel books. Send for a catalogue.

Map Store Inc., 1636 Eye St. NW, Washington, DC 20006 (tel. 202/628-2608). Maps and globes are the specialty here, but they also carry guidebooks.

Travel Merchandise Mart, 1425 "K" St. NW, Washington, DC 20005 (tel. 202/371-6633 or -6656). As the name indicates, this a good place to look for travel books and accessories of all types.

Florida

Map & Globe Store, 1120 E. Colonial Dr., Orlando, FL 32803 (tel. 305/425-0185 or toll free 800/227-7538); also 2328 Apalachee Pkwy., Suite 6, Tallahassee, FL 32301 (tel. 904/656-7723). "Everything in the way of maps and globes," including U.S. Survey quadrangle maps and nautical charts.

Georgia

Latitudes, 4400 Ashford Dunwoody Rd., Atlanta, GA 30346 (tel. 404/394-2772); also 3349 Peachtree Rd. NE, Atlanta, GA 30326 (tel. 404/237-6144). Here you'll find all manner of maps, globes, travel books, and travel accessories.

Illinois

Rand McNally Map Store, 23 E. Madison, Chicago, IL 60602 (tel. 312/332-4627 or toll free 800/323-1887). The famous map company also sells travel books and magazines, and some accessories.

Sandmeyer's Bookstore, 714 S. Dearborn St., Chicago, IL 60605 (tel. 312/922-2104). Sandmeyer's has over 6,000 items, including travel guides, maps, language learning aids, globes, atlases, and foreign newspapers and magazines.

The Savvy Traveller, 50 E. Washington St., Chicago, IL 60602 (tel. 312/263-2100). "Our aim is to provide everything a traveller needs to plan and take a trip, short of tickets," says Sandye Wexler. Guides both standard and offbeat, maps, novels, cookbooks, and photo books fill the shelves, as do money belts, clotheslines, games and puzzles, luggage, dual-voltage appliances, and currency and voltage converters.

Iowa

Travel Genie Map and Book Store, 113 Colorado Ave., Ames, IA 50010 (tel. 515/292-1070). Warren and Elaine Larson have travel and genealogy as their hobbies, and so their store is filled with 5,000 travel and genealogy books and guides, 4,000 maps, 15 globes, and travel aids such as small accessories, carry-on luggage, conversion calculators, language aids, cookbooks, and Iowa souvenirs. Their maps of many European countries are particularly detailed (1:50,000 and 1:100,000); they have genealogy forms as well. Ask for a free catalogue.

Maine

De Lorme Mapping Co., Lower Main St. (P.O. Box 298), Freeport, ME 04032 (tel. 207/865-4171 or toll free 800/227-1656; in ME 800/462-0029). This map publisher has a dozen state atlases, plus nautical charts and topographic maps of Maine, guides and globes, right near L. L. Bean.

Maryland

Passenger Stop, 732 Dulaney Valley Court, Towson, MD 21204 (tel. 301/821-5888). Send for their catalogue of travel gear.

Travel Books Unlimited, 4931 Cordell Ave., Bethesda, MD 20814 (tel. 301/951-8533). Owner Rochelle Jaffe's big store ("the Library of Congress of travel bookstores") covers 1,600 square feet and stocks 30,000 volumes: travel guides, literature, histories, archeology, art guides, geography, and how-to books. She also stock over 20,000 maps from all the leading cartography houses, as well as travel diaries, money exchange calculators, and other travel accessories. The Thomas Cook Timetables arrive monthly. A comprehensive catalogue is mailed out free annually; if you can't visit the store in person, you absolutely must write for the catalogue.

Massachusetts

Globe Corner Bookstore, 1 School St., Boston, MA 02108 (tel. 617/523-6658). Housed in Boston's famous

Old Corner Bookstore building at the corner of School and Washington Streets, this store specializes in travel books about New England and the world.

Harvard Square Map Store, 40 Brattle St., Cambridge, MA 02138 (tel. 617/497-6277) has an excellent selection of maps, and also carries several lines of travel guides. This store is located on the lower level of the Brattle Theatre building.

Michigan

Map & Globe Store, 1606 E. Michigan Ave., Lansing, MI 48912 (tel. 517/484-1978). This is the retail division of the Universal Map Company. Besides maps and globes, they have travel books.

Minnesota

Latitudes, 3801 Grand Ave. S., Minneapolis, MN 55409 (tel. 612/823-3742); they are also opening a store at 5101 Vernon Ave. S., Edina, MN 55436 (tel. 612/920-1848). Latitudes is a full-service travel store, carrying maps and guidebooks, globes and atlases, travel accessories and carry-on luggage. If they don't have the map you want, they'll order it specially.

Map Store, 348 N. Robert St., St. Paul, MN 55101 (tel. 612/227-1328). They carry travel guides and books, maps, and some accessories.

New Jersey

Geostat Map & Travel Center, 910 N. Route 73, Marlton, NJ 08053 (tel. 609/983-3600); also Routes 206 and 518, Skillman, NJ 08558 (tel. 609/924-2121), and

Caldor Shopping Center, Routes 10 & 202, Morris Plains, NJ 07950 (tel. 201/538-7707); and Wick Shopping Plaza, U.S. Route 1 and Plainfield Ave., Edison, NJ 08817 (tel. 201/985-1555). Travel books and maps.

New Mexico

Bookworks, 4022 Rio Grande Blvd., NW, Albuquerque, NM 87107 (tel. 505/344-8139). Travel is one of the specialties here, with photo books, guides, background books, globes and maps, and other travel-related resources.

Page One Inc., 11200 Montgomery Ave. NE, Albuquerque, NM 87111 (tel. 505/294-2026 or toll free in NM 800/521-4122). Though a general bookstore, Page One is a good place to pick up magazines and newspapers from foreign countries.

New York

British Travel Bookshop Ltd., 40 W. 57th St., New York, NY 10019 (tel. 212/765-0898). This well-established store specializes in books and maps of Great Britain.

Complete Traveller, 199 Madison Ave., New York, NY 10016 (tel. 212/685-9007). Founded by travel writers, this familiar and reliable store carries many, many travel guides, plus a selection of travel accessories such as electrical adapters and converters, travel irons, and hair dryers.

Hagstrom Map and Travel Center, 57 W. 43rd St., New York, NY 10036 (tel. 212/398-1222). A division of American Map Corporation, Hagstrom carries maps, guides, and charts produced by many companies.

They'll supply you with nautical charts of the entire east coast of North America including Canada and the Caribbean, topographic maps of the Northeast, aeronautical charts, maps of major U.S. and foreign cities, maps of foreign countries, and guidebooks. Send for an annotated list of the products they carry, and also a copy of their newsletter.

Traveller's Bookstore, 75 Rockefeller Plaza (22 W. 52nd St.), New York, NY 10019 (tel. 212/664-0995) is just what its name implies: a bookstore just for travelers. Jane Grossman, Candace Olmsted, and Martin Rapp are very well-informed, cordial, and efficient. They take orders by mail or phone. Their list extends beyond guidebooks to novels, collections of fairytales, and folklore of the various countries.

Travelore Books, 2 Elm St., Huntington Village, NY 11743 (tel. 516/673-6066). Leo Kornfeld's store is "Long Island's only travel bookstore," located off New York Avenue one block south of Main Street. Besides guidebooks by many companies, Leo carries travel videos, atlases, maps, globes, and ethnic and regional cookbooks.

Ontario

Gulliver's Travel Bookshop, 609 Bloor St. West, Toronto, ON M6G 1K5 (tel. 416/537-7700). Owner Louise Field, a history buff, carries travel guides, appropriate histories and literature, maps, and flags of different countries.

Oregon

Powell's Travel Store, Pioneer Courthouse Square, 701 S.W. Sixth Ave., Portland, OR 97204 (tel. 503/228-

1108). Powell's has several bookstores in Portland; this is the one that specializes in guidebooks, picture books, foreign language aids, maps, travel accessories, travelogues and history, some field guides, and also fiction relating to travel and foreign places.

Pennsylvania

Geostat Map & Travel Center, 125 S. 18th St., Philadelphia, PA 19103 (tel. 215/564-4700).

Travel Bound Bookstore, 815 S. Aiken Ave., Pittsburgh, PA 15232 (tel. 412/681-4100). Owner Shirley Stark runs a complete traveler's bookstore carrying several dozen guides series, maps by all of the big houses, cookbooks and food guides, language tapes and dictionaries. This store is especially strong in art, architecture, and museum guides, and it also carries rare offbeat historical guides, novels with a sense of place, and travel accessories. Ms. Stark is happy to do mail order, and will send you a copy of the store's catalogue for free.

Québec

Ulysses Bookstore, 1208 St-Denis, Montréal, QC H2X 3J5 (tel. 514/843-7135). Ulysses carries travel guides, maps, and travel-related books in both French and English, as well as travel accessories. Another branch of the store is at 560 Ave. du President Kennedy, Montréal, QC H3A 2S9.

Texas

Home-Garden and Travel Bookstore, 2476 Bolsover St., Houston, TX 77005 (tel. 713/527-0619); also 5868

Westheimer St., Houston, TX 77057 (tel. 713/789-2269). The Bolsover Street store has lots of cookbooks, travel books, photo books, and some travel accessories; the Westheimer Street store has many general interest books as well.

Travel Collection, 8235 Shoal Creek Blvd., Austin, TX 78758 (tel. 512/454-7151). Half of the store is filled with books and maps, the other half is devoted to travel accessories; and there's even a travel agency here, making it truly a one-stop travel shopping spot.

Whole Earth Provision Co., 2410 San Antonio St., Austin, TX 78705 (tel. 512/478-1577); also 4006 S. Lamar Blvd., Austin, TX 78704 (tel. 512/444-9974); and 8868 Research Blvd. Austin, TX 78758 (tel. 512/458-6333); and 2934 S. Shepherd St., Houston, TX 77098 (tel. 713/526-5226). Whole Earth will outfit you with travel guides and maps, binoculars, backpacks, camping equipment, and just about everything you need for a sojourn or a safari.

Utah

Sam Weller's Zion Book Store, 254 S. Main St., Salt Lake City, UT 84101 (tel. 801/328-2586); also 1076 E. Fort Union Blvd., Midvale, UT 84047 (tel. 801/566-0219); and 1600 S. Main St., Bountiful, UT 84010 (tel. 801/295-3921). The Main Street, Salt Lake City store has over a million and a half volumes, a third of them new, two-thirds used, including 1,000 new guides and travel books, and several thousand used travel narratives. Any title in the main store can be shipped overnight to the branch stores in Midvale or Bountiful. The map section is large as well, with lots of road maps for foreign countries, as well as detailed maps of Utah and the West. They also have language tapes and books.

Virginia

Book Gallery, 1207 Emmet St., Charlottesville, VA 22901 (tel. 804/977-2892); also 1601 Willow Lawn Dr., Richmond, VA 23230 (tel. 804/673-9613). A general bookstore with a very good selection of travel books (including many offbeat ones) and globes.

Travel Merchandise Mart, 2102 Crystal Plaza, Arlington, VA 22202 (tel. 703/685-1676 or toll free 800/446-2424; in VA 800/572-1717). Books, maps, and accessories.

Washington

International Books, 3237 Eastlake Ave., East, Seattle, WA 98102-3826 (tel. 206/323-5667). Language learning aids are the specialty here, with language guides and cassette tapes "from Arabic to Yoruba" on sale.

Metsker Maps of Seattle, 702 First Ave., Seattle, WA 98104 (tel. 206/623-8747). Besides travel guides, look here for planespheres for reckoning the stars and planets from various latitudes, plus inflatable globes, world maps, foreign country and city maps, and nautical charts (including those to Canadian waters).

Pioneer Maps, 14125 N.E. 20th St., Bellevue, WA 98007 (tel. 206/746-3200). Look here for travel maps and books, especially for Asia, and particularly the offbeat guides; also, there's a good selection of books for Mexico and Latin America. The map selection is quite complete for the world, and includes atlases, globes, topographic maps, and nautical charts as well as highway, country, and city maps.

Travel Accessories Market, 1419 First Ave., Seattle, WA 98101 (tel. 206/447-9468). They have a good selection of books and maps for foreign destinations, plus a vast selection of travel accessories and convenience items, including convertible suitcase/backpacks, lightweight rainwear and other easily-packable articles of clothing.

Wide World Books and Maps, 401 N.E. 45th St., Seattle, WA 98105 (tel. 206/634-3453), will send you a free catalogue, and will fill orders by mail; but drop in to look over their whole collection of more than 3,500 titles. Wide World Books publishes *How to Travel Inexpensively*, "a newsletter and catalog of hard-to-find travel information." They specialize in the offbeat guidebook series, and in little-known guidebooks that may not be available elsewhere.

APPENDIX 4:
CAR RENTAL COMPANIES

It's easy to do comparison-shopping among car rental companies—if you know they exist. But most people think there are only about four or five large companies, so they miss some of the best rental prices.

Here is a list of the major car rental companies. Though not every company will have rental facilities in every location, by making a few quick toll-free calls you can determine which companies rent cars where, and which company offers the best deal.

(Note: the first number given for each company is that of the corporate headquarters and is a toll call; use it for special questions or complaints. If you want to ask about prices or to make a reservation, be sure to call the toll-free reservation number.)

Before calling, get pencil and paper ready. Review the strategies in Chapter 8, and remember to ask about such things as Collision Damage Waiver, mileage charges, "full tank" or "empty tank" basis, taxes, weekend packages, and discounts (like the ever-present 10%). Know what your own automobile insurance and health policies already cover, so that you won't have to pay twice for insurance costs. You'll get a great price on your rental car, whether you rent a Volkswagen or a Lincoln.

For more information about car rental companies, contact the American Car Rental Association, 2011 Eye St. NW, Fifth Floor, Washington, DC 20006 (tel. 202/223-2118).

If you're interested in buying or renting a recreational vehicle (camper, conversion van, travel trailer, etc.), get in touch with the Recreation Vehicle Industry Association, 1896 Preston White Dr., P.O. Box 2999, Reston, VA 22090 (tel. 703/620-6003). They've got all sorts of useful brochures, booklets, and flyers for you, free of charge.

North American Rentals:

AGENCY RENT-A-CAR, 30000 Aurora Rd., Solon, OH 44139 (tel. 216/349-1000; for reservations, toll free 800/321-1972; in OH toll free 800/362-1794). Agency has 18,000 cars in 200 locations in 38 states.

AJAX RENT-A-CAR, 4121 N.W. 25th St., Miami, FL 33142 (tel. 305/871-5050; for reservations, toll free 800/352-2592). Ajax has 11,000 cars at 48 locations in 18 states.

ALAMO RENT-A-CAR, 1401 S. Federal Hwy., Fort Lauderdale, FL 33316 (P.O. Box 22776, Fort Lauderdale, FL 33335) (tel. 305/522-0000; for reservations, toll free 800/327-9633; in FL toll free 800/432-4320). Alamo operates in 13 states with 60,000 cars at 59 locations.

AMERICAN INTERNATIONAL RENT-A-CAR, 1 Harborside Dr., East Boston, MA 02128 (tel. 617/561-1000; for reservations, toll free 800/527-0202). AI has 38,000 cars at 317 locations in 44 states.

AUTO DRIVE A WAY, 310 S. Michigan Ave., Chicago, IL 60604 (tel. 312/939-3600; for reservations, toll free 800/621-4155). This is a "driveaway" company (see Chapter 8 under "Driveaways") with some rental cars as well, in eight states.

AVIS RENT-A-CAR SYSTEM, 900 Old Country Rd., Garden City, NY 11530 (tel. 516/222-3000; for reservations, toll free 800/331-1212; in OK toll free 800/482-4554; in AK and HI toll free 800/331-1717). Avis has 135,000 cars in 1,200 locations in the U.S., and operates worldwide.

BUDGET RENT-A-CAR, 200 N. Michigan Ave., Chicago, IL 60601 (tel. 312/580-5000; for reservations, toll free 800/527-0700). Budget has 110,000 cars at 1,130 locations, nationwide; it's the same operation as Sears Rent-A-Car. They can reserve a car for you in many foreign countries as well.

DOLLAR RENT-A-CAR, 6141 W. Century Blvd., Los Angeles, CA 90045 (tel. 213/776-8100; for reservations, toll free 800/421-6868; in CA toll free 800/262-1520; in AK and HI 800/421-2624). Dollar has 46,000 cars at 450 locations, nationwide.

ENTERPRISE RENT-A-CAR, 35 Hunter Ave., St. Louis, MO 63124 (tel. 314/863-7000; for reservations, toll free 800/325-8007). Enterprise operates in 15 states.

GENERAL RENT-A-CAR, 1600 N.W. Lejeune Rd., Miami, FL 33126 (tel. 305/871-4440; for reservations, toll free 800/327-7607; in FL call locally). General operates in 10 states, with 20,000 cars at 30 locations.

HERTZ CORPORATION, 660 Madison Ave., New York, NY 10021 (tel. 212/980-2121; for reservations, toll free 800/654-3131; in OK toll free 800/522-3711; in AK and HI toll free 800/654-8200). Hertz operates worldwide, with 150,000 cars at 1,800 locations in the U.S.

KEMWEL GROUP, 106 Calvert St., Harrison, NY 10528 (tel. 914/835-5454; for reservations, toll free 800/468-0468). Kemwel operates in 42 states and several foreign countries.

NATIONAL CAR RENTAL, 7700 France Ave. S., Minneapolis, MN 55435 (tel. 612/830-2121; for reservations, toll free 800/328-4567). National has 110,000 cars at 1,100 locations, nationwide. National has affiliates in many other countries.

PAYLESS RENT-A-CAR, 5510 Gulfport Blvd., St. Petersburg, FL 33707 (tel. 813/381-2758; for reservations, toll free 800/237-2804; in FL, call locally). Payless operates in 36 states.

RENT-A-WRECK, 1100 Glendon St., Los Angeles, CA 90024 (tel. 213/208-7712; for reservations, toll free 800/421-7253; in CA 800/535-1391). Rent-a-Wreck rents cars in 43 states.

SEARS RENT-A-CAR, 200 N. Michigan Ave., Chicago, IL 60601 (tel. 312/580-5000; for reservations, toll free 800/527-0770). This is the same company as Budget Rent-a-Car.

SNAPPY RENT-A-CAR, 3601 Green Rd., Suite 100, Beachwood, OH 44122 (tel. 216/831-6340; for reservations, toll free 800/762-7791). Snappy has 16,000 cars in 206 locations in 45 states.

THRIFTY RENT-A-CAR, 4608 S. Garnett Rd., Tulsa, OK 74146 (P.O. Box 35250, Tulsa, OK 74153) (tel. 918/665-3930; for reservations, toll free 800/367-2277). Thrifty has 35,000 cars in 400 locations in 48 states, plus affiliates in foreign countries.

TROPICAL RENT-A-CAR, 550 Paiea St., Suite 203, Honolulu, HI 96819 (tel. 808/836-0788; for reservations, toll free 800/367-5140). Tropical operates in eight states.

VALUE RENT-A-CAR, P.O. Box 8664, Deerfield Beach, FL 33441 (tel. 305/429-8300; for reservations, toll free 800/327-2501). Formerly Greyhound Rent-a-Car. Value has 30,000 cars at 37 locations in eight states.

Foreign Rentals:

To rent or lease a car overseas, contact these companies, listed above: Avis, Budget, Hertz, Kemwel, National, or Thrifty. In addition, the following companies may be helpful to you:

CONVOYS CAR RENTAL/INTER-EUROPEAN HIRE, 1133 Broadway, New York, NY 10010 (tel. 212/929-0920).

EUROPE BY CAR, 1 Rockefeller Plaza, New York, NY 10020 (tel. 212/234-1713 or 581-3040; or toll free 800/

223-1516; other U.S. cities have local branches of this company, so check your local directory).

FOREMOST EURO-CAR, 5430 Van Nuys Blvd., Van Nuys, CA 91401 (tel. 213/872-2226).

Index

Notes

Notes

Notes

Notes

Notes

Notes

Notes

Notes

Notes

NOW!
ARTHUR FROMMER LAUNCHES HIS SECOND TRAVEL REVOLUTION
with

The New World of Travel

The hottest news and latest trends in travel today—heretofore the closely guarded secrets of the travel trade—are revealed in this new sourcebook by the dean of American travel. Here, collected in one book that is updated every year, are the most exciting, challenging, and money-saving ideas in travel today.

You'll find out about hundreds of alternative new modes of travel—and the many organizations that sponsor them—that will lead you to vacations that cater to your mind, your spirit, and your sense of thrift.

Learn how to fly for free as an air courier; travel for free as a tour escort; live for free on a hospitality exchange; add earnings as a part-time travel agent; pay less for air tickets, cruises, and hotels; enhance your life through cooperative camping, political tours, and adventure trips; change your life at utopian communities, low-cost spas, and yoga retreats; pursue low-cost studies and language training; travel comfortably while single or over 60; sail on passenger freighters; and vacation in the cheapest places on earth.

And in every yearly edition, Arthur Frommer spotlights the 10 GREATEST TRAVEL VALUES for the coming year. 384 pages, large-format with many, many illustrations. All for $12.95!

ORDER NOW
TURN TO THE LAST PAGE OF THIS BOOK FOR ORDER FORM.

NOW, SAVE MONEY ON ALL YOUR TRAVELS!
Join Arthur Frommer's $35-A-Day Travel Club™

Saving money while traveling is never a simple matter, which is why, over 26 years ago, the **$35-A-Day Travel Club** was formed. Actually, the idea came from readers of the Arthur Frommer Publications who felt that such an organization could bring financial benefits, continuing travel information, and a sense of community to economy-minded travelers all over the world.

In keeping with the money-saving concept, the annual membership fee is low—$18 (U.S. residents) or $20 U.S. (Canadian, Mexican, and foreign residents)—and is immediately exceeded by the value of your benefits which include:

(1) The latest edition of any TWO of the books listed on the following pages.

(2) An annual subscription to an 8-page quarterly newspaper *The Wonderful World of Budget Travel* which keeps you up-to-date on fastbreaking developments in low-cost travel in all parts of the world—bringing you the kind of information you'd have to pay over $35 a year to obtain elsewhere. This consumer-conscious publication also includes the following columns:

Hospitality Exchange—members all over the world who are willing to provide hospitality to other members as they pass through their home cities.

Share-a-Trip—requests from members for travel companions who can share costs and help avoid the burdensome single supplement.

Readers Ask . . . Readers Reply—travel questions from members to which other members reply with authentic firsthand information.

(3) A copy of *Arthur Frommer's Guide to New York.*

(4) Your personal membership card which entitles you to purchase through the Club all Arthur Frommer Publications for a third to a half off their regular retail prices during the term of your membership.

So why not join this hardy band of international budgeteers NOW and participate in its exchange of information and hospitality? Simply send $18 (U.S. residents) or $20 U.S. (Canadian, Mexican, and other foreign residents) along with your name and address to: $35-A-Day Travel Club, Inc., Gulf + Western Building, One Gulf + Western Plaza, New York, NY 10023. Remember to specify which *two* of the books in section (1) above you wish to receive in your initial package of member's benefits. Or tear out the next page, check off any two of the books listed on either side, and send it to us with your membership fee.

Date_____

FROMMER BOOKS
PRENTICE HALL PRESS
ONE GULF + WESTERN PLAZA
NEW YORK, NY 10023

Friends:

Please send me the books checked below:

FROMMER'S $-A-DAY GUIDES™
(In-depth guides to sightseeing and low-cost tourist accommodations and facilities.)

☐ Europe on $30 a Day	$13.95	☐ New Zealand on $40 a Day	$11.95
☐ Australia on $30 a Day	$11.95	☐ New York on $50 a Day	$10.95
☐ Eastern Europe on $25 a Day	$10.95	☐ Scandinavia on $50 a Day	$10.95
☐ England on $40 a Day	$11.95	☐ Scotland and Wales on $40 a Day	$11.95
☐ Greece on $30 a Day	$11.95	☐ South America on $30 a Day	$10.95
☐ Hawaii on $50 a Day	$11.95	☐ Spain and Morocco (plus the Canary Is.) on $40 a Day	$10.95
☐ India on $25 a Day	$10.95	☐ Turkey on $25 a Day	$10.95
☐ Ireland on $30 a Day	$10.95	☐ Washington, D.C., & Historic Va. on $40 a Day	$11.95
☐ Israel on $30 & $35 a Day	$11.95		
☐ Mexico (plus Belize & Guatemala) on $20 a Day	$10.95		

FROMMER'S DOLLARWISE GUIDES™
(Guides to sightseeing and tourist accommodations and facilities from budget to deluxe, with emphasis on the medium-priced.)

☐ Alaska	$12.95	☐ Cruises (incl. Alaska, Carib, Mex, Hawaii, Panama, Canada, & US)	$12.95
☐ Austria & Hungary	$11.95	☐ California & Las Vegas	$11.95
☐ Belgium, Holland, Luxembourg	$11.95	☐ Florida	$11.95
☐ Egypt	$11.95	☐ Mid-Atlantic States	$12.95
☐ England & Scotland	$11.95	☐ New England	$12.95
☐ France	$11.95	☐ New York State	$12.95
☐ Germany	$12.95	☐ Northwest	$11.95
☐ Italy	$11.95	☐ Skiing in Europe	$12.95
☐ Japan & Hong Kong	$13.95	☐ Skiing USA—East	$11.95
☐ Portugal, Madeira, & the Azores	$12.95	☐ Skiing USA—West	$11.95
☐ South Pacific	$12.95	☐ Southeast & New Orleans	$11.95
☐ Switzerland & Liechtenstein	$12.95	☐ Southwest	$11.95
☐ Bermuda & The Bahamas	$11.95	☐ Texas	$11.95
☐ Canada	$12.95		
☐ Caribbean	$13.95		

FROMMER'S TOURING GUIDES™
(Color illustrated guides that include walking tours, cultural & historic sites, and other vital travel information.)

☐ Egypt	$8.95	☐ Paris	$8.95
☐ Florence	$8.95	☐ Venice	$8.95
☐ London	$8.95		

TURN PAGE FOR ADDITIONAL BOOKS AND ORDER FORM.

THE ARTHUR FROMMER GUIDES™

(Pocket-size guides to sightseeing and tourist accommodations and facilities in all price ranges.)

☐ Amsterdam/Holland	$5.95	☐ Mexico City/Acapulco	$5.95
☐ Athens	$5.95	☐ Minneapolis/St. Paul	$5.95
☐ Atlantic City/Cape May	$5.95	☐ Montreal/Quebec City	$5.95
☐ Boston	$5.95	☐ New Orleans	$5.95
☐ Cancún/Cozumel/Yucatán	$5.95	☐ New York	$5.95
☐ Dublin/Ireland	$5.95	☐ Orlando/Disney World/EPCOT	$5.95
☐ Hawaii	$5.95	☐ Paris	$5.95
☐ Las Vegas	$5.95	☐ Philadelphia	$5.95
☐ Lisbon/Madrid/Costa del Sol	$5.95	☐ Rome	$5.95
☐ London	$5.95	☐ San Francisco	$5.95
☐ Los Angeles	$5.95	☐ Washington, D.C.	$5.95

SPECIAL EDITIONS

☐ A Shopper's Guide to the Caribbean	$12.95	☐ Motorist's Phrase Book (Fr/Ger/Sp)	$4.95
☐ Bed & Breakfast—N. America	$8.95	☐ Swap and Go (Home Exchanging)	$10.95
☐ Guide to Honeymoon Destinations (US, Canada, Mexico, & Carib)	$12.95	☐ The Candy Apple (NY for Kids)	$11.95
		☐ Travel Diary and Record Book	$5.95
☐ Beat the High Cost of Travel	$6.95	☐ Where to Stay USA (Lodging from $3 to $30 a night)	$10.95
☐ Marilyn Wood's Wonderful Weekends (NY, Conn, Mass, RI, Vt, NH, NJ, Del, Pa)	$11.95		

☐ Arthur Frommer's New World of Travel (Annual sourcebook previewing: new travel trends, new modes of travel, and the latest cost-cutting strategies for savvy travelers) $12.95

SERIOUS SHOPPER'S GUIDES

(Illustrated guides listing hundreds of stores, conveniently organized alphabetically by category.)

☐ Italy	$15.95	☐ Los Angeles	$14.95
☐ London	$15.95	☐ Paris	$15.95

ORDER NOW!

In U.S. include $1.50 shipping UPS for 1st book; 50¢ ea. add'l book. Outside U.S. $2 and 50¢, respectively.

Enclosed is my check or money order for $_____

NAME _____

ADDRESS _____

CITY _____ STATE _____ ZIP _____